CREATIVE COOKING
PASTA

Copyright © 1992 Ottenheimer Publishers, Inc.

Compiled and edited by Marian Hoffman.
Designed by Ruth Ann Thompson.

All Rights Reserved.

Printed and bound in the United States of America.

TABLE OF CONTENTS

INTRODUCTION

For generations, families have enjoyed delicious pasta dishes ranging from appetizers to desserts. Pasta's versatility is perhaps its greatest quality. It can be served with a sauce, stuffed and baked, or used as a soup or salad ingredient. Pasta can be combined with virtually any fresh ingredient for a terrific dish or it can be combined with leftover foods to create an entirely new dish. The possibilities are endless.

◆ Pasta is usually purchased dried and can be stored in a cool dry place for up to two years. Fresh pasta can also be purchased in many food stores, but must be refrigerated and can only be stored for a few days. Whether pasta is fresh or dried, however, be sure that the pasta is not stored too close to foods with very strong flavors since the pasta could pick up odors or change flavor.

◆ Pasta is available in many varieties. Traditional pasta is made from white flour, but it can be made with whole-wheat flour, rye flour, or mixtures of both. There are also many flavored pastas on the market today. Some pastas are flavored with vegetables such as spinach and carrots and others are made with strawberries and even blueberries. In addition to adding a delightful taste twist, these flavored pastas come in different colors that make any dish more exciting. Try substituting a flavored pasta for one that is listed in the recipes that follow for a change of pace.

◆ Italian pasta dishes are perhaps the most widely known but pasta is found in traditional dishes from around the world. From appetizers to desserts, explore all of the delectable possibilities contained in this cookbook.

◆ Pasta is available in many shapes and sizes and can be used interchangeably without any trouble. Some pasta is long and thin, such as spaghetti, vermicelli, and angel hair; some pastas like linguine and fettuccine are long and flat. Pasta shells, wheels, spirals, butterflies, tubes, and rice make any dish fun to look at as well as good to eat. The pasta type recommended in each recipe that follows is only a suggestion; feel free to experiment with different pasta shapes as well as flavors.

◆ Pasta is nutritious, wholesome, and low in fat. Because it is a good source of carbohydrates, pasta is considered to be a high-energy food; it is often eaten in great quantities by athletes preparing for important races or games to help them build up large reserves of energy. Pasta is also high in protein, magnesium, phosphorous, zinc, and several B vitamins.

◆ Pasta can be fattening if prepared with ingredients that are high in calories, such as butter and high-fat cheeses. Try serving pasta with low-calorie, high-protein foods such as chicken, or with vegetables or low-fat cheeses. By choosing carefully which foods to combine with pasta, you can prepare a dish that can be easily incorporated into a low-calorie diet.

- One of the beauties of pasta is that it is easy to prepare. Here are a few hints that will make cooking pasta easy:
  - ✓ Use plenty of boiling water when cooking pasta; add 1 tablespoon salt for every 4 quarts of water.
  - ✓ Boil water rapidly over high heat.
  - ✓ Add a dash of cooking oil to boiling water so that the pasta doesn't stick to the pot.
  - ✓ Do not overcook pasta. Whenever possible, cook until just tender, or al dente.
  - ✓ Slightly undercook pasta if a recipe calls for pasta to be cooked again.
  - ✓ Pasta should be eaten as soon as it is cooked, unless it will be used in a casserole, stew, or salad.
  - ✓ If a recipe calls for grated cheese, grate the cheese just before using.
  - ✓ Whenever possible, use fresh herbs instead of dried herbs to get delicious flavor.
  - ✓ Use only fresh eggs when making your own pasta dough.
  - ✓ Don't use spices that have been stored for a long time.
  - ✓ In recipes that call for pepper, use freshly grated pepper for the most flavor.
  - ✓ Melted butter should be golden when drizzled over pasta; otherwise, the dish might taste bitter.
- The more than 500 recipes in this book are designed to be easy-to-follow and simple-to-prepare and should provide many hours of eating enjoyment. So go ahead. Enjoy!

Beef and Bean Soup with Pasta

Serves 8

2¹/₂ quarts water
1 teaspoon salt
2¹/₄ pounds beef ribs
2 soup bones
1 onion
1 bay leaf
2¹/₄ cups string beans, cut into 2-inch pieces
1 cup vermicelli
1 clove garlic, peeled and finely chopped
¹/₂ cup finely chopped fresh chives or 1 tablespoon dried chives
¹/₂ cup finely chopped parsley
Salt and pepper to taste

1. Place water and salt in stock pot and bring to a boil. Add meat, bones, onion, and bay leaf. Simmer gently for 2 hours, skimming froth as needed during first 15 minutes of cooking time.
2. Place green beans in saucepan and cover with salted water; bring to a boil, then cover and simmer for 15 minutes.
3. Cook vermicelli in boiling salted water according to package directions; drain and let cool.
4. Remove bones from stock. Trim fat from meat, then dice meat and set aside. Strain stock. Add garlic, string beans, diced meat, and pasta to stock. Sprinkle with chives and parsley, season with salt and pepper, and serve.

Beef Broth with Dumplings

Serves 4

Beef Broth

2 pounds beef shank
6 cups cold water
2 teaspoons salt
¹/₄ teaspoon pepper
2 cloves
5 medium potatoes, sliced
1 large carrot, sliced
2 onions, sliced
Chopped parsley

Dumplings

1¹/₂ tablespoons butter
¹/₄ cup flour
1²/₃ cups milk
2 egg yolks
2 tablespoons grated Parmesan cheese
Pinch of grated cardamom or a drop of almond extract
4 to 6 cups salted water

1. To make broth, cover meat with cold water and bring slowly to a boil; skim as needed. Season with salt, pepper, and chives; cover and simmer for 45 minutes. Add potatoes, carrot, and onions. Continue simmering until meat and vegetables are tender.
2. While broth is cooking, make dumplings. Melt butter in saucepan over low heat; stir in flour. Add milk, stirring constantly until sauce thickens. Remove from heat. In small bowl, beat egg yolks and 1 to 2 tablespoons milk together; add 2 tablespoons sauce to this mixture and blend well. Pour egg yolk mixture into remaining sauce and cook over low heat, stirring vigorously, until sauce is hot, thick, and well blended. Stir in cheese and car-

damom or almond extract. Let cool.
3. Form dumpling dough into balls the size of a quarter. Bring water to a boil in large pot. Reduce heat, then gently drop dumplings into hot water; simmer for 5 minutes. Remove dumplings, drain, and set aside.
4. Remove meat from broth, discard any fat, and cut meat off the bone into bite-size pieces; return meat to broth.
5. Add dumplings to broth and simmer until heated thoroughly. Sprinkle with chopped parsley, and serve.

Beef Vegetable Soup with Noodles

Serves 6

1 pound ground beef
2 stalks celery, finely chopped
3 carrots, thinly sliced
2 medium onions, chopped
6 cups water
1 beef bouillon cube
1 (8-ounce) can tomato sauce
¹/₂ cup small pasta shells
1 (28-ounce) can tomatoes, undrained, chopped
2 bay leaves
1¹/₂ teaspoons basil
Salt and pepper to taste
1 (10¹/₂-ounce) package frozen green beans or peas

1. Brown ground beef in large saucepan. Add celery, carrots, and onions; saute for 5 minutes, stirring frequently. Add remaining ingredients, except green beans or peas, and bring to a boil. Cover and simmer for 50 minutes.
2. Add green beans or peas and continue simmering until vegetables and pasta are tender. Discard bay leaves, and serve.

Beef Balls with Noodles

Serves 6

Beef Balls

1 tablespoon oil
2 onions, grated
2 cloves garlic, peeled and crushed
1½ pounds ground beef
4 slices slightly stale bread, diced
1 egg, lightly beaten
½ teaspoon nutmeg
1 teaspoon salt
¼ teaspoon pepper

Broth

1 tablespoon oil
1 onion, peeled and thinly sliced
2 cloves garlic, peeled and crushed
1 tablespoon oil
4 cups chicken stock
1-inch piece fresh ginger, peeled
4 shallots, peeled and sliced
4 stalks celery, sliced
4 cabbage leaves, finely shredded
Celery leaves or parsley, for garnish
12 ounces egg noodles

1. Heat oil in small skillet. Add onions and garlic; saute until lightly browned. Combine onions, garlic, and remaining beef ball ingredients in mixing bowl; blend well. Form into 18 small balls and set aside.
2. To make broth, heat oil in large saucepan. Add onion and garlic; saute until onion is translucent. Add chicken stock and ginger; bring to a boil. With slotted spoon, lower meatballs into stock and return to a boil. Reduce heat to medium and cook for 15 minutes, or until meat is thoroughly cooked. Add shallots, celery, and cabbage leaves; cook 5 minutes longer, or until vegetables are crisp-tender.
3. Cook noodles in boiling water according to package directions; drain. Divide noodles among 6 individual soup bowls. Put 3 meat-balls and some vegetables in each bowl. Fill to the top of bowl with broth. Garnish with celery leaves or parsley, and serve.

Beef-Noodle Soup

Serves 6

1¼ pounds beef short ribs
1 tablespoon salt
6 cups water
2 beef bouillon cubes
1 cup chopped celery with leaves
4 ounces egg noodles

1. Combine beef, salt, and water in large pot. Simmer, covered, for 2 hours, or until meat is tender; skim off excess fat. Remove meat from bones and cut into small pieces.
2. Add bouillon, celery, and cut-up meat to broth. Cover and simmer for 10 minutes. Stir in noodles, cover, and simmer for 7 to 10 minutes, or until noodles and celery are tender.
3. If thinner soup is desired, add a little hot water to broth. Spoon soup into individual soup bowls, and serve.

Cabbage and Bean-Thread Soup

Serves 6

2 ounces pork, thinly sliced into small pieces
1¼ teaspoons soy sauce
1 teaspoon cornstarch
½ ounce transparent (cellophane) noodles
2 tablespoons oil
1 teaspoon salt
3 cups water
¼ cup thinly sliced Chinese cabbage
½ cup thinly sliced cucumber
1 tablespoon chopped scallion
¼ teaspoon pepper
½ teaspoon sesame oil

1. Mix pork with 1 teaspoon soy sauce and cornstarch. Set aside.
2. Place noodles in bowl with just enough hot water to cover; let stand for 5 minutes.
3. Heat oil in frying pan. Saute pork over moderate heat for 5 minutes; remove from pan.
4. Add salt and water to large saucepan; bring to a boil. Add noodles, pork, cabbage, and cucumber, and boil for 5 minutes. Mix scallion, pepper, sesame oil, and remaining ¼ teaspoon soy sauce together; add to soup, mixing well. Simmer until soup is thoroughly heated, and serve.

Sicilian Sausage Soup with Orzo

Serves 4

¼ pound sweet Italian sausage, with casing removed
½ cup finely chopped onion
¼ cup chopped peeled carrots
¼ cup chopped celery
2 tablespoons chopped parsley
1 (16-ounce) can Italian-style tomatoes, drained and broken up with a fork
1 (13¾-ounce) can chicken broth
½ teaspoon basil
¼ cup rice-shaped pasta (orzo)
Salt and pepper to taste

1. Brown sausage in medium frying pan, breaking it into small pieces as it cooks. Remove sausage from pan with slotted spoon. Place into large saucepan.
2. Add onion to same frying pan and saute in sausage drippings until translucent. Remove onion with slotted spoon and add to sausage. Add vegetables, chicken broth, and basil to sausage mixture. Bring soup to a boil; stir well. Cook over moderate heat for 15 minutes.
3. Stir in orzo, salt, and pepper. Reduce heat to low, cover, and simmer for 20 minutes, or until sausage is done and orzo is tender. Spoon into soup bowls, and serve.

Dry Soup
with Vermicelli

Serves 6

1/2 pound chorizo (Mexican pork
  sausage)
6 tablespoons olive oil
1/2 pound vermicelli
1 small onion, chopped
1 cup canned tomatoes,
  drained
2 cups chicken broth
Salt and pepper to taste
Grated Parmesan cheese
  to taste
Chopped parsley, for garnish

1. Brown chorizo in frying pan;
remove from pan, drain on paper
towels, and set aside.
2. Heat oil in heavy skillet. Saute
vermicelli over medium heat until
golden brown. Drain vermicelli on
paper towels, then place in bottom
of 2-quart casserole dish.
3. Preheat oven to 350 degrees.
4. Drain off all except 1 tablespoon
oil from skillet. Add onion and saute
until translucent. Add tomatoes,
chicken broth, salt, and pepper.
Bring to a boil, then pour mixture
over vermicelli. Add chorizo and stir
well. Cover and bake for 15 minutes.
Sprinkle with Parmesan cheese and
parsley, and serve.

Chicken Noodle Soup

Serves 4 to 6

4 to 5 cups chicken stock
8 ounces thin egg noodles
Salt and pepper to taste
1 cup diced cooked chicken
2 tablespoons finely chopped
  parsley

1. Bring stock to boil in large
saucepan. Add noodles, stirring
constantly. Cook noodles according
to package directions. Season to
taste. Add chicken and cook until
heated thoroughly.
2. Serve soup hot, sprinkled liberally
with parsley.

Chicken and
Vegetable Soup
with Noodles

Serves 4

2 tablespoons butter
2 carrots, peeled and sliced
2 stalks celery, sliced
1/2 cup chopped green pepper
1 small onion, peeled and
  chopped
4 cups chicken broth
1 1/2 cups chopped cooked
  chicken
1 large tomato, skinned and
  chopped
Salt and pepper to taste
1/2 cup frozen peas
8 ounces egg noodles, broken
  into small pieces

1. Heat butter in large saucepan.
Add carrots, celery, green pepper,
and onion; saute for 6 minutes,
stirring occasionally. Add chicken
broth, chicken, tomato, salt, and
pepper; simmer for 20 minutes.
2. Add peas to soup. Stir well, then
simmer for 5 minutes longer. Add
small pieces of noodles and simmer
for 5 minutes, stirring occasionally.
Remove from heat and serve.

Chicken Broth with
Filled Pasta

Serves 8

Pasta

Homemade Egg Noodles
  (see Index)

Filling

3/4 cup ricotta cheese
1/4 cup grated Parmesan cheese
2 tablespoons chopped parsley
Salt and pepper, to taste
Soup
3 (10 3/4-ounce) cans condensed
  chicken broth
3 soup-cans water or 8 cups
  homemade chicken stock

1. Make pasta. Cover with plastic
wrap and let stand for 30 minutes.

2. In small mixing bowl, mix ricotta
and Parmesan cheeses, parsley, salt,
and pepper together well.
3. On lightly floured surface, roll
dough out, a quarter at a time, until
paper-thin; keep remaining dough
tightly covered until ready to use. If
using pasta machine, roll to slightly
less than 1/16 of an inch. Cut into 2-
inch rounds with floured biscuit
cutter. Top each pasta round with 1/4
teaspoon of cheese filling. Dampen
edge of pasta circle with a small
amount of water and fold into half-
moon shape. Place filled pasta on
plate or tray and cover until all are
completed.
4. Combine chicken broth and water
in large saucepan and bring to a boil.
Add filled pasta and boil for 5 to 10
minutes, or until tender. Ladle broth
and pasta in soup bowls, and serve
with grated cheese.
5. The pasta can be made in
advance and frozen, uncooked, in a
single layer on a cookie sheet.
Transfer to a freezer bag and keep
frozen until ready to cook.

Japanese
Chicken Noodle Soup

Serves 4

5 cups chicken broth
1 (4-ounce) can mushroom stems
  and pieces, drained, reserve
  liquid
2 teaspoons soy sauce
1 cup cooked thin egg noodles
1 cooked boneless chicken
  breast, thinly sliced
4 thin slices lemon with rind

1. Bring chicken broth to a boil in
large saucepan. If there are not 5
cups of broth, add enough reserved
mushroom liquid to make 5 cups.
Simmer, covered, for 5 minutes. Add
mushrooms, soy sauce, and noodles.
Stir well and simmer for 3 minutes,
or until heated thoroughly.
2. Divide sliced chicken among 4
soup bowls. Pour soup into bowls.
Garnish each with thin slice of
lemon, and serve.

Chicken Soup with Vermicelli

Serves 6

6 cups chicken stock
1 whole chicken breast, split
¼ cup vegetable oil
¼ pound vermicelli, broken into 2-inch lengths
1 large tomato, skinned, seeded, and chopped
1 ripe avocado, peeled, pitted, and cut into chunks
2 hot green chilies, chopped
Salt and pepper to taste

1. At least 6 hours before serving, heat stock to boiling in large saucepan. Add chicken, reduce heat to low, and simmer for 25 minutes. Remove chicken from broth and set aside to cool. When chicken is cool enough to handle, remove skin and bones; shred chicken meat. Refrigerate chicken and stock until ready to use.
2. Heat oil in small skillet. Add pasta and cook until lightly browned. Remove from pan and drain on paper towels.
3. Reheat stock to boiling. Add vermicelli and cook until tender. Add tomato and shredded chicken; heat thoroughly. Add avocado, chilies, salt, and pepper; heat thoroughly. Serve soup piping hot.

Egg Drop Noodle Soup

Serves 4

4 cups chicken stock
½ cup uncooked thin egg noodles
2 eggs, beaten
1 tablespoon lemon juice
Salt and pepper to taste
½ cup finely chopped scallions

1. Place chicken stock in large saucepan and bring to a boil. Add noodles; boil for 5 minutes, or until noodles are just tender. Reduce heat to simmer.

2. Stir eggs, lemon juice, salt, and pepper together well. Slowly add eggs to stock in a thin stream, stirring gently with a fork. Simmer for 1 minute, or until egg has set.
3. Sprinkle soup with chopped scallions, and serve hot.

Chicken Corn Chowder

Serves 8

3 quarts chicken broth
8 ounces egg noodles
2 cups diced cooked chicken
½ teaspoon nutmeg
2 (17-ounce) cans cream-style corn
2 hard-cooked eggs, shelled and chopped, optional

1. Place broth in large saucepan and bring to a boil. Add noodles, chicken, nutmeg, and corn. Cook, stirring occasionally, for 10 minutes, or until noodles are tender.
2. Garnish with chopped egg, if desired, and serve.

Vermicelli Chicken Soup

Serves 4

½ stewing chicken, about 1½ pounds
1½ teaspoons salt
6 whole peppercorns
1 stalk celery
1 carrot
1 large onion
1 clove garlic, peeled
1 tomato, quartered
½ cup shelled peas
½ cup cauliflower florets
½ cup julienne-sliced celery
½ cup julienne-sliced carrots
½ cup vermicelli

1. Place chicken in large pot, cover with cold water, and bring to a boil; skim as needed. Add salt, peppercorns, celery stalk, carrot, onion, garlic, and tomato to chicken; boil for 1 hour.
2. Place peas, cauliflower florets, and julienne strips of celery and carrot in saucepan with 1 cup water; boil for 10 minutes. Drain vegetables and set aside.
3. Cook vermicelli for 3 minutes in 2 cups boiling water; drain.
4. Remove chicken from stock. Remove skin and bones, then dice chicken meat. Combine diced chicken, vermicelli, and vegetables in soup tureen. Strain stock into tureen, and serve.

Turkey Vegetable Noodle Soup

Serves 6 to 8

2½ cups chicken broth
½ cup diced carrots
½ cup diced celery
1 onion, diced
Salt and pepper to taste
½ cup frozen peas
½ cup egg noodles
1 (8-ounce) can corn
1 (8-ounce) can whole tomatoes, drained
1½ cups diced cooked turkey
Chopped parsley, for garnish

1. Place all ingredients in large saucepan and bring to a boil. Reduce heat and simmer for 45 minutes.
2. Remove from heat and spoon into individual soup bowls. Sprinkle with chopped parsley, and serve.

Turkey and Pasta Soup

Serves 4

2 turkey wings, about
   1³/₄ pounds
6 cups water
1 teaspoon salt
1 bay leaf
5 peppercorns
1 teaspoon basil
³/₄ cup diced carrots
³/₄ cup broccoli florets
³/₄ cup leeks, white part only,
   cut into rings
³/₄ cup sliced mushrooms
¹/₄ cup butter
³/₄ cup spaghetti, broken into
   small pieces
2 teaspoons seasoned salt
2 tablespoons chopped parsley

1. Place turkey, water, salt, bay leaf, peppercorns, and basil in large pot and simmer for 45 minutes. Remove turkey wings from stock; discard skin and bones, and chop turkey meat into chunks. Strain broth, then return to pot and reheat.
2. Heat butter in frying pan. Add carrots, broccoli, leeks, and mushrooms; saute for 2 minutes, stirring frequently.
3. Bring stock to a boil. Add sauteed vegetables and pasta, stir, and cook for 5 minutes, or until pasta is just tender. Add turkey and seasoned salt; cook until heated thoroughly. Garnish with parsley, and serve.

Stracciatella

Serves 4

¹/₄ cup fine semolina
3 eggs, beaten
1 tablespoon chopped parsley
3 tablespoons grated Parmesan
   cheese
2 quarts beef stock
Salt to taste
Pinch of nutmeg

1. Combine semolina, eggs, parsley, and 2 tablespoons Parmesan cheese together; mix well. Stir in 1 cup cold beef stock, salt, and nutmeg.
2. Place remaining beef stock in large saucepan. Add egg-semolina mixture; cook over medium heat for 3 to 4 minutes, stirring constantly until thin egg shreds form. Sprinkle with remaining Parmesan cheese, and serve immediately.

Chinese Noodle Soup

Serves 6

2 tablespoons dried Chinese
   mushrooms
2 tablespoons sherry
2 tablespoons soy sauce
Salt and pepper to taste
Pinch of ground ginger
¹/₂ pound boneless pork,
   cut into thin strips
4 cups salted water
8 ounces transparent
   (cellophane) noodles
5 ounces bamboo shoots,
   drained and thinly sliced
2 quarts chicken broth
3 tablespoons vegetable oil
¹/₂ cup diced cooked chicken
5 ounces ham steak, diced
¹/₂ cup chopped watercress

1. Soak mushrooms in water to cover for 30 minutes; drain, slice, and set aside.
2. Combine sherry, soy sauce, salt, pepper, and ginger in mixing bowl. Add pork and let stand, covered, for 1 hour.
3. Bring salted water to a boil in large saucepan. Add noodles and cook for 10 minutes; drain and set aside. Add mushrooms, bamboo shoots, and noodles to chicken broth; simmer for 2 minutes.
4. Remove pork from soy sauce mixture; pat dry. Saute pork in vegetable oil for 2 minutes. Add pork, chicken, ham, and watercress to broth. Heat thoroughly, then spoon broth into individual soup bowls and serve.

Yogurt and Noodle Soup

Serves 4 to 6

3 cups unflavored yogurt
1 egg, beaten
3 cups chicken or beef broth
1 cup broad egg noodles,
   broken into small pieces
1 teaspoon salt
3 tablespoons butter
1 medium onion, finely chopped
1 tablespoon crushed dried mint

1. Combine yogurt and egg in saucepan. Bring almost to a boil, stirring constantly in one direction to prevent curdling. Stir in broth, noodles, and salt. Bring to a boil, then simmer for 10 minutes or until noodles are tender.
2. While soup simmers, melt butter in small frying pan. Add onion and saute until lightly browned. Stir in mint. Add onion mixture to soup, stir, and serve hot.

Winter Vegetable Soup with Pasta

Serves 4

1 tablespoon oil
1 large onion, chopped
1 small rutabaga, peeled and
   thickly sliced
1 cup sliced celery
1 cup sliced carrots
¹/₄ head white cabbage,
   shredded
4 cups hot beef broth
¹/₂ cup vermicelli
1 tablespoon chopped parsley
¹/₄ cup sour cream, optional

1. Heat oil in large saucepan. Add onions and saute until translucent. Add remaining vegetables and saute for 1 minute longer. Add beef broth and simmer, covered, for 20 minutes.
2. Add vermicelli, stir soup well, and cook for about 4 minutes, or until pasta is just tender. Serve each portion garnished with chopped parsley and 1 tablespoon sour cream, if desired.

Minestrone

Serves 6

1/2 pound dry white beans, soaked in water overnight
3 quarts salted water
4 teaspoons olive oil
1 onion, chopped
1 clove garlic, peeled and minced
1 leek, diced
1 tablespoon chopped parsley
2 teaspoons basil
1 teaspoon oregano
1 tablespoon tomato paste
2 small tomatoes, skinned and chopped or 1 (28-ounce) can crushed tomatoes, undrained
3 stalks celery, chopped
2 carrots, sliced
2 potatoes, diced
1 small turnip, peeled and diced
1 medium zucchini, diced
1/2 cup shredded cabbage
6 cups water
Salt and pepper to taste
4 ounces rotelle or tubular pasta
1/2 cup grated Parmesan cheese

1. Drain beans and boil them in salted water for 1 hour, until tender; drain and set aside.
2. Heat olive oil in large, heavy pot. Add onion, garlic, and leek; saute for 5 minutes. Add parsley, basil, oregano, and tomato paste thinned with a little water; cook for 5 minutes more. Add tomatoes, celery, carrots, potatoes, turnip, zucchini, cabbage, water, salt, and pepper; cook over low heat for 45 minutes. Add beans.
2. Add rotelle or tubular pasta to mixture; cook for 15 minutes, or until tender. Spoon into soup bowls, and serve sprinkled with grated Parmesan cheese.

Genoese Vegetable Soup

Serves 4

2 tablespoons olive oil
2 medium onions, finely chopped
1 cup finely chopped zucchini
1/2 cup finely chopped carrots
3/4 cup string beans, broken into small pieces
6 cups vegetable broth
Salt and pepper to taste
3 cloves garlic, finely chopped
1 cup rice-shaped pasta (orzo)
1/4 cup chopped fresh basil leaves
1/4 cup chopped parsley
1 tablespoon grated Pecorino or Parmesan cheese

1. Heat olive oil in saucepan. Add onions and saute until translucent. Add zucchini, carrots, and string beans; saute for 10 minutes longer, stirring frequently.
2. Add vegetable broth and simmer for 15 minutes. Season with salt and pepper. Add garlic and simmer for 2 minutes longer; remove garlic from soup.
3. Add pasta and simmer for 2 or 3 minutes, until pasta is just tender. To serve, garnish soup with fresh basil and parsley; sprinkle with grated cheese.

Neapolitan Pasta Soup

Serves 4

1/2 cup butter beans
8 cups water
1 bay leaf
4 teaspoons powdered vegetable bouillon
1/2 cup whole-wheat noodles
1 teaspoon salt
1 clove garlic, peeled and finely chopped
6 tablespoons olive oil
2 1/4 cups diced tomatoes, drained if canned
1/2 teaspoon oregano
Pinch of cayenne pepper

1. Soak beans in 4 cups water overnight. Drain, then place beans in large saucepan with 4 cups fresh water, bay leaf, and 2 teaspoons vegetable bouillon powder. Simmer, covered, for 45 minutes.
2. Cook noodles in boiling, salted water until just tender, according to package directions; drain and set aside.
3. In frying pan, saute garlic in olive oil until transparent. Add tomato, oregano, and cayenne pepper; simmer, stirring constantly, for 5 minutes. Pour tomato mixture into bean soup. Add noodles.
4. Reheat soup briefly. Add remaining vegetable bouillon powder, stirring well. Serve hot.

Pasta Shell Vegetable Soup

Serves 4

2 1/2 cups water
1 cup canned tomatoes, drained and cut into pieces
2 cups cabbage, shredded
1 onion, sliced
1 clove garlic, peeled and minced
1/2 cup uncooked small pasta shells
1 (10-ounce) can condensed beef broth
1 (10-ounce) can condensed vegetable soup
1/2 teaspoon caraway seed
2 tablespoons Parmesan cheese

1. Combine all ingredients, except Parmesan cheese, in large saucepan. Bring to a boil. Reduce heat and simmer, stirring occasionally, for 30 minutes, or until vegetables and pasta are tender.
2. Sprinkle soup with grated Parmesan cheese, and serve.

Neapolitan Minestrone

Serves 6

1 1/2 pounds beef shanks
1 onion, quartered
2 celery stalks, chopped
1 carrot, chopped
1 turnip, chopped
1 potato, peeled and chopped
1 tablespoon chopped parsley
1 small bay leaf
2 whole peppercorns
1 clove

1½ teaspoons salt
6 cups water
¼ pound ham, cut into thin
strips
2 ounces penne or elbow
macaroni
3 tablespoons tomato paste
1 teaspoon dried chervil
¼ cup grated Parmesan cheese

1. Place beef shanks, onion, celery, carrot, turnip, potato, parsley, bay leaf, peppercorns, clove, and salt in large Dutch oven. Add water and bring to a boil; skim as needed. Reduce heat to low, cover, and simmer for 1½ to 2 hours. Remove meat and let cool; dice meat. Strain broth and skim off fat; return broth to pot.
2. Cook penne or macaroni in boiling, salted water until tender, following package directions; drain.
3. Bring broth to a boil. Combine tomato paste with 1 cup hot broth, stirring until well mixed. Add tomato mixture to broth in pot, along with diced beef and ham. Cover and simmer for 15 minutes.
4. Add pasta and chervil to soup and cook until heated thoroughly. Sprinkle with Parmesan cheese, and serve.

Roman-Style Vegetable Soup

Serves 4 to 6

½ cup finely chopped salt pork
1 large onion, diced
1 clove garlic, peeled
3 carrots, peeled and diced
2 stalks celery, sliced
1 parsnip, peeled and diced
½ cup chopped parsley
2 large tomatoes, chopped
4 cups beef broth
1 (16-ounce) can red kidney
beans, drained
1 teaspoon basil
Salt and pepper to taste
1½ cups broad egg noodles
Grated Parmesan cheese

1. Saute salt pork in large pan over moderate heat to render fat. Add onion and garlic; saute until onion is translucent. Add carrots, celery, parsnip, parsley, and tomatoes, stirring well. Add beef broth, beans, basil, salt, and pepper. Bring to a boil, then cover and cook over low heat for 1 hour.
2. Add noodles and simmer for 15 minutes, or until noodles are tender. Sprinkle soup with grated Parmesan cheese, and serve.

Hearty Vegetable Soup

Serves 4

2 tablespoons oil
2 slices bacon, chopped
3 carrots, peeled and chopped
2 onions, chopped
3 tomatoes, skinned and chopped
2 stalks celery, chopped
½ small head cabbage, shredded
5 cups water or stock
Salt and pepper to taste
1 bay leaf
½ cup elbow macaroni
Chopped parsley
Grated Parmesan cheese

1. Heat oil in large saucepan. Add chopped bacon and vegetables; saute for 5 minutes. Add water or stock, salt, pepper, and bay leaf. Cover and simmer for 30 minutes.
2. Add macaroni to soup and simmer for 20 minutes longer, or until macaroni is tender. Remove bay leaf. Adjust seasoning and sprinkle with parsley. Serve grated cheese separately.

Chinese Vegetable Soup with Noodles

Serves 4 to 6

1 tablespoon oil
1 small onion, chopped
¼ head savoy cabbage or green
cabbage, sliced
1 leek, white part only, sliced
2 ounces mushrooms, sliced

1 celery stalk, sliced
5 cups beef broth
2 ounces frozen peas
4 ounces thin egg noodles
Salt and pepper to taste
1 tablespoon soy sauce
3 tablespoons dry sherry

1. Heat oil in large saucepan. Add onion and saute until golden. Add sliced vegetables and saute for 5 minutes. Add broth and bring to a boil. Add peas and noodles, then simmer for 15 minutes.
2. Season soup with salt, pepper, soy sauce, and sherry. Serve immediately.

Zucchini and Pasta Soup

Serves 4

¼ cup olive oil
1 onion, chopped
2¼ cups diced zucchini
2 ripe tomatoes, skinned and
chopped
6 cups hot beef broth
¾ cup spaghetti, broken into
small pieces
¼ cup chopped fresh basil leaves
or 1 teaspoon dried basil
¼ cup chopped parsley
Salt and pepper to taste
2 tablespoons grated Pecorino or
Parmesan cheese

1. Heat oil in large saucepan. Add onion and saute until translucent. Add zucchini and tomatoes; saute, stirring constantly, for 2 minutes longer. Add beef broth and bring to a boil.
2. Add pasta to soup, stir once, and cook for 6 minutes, or until just tender.
3. Stir herbs into soup and season with salt and pepper. Sprinkle with grated cheese just before serving.

Vegetable-Noodle Soup with Garlic

Serves 6 to 8

1/4 cup butter
1 large onion, sliced
3 potatoes, sliced
2 large ripe tomatoes, skinned and chopped
6 to 7 cups beef stock
Chopped parsley
1/8 teaspoon oregano
Salt and pepper to taste
1 cup sliced green beans
1/4 cup vermicelli, broken into small pieces
2 to 3 cloves garlic, peeled and crushed
3 sprigs fresh basil or 2 teaspoons dried basil
2 slices tomatoes, broiled
Grated Parmesan cheese

1. Melt butter in large saucepan. Add onion and potatoes; saute gently for 5 to 6 minutes, without browning. Add tomatoes and saute for 1 minute longer. Add stock and bring to a boil. Add chopped parsley and oregano, salt, pepper, beans, and vermicelli. Cook over low heat for about 10 minutes, or until beans and noodles are tender.
2. Meanwhile, prepare garlic paste by mixing crushed garlic with basil and broiled tomato slices. Pound all together to make smooth paste, adding a little soup to moisten.
3. Just before serving, add garlic paste to soup and mix well. Serve hot, with grated cheese in separate dish.

Pasta Tomato Soup

Serves 4

4 cups water
2 vegetable bouillon cubes
4 large ripe tomatoes, skinned
1 teaspoon oil
1/2 cup vermicelli
3 eggs, separated
2 teaspoons lemon juice
2 tablespoons chopped parsley or fresh basil

1. Place water in large saucepan and bring to a boil. Add bouillon cubes, stirring until dissolved. Sieve or puree tomatoes in food processor or blender; add tomato puree and oil to stock.
2. Bring soup to a boil, then add vermicelli and cook about 4 minutes, until noodles are just tender. Remove soup from heat, cover, and keep warm.
3. Beat egg whites with lemon juice until stiff. Whisk yolks into whites, one at a time. Gradually stir 1/2 cup hot soup into egg mixture. Then blend egg mixture into remaining soup.
4. Serve soup hot, garnished with chopped parsley or basil.

Lo-Mein Soup

Serves 4 to 6

8 cups water
1 teaspoon salt
1 cup fresh Chinese noodles
2 tablespoons sesame oil
1/2 pound boneless pork, cut into thin strips
3 scallions, shredded
1 1/4 cups Chinese cabbage leaves, shredded
4 cups hot chicken broth
1/8 teaspoon salt
1/8 teaspoon pepper

1. Place water and salt in large saucepan and bring to a boil. Add noodles and boil for about 8 minutes, or until noodles are tender; drain and set noodles aside.
2. Heat oil in frying pan. Add pork strips and saute until browned. Add scallions and Chinese cabbage; saute for 2 minutes longer. Add pork-vegetable mixture and noodles to chicken broth. Season with salt and pepper. Serve in warmed soup bowls.

Herb Soup with Pasta

Serves 4

4 cups chicken broth
1/2 cup rotelle
1/2 cup peas
1/2 head leaf lettuce, cut into thin strips
1/4 cup finely chopped fresh chives
1/4 cup finely chopped fresh dill
1/4 cup finely chopped parsley
1 teaspoon butter
Salt and pepper to taste
Pinch of freshly grated nutmeg
Fresh basil leaves, for garnish

1. Bring chicken broth to a boil in large saucepan. Add pasta and peas. Cook, partially covered, over moderate heat until pasta is tender.
2. Add lettuce strips, chopped herbs, and butter to soup; heat briefly. Season with salt, pepper, and nutmeg. Pour soup into individual soup bowls. Sprinkle with basil and serve at once.

Fettuccine and Chickpea Soup

Serves 4

2 cups dried chickpeas
3 cloves garlic, peeled
2 sprigs fresh rosemary or 1 teaspoon dried rosemary
3 ounces lean bacon, chopped
4 cups clear beef bouillon
3/4 cup fettuccine, broken into small pieces
Salt and pepper to taste
1/4 cup grated Parmesan cheese

1. Cover chickpeas with lukewarm water and let soak for 12 hours.
2. Drain, then place in saucepan with fresh salted water to cover; bring to a boil. Add 1 garlic clove and 1 sprig rosemary (or 1/4 teaspoon dried rosemary); cover and cook over moderate heat for 1 1/2 hours. Strain cooked chickpeas, reserving cooking liquid. Cover chickpeas and keep warm; discard rosemary sprig and garlic.

3. Finely chop remaining garlic and rosemary. Add reserved cooking liquid to beef bouillon to make 6 cups, and bring to a boil. Add chopped rosemary, garlic, and bacon. Add fettuccine and cook until just tender according to package directions.

4. Season soup with salt and pepper. Add chickpeas to soup and simmer until hot but not boiling. Serve with grated Parmesan cheese.

Pasta Soup with Basil

Serves 4

1½ cups diced, peeled potatoes
6 cups vegetable broth
2 tomatoes, skinned and diced
¾ cup spaghetti, broken into
    small pieces
½ tablespoon virgin olive oil
Salt and white pepper to taste
2 tablespoons grated Parmesan
    cheese
½ cup chopped fresh basil
    leaves

1. Simmer potatoes in vegetable broth for about 25 minutes, adding tomatoes for last 10 minutes of cooking time. Add spaghetti and simmer for 5 minutes, until spaghetti is just cooked but not too soft.

2. Stir olive oil into soup. Season with salt and pepper. Simmer soup until heated thoroughly.

3. Spoon soup into 4 soup bowls. Divide basil leaves among the 4 bowls. Sprinkle with grated Parmesan cheese, and serve.

Tomato Soup with Ricotta Gnocchi

Serves 4

2 tablespoons butter
3 tablespoons plus 1 teaspoon
    whole-wheat flour
2 tomatoes, skinned and chopped
4 cups hot vegetable broth
Salt and pepper to taste

2 sprigs fresh thyme or
    ½ teaspoon dried thyme
1 sprig rosemary or ¼ teaspoon
    dried rosemary
2 hard-boiled eggs, shelled and
    mashed
¼ cup butter
1 egg, lightly beaten
2 tablespoons ricotta cheese
Pinch of nutmeg

1. Melt butter in large saucepan. Add flour and cook, stirring constantly, until golden. Add tomatoes and vegetables. Season with salt, pepper, thyme, and rosemary; simmer for 10 minutes.

2. To make gnocchi, combine mashed hard-boiled eggs, butter, beaten egg, ricotta, and 3 tablespoons flour to form smooth, pliable, but firm dough. Season with pinch of salt and nutmeg.

3. Dip teaspoon in hot water and use to shape gnocchi into 1-inch balls; press each ball in with thumb. Add gnocchi to simmering soup and cook until they rise to the surface. Spoon some soup and gnocchi into each soup bowl, and serve.

Kreplach Soup

Serves 4

2 eggs
½ teaspoon salt
1 tablespoon oil
¾ to 1 cup flour, sifted
1 cup finely minced cooked
    chicken
2 tablespoons chopped parsley
1 small onion, peeled and finely
    chopped
1 tablespoon melted butter
½ teaspoon salt
Pinch of pepper
Pinch of powdered ginger
4 cups chicken broth

1. Combine eggs with salt and oil. Gradually add enough flour to make firm dough.

2. Combine chicken and 1 tablespoon chopped parsley. Add onion, butter, salt, pepper, and ginger.

3. Roll out dough to ⅛ inch thick and cut into 2-inch squares. Place meat filling in center of each square. Fold each square in half diagonally, and use a fork to crimp edges together firmly. Leave stuffed pasta to dry on floured cloth for 1 hour.

4. Bring chicken broth to a boil in large saucepan. Add filled pasta and cook gently for 20 minutes. Serve soup garnished with remaining chopped parsley.

Noodles in Broth

Serves 4 to 6

2 cloves garlic, peeled and
    thinly sliced
1 onion, thinly sliced
1 tablespoon oil
7 cups water
2 slices fresh ginger, peeled
1 pound chicken breast
Salt and pepper to taste
8 ounces egg noodles
4 cabbage leaves, shredded
1 cup bean sprouts, cleaned
    and drained
2 scallions, cut into ½-inch
    pieces
Celery leaves, for garnish

1. Saute garlic and onion in oil in bottom of deep saucepan. Add water, ginger, chicken, salt, and pepper. Bring to a boil, then simmer for 20 minutes, or until chicken is tender. Remove chicken and let cool. Remove skin and bones, and cut chicken meat into strips; set aside.

2. Cook noodles in boiling, salted water until just tender; drain and set aside.

3. Add cabbage leaves, bean sprouts, and scallions to stock; simmer for 2 minutes. Add chicken strips and simmer until chicken is hot. Adjust seasoning.

4. Divide noodles into individual soup bowls. Fill each bowl with piping hot soup and garnish with celery leaves. Serve at once.

Wonton Soup

Serves 6

1³/₄ cups flour
1 egg, beaten
¹/₂ cup water
3 teaspoons salt
2 scallions, finely chopped
¹/₂ cup canned bamboo shoots, drained and finely chopped
¹/₄ pound boneless pork, finely chopped
¹/₄ pound boneless chicken breast, finely chopped
1 tablespoon soy sauce
1 tablespoon sake (rice wine) or dry sherry
¹/₈ teaspoon pepper
1 egg white, beaten with 1 tablespoon water
3 quarts water
4 cups chicken broth
¹/₄ cup chopped watercress

1. Sift flour into mixing bowl. Add egg, water, and 1 teaspoon salt; mix to form dough. Knead dough until smooth, then cover and set aside to rest for 1 hour.
2. Mix half the scallions, bamboo shoots, pork, chicken, soy sauce, sake, and pepper together well to form smooth filling.
3. Roll dough out thinly onto floured board and cut out circles 3 inches in diameter. Place filling in center of each circle. Paint edges of each circle with egg white mixture. Fold each circle in half, and press edges together with fork.
4. Bring water and 2 teaspoons salt to a boil in large pot. Add wontons and cook for 5 minutes. Remove wontons from pot, drain in colander, and set aside.
5. Heat chicken broth in large saucepan. Divide wontons and remaining scallions among 6 soup bowls. Pour chicken stock on top, and garnish with watercress.

Nabeyaki-Udon Soup

Serves 4

4 cups chicken broth
²/₃ cup Udon noodles (Japanese whole-wheat pasta) or thin spaghetti
¹/₂ pound boneless chicken breast, cut into thin strips
1 cup sliced mushrooms
3 scallions, sliced
4 eggs
2 tablespoons soy sauce
¹/₂ cup finely chopped parsley

1. Bring chicken broth to a boil in large saucepan. Add noodles and cook for about 3 minutes, until noodles are half-cooked. Add chicken, mushrooms, and scallions; cook for 1 minute longer.
2. Break eggs, one by one, into a cup; slide each egg into gently simmering soup and cook for 3 minutes. Carefully remove eggs with slotted spoon and place one in each soup bowl.
3. Stir soy sauce and parsley into soup. Pour soup over eggs, and serve immediately.

Takko Mein Soup

Serves 4

¹/₂ cup warm water
6 dried Chinese mushrooms
8 cups water
1 teaspoon salt
1 teaspoon oil
1 cup fresh Chinese noodles
4 cups chicken broth
2 ounces lean uncooked ham, cut into thin strips
1¹/₄ cups chopped spinach leaves
1 (8-ounce) can oysters, undrained
1¹/₄-inch piece fresh ginger, peeled and finely grated
Salt to taste

1. Pour warm water over dried mushrooms and leave to soak for 30 minutes. Drain and thinly slice mushrooms.
2. Place water, salt, and oil in large pot and bring to a boil. Add noodles and cook for 8 minutes; drain noodles and cover to keep warm.
3. Bring chicken broth to a boil in large saucepan. Add ham strips and simmer for 5 minutes. Stir in spinach, drained mushrooms, and oysters with can liquid. Simmer for 2 minutes. Add noodles and grated ginger; cook until heated thoroughly. Season with salt, and serve.

Cold Noodle Soup

Serves 4 to 6

1 pound whole-wheat noodles
¹/₂ pound cooked beef brisket or top round, cut into thin strips
4 cups chicken stock
8 black peppercorns
2-inch piece fresh ginger, peeled
1 teaspoon salt
1 teaspoon soy sauce
4 dried chilies
1 cucumber, sliced
1 large, hard pear, peeled, cored, and thinly sliced
3 hard-boiled eggs, shelled and halved lengthwise
Prepared mustard and vinegar to taste

1. Cook noodles in boiling salted water following package directions; drain and set aside to cool.
2. Place all ingredients except noodles in large saucepan. Bring to a boil, then reduce heat and simmer for 5 minutes. Remove from heat and refrigerate until chilled. Remove peppercorns, ginger, and chilies.
3. Divide noodles among individual soup bowls. Divide cucumber and pear slices among the bowls as well, alternating slices in layers on top of noodles. Place half an egg on top of each bowl. Spoon soup on top, add mustard and vinegar to taste, and serve cold.

Tortellini Salad

Serves 4

8 ounces cheese-filled
  tortellini
1 red pepper, seeded and
  chopped
1 onion, chopped
2 stalks celery, chopped
1/4 cup sliced pitted black
  olives
1/4 cup mayonnaise
1 tablespoon lemon juice
2 dashes Tabasco sauce
Lettuce
Parsley sprigs, for garnish

1. Cook tortellini in boiling, salted water following package directions; drain.
2. Combine red pepper, onion, celery, and olives; add mixture to tortellini and toss well.
3. Combine mayonnaise, lemon juice, and Tabasco sauce. Add dressing to pasta salad and toss gently until well coated. Refrigerate until well chilled.
4. To serve, spoon tortellini salad onto bed of lettuce. Garnish with parsley sprigs.

Green Fettuccine Salad

Serves 4

1 pound green fettuccine
  noodles, cooked, drained,
  and chilled
3 tablespoons vinaigrette
  dressing

1 cup chopped cooked asparagus
6 medium-size mushrooms,
  thinly sliced
6 cherry tomatoes, sliced
2 tablespoons chopped parsley
Pinch of fresh basil
4 large cabbage leaves

1. Combine noodles, vinaigrette dressing, asparagus, mushrooms, tomatoes, parsley, and basil. Refrigerate for 15 minutes.
2. Spoon onto cabbage leaves, and serve.

Amsterdam Pasta Salad

Serves 4

8 ounces rigatoni
4 hard-boiled eggs, shelled and
  quartered
6 small tomatoes, sliced
2 small cucumbers, sliced
1 red pepper, seeded and cut into
  thin strips
1/2 pound corned beef, sliced
2 tablespoons vinegar
3 tablespoons oil
Salt and pepper to taste
Pinch of sugar
Pinch of garlic powder
1/2 cup chopped parsley

1. Cook pasta in boiling, salted water until just tender, following package directions; drain.
2. Mix pasta, eggs, vegetables, and corned beef together in bowl.
3. Combine vinegar, oil, salt, pepper, sugar, and garlic powder to form dressing. Add dressing to pasta salad and toss well. Cover and let sit at room temperature for 30 minutes. Sprinkle parsley, and serve.

Colorful Pasta Salad

Serves 4

8 ounces tri-colored pasta
  twists
2 cups low-fat plain yogurt
3 tablespoons lemon juice
2 teaspoons sugar
Pinch of salt
1 cup whipping cream
1 3/4 cups Emmenthaler cheese,
  rind removed and cut into
  thin strips
1/3 cup chopped walnuts
1 1/4 cups seedless red grapes,
  halved
1 pear, sliced
1 red apple, sliced
1/2 head endive

1. Cook pasta in boiling, salted water until just tender, following package directions; drain.
2. Mix yogurt, lemon juice, sugar, and a pinch of salt together. Whip cream until stiff and stir into yogurt mixture.
3. Combine cheese, walnuts, fruits, pasta, and yogurt mixture in bowl. Separate endive into leaves, then tear into pieces. Arrange endive pieces on 4 salad plates. Spoon pasta salad on top, and serve.

Ellen's
Pasta Twists Salad

Serves 4

8 ounces tri-colored pasta twists
³/₄ cup frozen broccoli
³/₄ cup frozen carrots
³/₄ cup frozen cauliflower
1¹/₂ cups diced Cheddar cheese
²/₃ cup bottled Parmesan cheese
   dressing
¹/₂ teaspoon basil
Salt and pepper to taste

1. Cook pasta and frozen vegetables in boiling, salted water for about 7 minutes, or until pasta and vegetables are just tender; drain and let cool.
2. Combine diced cheese, salad dressing, basil, salt, and pepper. Add pasta and vegetables; toss well. Cover and refrigerate, or serve at once.

Green
Spaghetti Salad

Serves 8

1 pound green spaghetti, broken
   into 4-inch long pieces
¹/₂ cup mixed fresh parsley and
   chervil
¹/₂ cup tarragon vinegar
¹/₂ cup olive oil
4 shallots, peeled and chopped
4 cloves garlic, peeled and
   chopped
¹/₄ pound freshly grated
   Parmesan cheese
¹/₂ teaspoon white pepper
¹/₄ cup pine nuts

1. Cook spaghetti in boiling, salted water until just tender, following package directions; drain.
2. Remove tough stems from fresh herbs. Puree herbs, vinegar, and oil together in blender or food processor. Add shallots and garlic to pureed herb mixture. Add grated cheese and pepper.
3. Toss pasta with pureed mixture. Add pine nuts; mix well. Cover and refrigerate for 1 hour before serving.

Roman Pasta Salad

Serves 4

8 ounces rigatoni
2 cups fresh green beans, cut
   into pieces
2 carrots, sliced
2 cups green peas
3 tomatoes, cut into eighths
¹/₄ pound Italian salami, thinly
   sliced
2 tablespoons halved pitted
   green olives
2 tablespoons halved pitted
   black olives
6 anchovies, chopped
2 tablespoons capers
3 tablespoons vinegar
¹/₄ cup oil
Salt and pepper to taste
Pinch of sugar
3 tablespoons chopped chives

1. Cook pasta in boiling, salted water until just tender, following package directions; drain and set aside.
2. Boil green beans in salted water for 12 minutes; add carrots and peas for last 5 minutes of cooking time; drain.
3. Mix pasta, vegetables, tomatoes, salami, and olives together. Combine anchovies, capers, vinegar, oil, salt, pepper, and sugar. Add dressing to pasta mixture and toss well. Add chives, cover, and let stand for 1 hour before serving.

Pesto Salad

Serves 4

8 ounces small pasta shells
2 cups fresh basil leaves
1 cup fresh parsley
2 tablespoons pine nuts
2 cloves garlic, peeled
1 teaspoon salt
¹/₃ cup extra-virgin olive oil
¹/₂ cup freshly grated Parmesan
   cheese
1. Cook pasta in boiling, salted water until just tender, following package directions; drain.
2. Place basil, parsley, pine nuts,

garlic, salt, and oil in food processor or blender; process until smooth. Transfer to mixing bowl and blend in Parmesan cheese. Refrigerate until ready to serve.
3. Toss pasta with basil mixture, and serve.

Chickpea
and Pasta Salad

Serves 4

1 cup chickpeas
1 quart cold water
2 teaspoons vegetable broth
¹/₂ bay leaf
8 ounces pasta twists
1³/₄ cups cottage cheese
1 cup heavy whipping cream
Salt to taste
¹/₄ teaspoon curry powder
2 tablespoons lemon juice
2 cans mandarin oranges,
   drained
1¹/₄ cups peeled roasted
   almonds, cut into thin
   pieces

1. Soak chickpeas overnight in cold water. The next day, place chickpeas and soaking liquid, vegetable broth, and bay leaf in large saucepan; simmer for 40 minutes; drain.
2. Cook pasta in boiling, salted water until just tender, following package directions; drain.
3. Mix cottage cheese, cream, salt, curry powder, and lemon juice together in large bowl. Add remaining ingredients, mix well, and serve.

Danish Pasta Salad

Serves 4

8 ounces pasta bow ties
³/₄ cup frozen peas
³/₄ cup frozen carrots
1³/₄ cups mayonnaise
3 tablespoons lemon juice
2 tablespoons pineapple juice
3 tablespoons milk
¹/₂ teaspoon curry powder

Salt and pepper to taste
½ cup diced pineapple
1 large dill gherkin, diced
1¼ cups cooked ham, fat removed

1. Cook pasta in boiling, salted water until tender, following package directions; drain.
2. Boil peas and carrots in ¼ cup water for 4 minutes; drain and cool.
3. Mix mayonnaise, lemon juice, pineapple juice, milk, curry powder, salt, and pepper together; toss pasta with mixture. Add peas, carrots, diced pineapple, pickle, and ham together. Cover and refrigerate for 1 hour. Check seasoning before serving.

Pasta Primavera Salad

Serves 8 to 10

1 pound pasta shells
¾ cup virgin olive oil
2 tablespoons red wine vinegar
2 cloves garlic, peeled and crushed
3 tablespoons minced parsley
2 cups broccoli florets, cooked until crisp-tender and chilled
4 scallions, finely minced
1 cup finely diced Mozzarella cheese
1 large pimento, sliced
Salt and pepper to taste
Cherry tomatoes, halved, for garnish

1. Cook pasta in boiling, salted water until just tender, following package directions; drain.
2. Combine olive oil, vinegar, and garlic in small jar; shake well to blend. Set aside.
3. In large bowl or serving dish, combine parsley, cooked broccoli, scallions, pasta, cheese, and pimento. Toss with dressing until well blended. Season with salt and pepper. Refrigerate for at least 3 hours to blend flavors.
4. To serve, adjust seasonings and garnish with cherry tomatoes.

Pasta Salad with Peas and Corn

Serves 8

1 pound penne
½ cup chopped parsley
½ cup chopped fresh chives or basil
4 teaspoons vinegar
Salt and pepper to taste
½ teaspoon paprika
Pinch of garlic powder
5 tablespoons oil
2¼ cup cooked peas
1 red pepper, seeded and diced
½ pound cooked ham, diced
2¼ cups canned sweet corn, drained
2 hard-boiled eggs, shelled and cut into eighths
¼ cup sliced radishes

1. Cook penne in boiling, salted water until just tender, following package directions; drain.
2. Set aside 1 tablespoon of chopped herbs, then mix remaining herbs with vinegar, salt, pepper, paprika, garlic powder, and oil.
3. In large salad bowl, mix pasta, peas, diced red pepper, ham, corn, and half the radishes together; add dressing, tossing well. Place eggs and remaining radish slices on top. Sprinkle with reserved tablespoon of chopped herbs, and serve.

Pasta and Broccoli Salad

Serves 4

4 ounces spaghetti
1¼ cups broccoli, cut into 1¼-inch pieces
4 cups salted water
1 zucchini, cut into pieces
2 tomatoes, cut into pieces
2 hard-boiled eggs, shelled and finely chopped
¼ cup chopped walnuts
1 cup heavy whipping cream
1 tablespoon lemon juice
Salt and pepper to taste
1 tablespoon chives

1. Cook pasta and broccoli in boiling, salted water for 10 minutes, or until both are just tender; drain.
2. Mix pasta and broccoli, zucchini, tomatoes, eggs, and nuts together. Combine cream, lemon juice, salt, and pepper; toss with pasta-broccoli salad.
3. Sprinkle salad with chives and let stand for 5 minutes. Add more lemon juice, salt, and pepper to taste, if desired; serve.

Hot Pasta Salad

Serves 4

8 ounces thin spaghetti
1 quart water
1 teaspoon salt
1¼ cups broccoli
Pinch of nutmeg
1 clove garlic, peeled and finely chopped
6 tablespoons olive oil
¼ cup vinegar
¾ cup diced Pecorino cheese or Parmesan cheese

1. Cook spaghetti in boiling, salted water until just tender, following package directions; drain.
2. Place remaining quart water and 1 teaspoon salt in separate saucepan and bring to a boil. Boil broccoli for 2 minutes; drain and sprinkle with nutmeg.
3. Saute garlic in 1 tablespoon olive oil for 30 seconds; remove from heat and add vinegar and remaining oil. Mix all ingredients together in salad bowl. Serve warm.

Pasta and Bacon Salad

Serves 4

8 ounces whole-wheat or
   regular pasta twists
1/2 pound lean bacon
1 tablespoon oil
1 onion, diced
2 to 4 tablespoons vinegar
Pinch of cayenne pepper
1 small endive, cut into thin
   strips
1/2 cup chopped fresh chives
   or 1 tablespoon dried chives

1. Cook pasta in boiling, salted water until just tender, following package directions; drain.
2. Cook bacon until crisp; drain on paper towels. Heat oil in saucepan. Add onion and saute until translucent. Remove from heat; add vinegar and cayenne pepper.
3. Mix pasta, endive, chives, and warm dressing together in salad bowl. Sprinkle with crisp bacon, and serve at once.

Gnocchi Salad
with Cream and Herbs

Serves 4

1 cup gnocchi
5 hard-boiled eggs, shelled and
   halved
1/2 cup oil
1 tablespoon chopped fresh dill
   or 1 teaspoon dried dill
1 tablespoon chopped parsley
1 teaspoon cardamom
1 tablespoon prepared mustard
1/4 cup low-fat plain yogurt
1 clove garlic, peeled and finely
   chopped
Salt and pepper to taste
2 1/4 cups sliced red peppers
1 (7-ounce) can tuna fish,
   drained and flaked
2 small onions, cut into rings
1/2 cup pitted green olives

1. Cook gnocchi in boiling, salted water following package directions; drain.
2. Remove yolks from eggs and mix whites with oil. Combine egg yolks, herbs, mustard, yogurt, and garlic. Season with salt and pepper.
3. In salad bowl, combine egg white mixture, yogurt dressing, pasta, red peppers, tuna fish, onion rings, and olives. Refrigerate for 2 hours before serving.

Tagliatelle Verde Salad

Serves 4

8 ounces green tagliatelle or
   other green pasta
8 tablespoons olive oil
1 1/4 cups thinly sliced zucchini
Salt and pepper to taste
3 ounces lean bacon, diced
1 clove garlic, peeled and
   crushed
1/4 cup vinegar
1 tablespoon capers
3 tablespoons chopped parsley
1 tablespoon chopped fresh basil
   or 1 teaspoon dried basil
Pinch of sugar
1 tablespoon grated Parmesan
   cheese
2 1/4 cups cooked asparagus, cut
   into 3/4-inch long pieces

1. Cook tagliatelle in boiling, salted water until just tender, following package directions; drain.
2. Heat 2 tablespoons oil in small frying pan; saute zucchini for 5 minutes. Season with salt and pepper. Remove from pan and set aside to cool.
3. Heat 1 tablespoon oil in frying pan. Cook bacon until crisp; drain on paper towels.
4. Mix garlic, vinegar, capers, parsley, basil, sugar, and Parmesan cheese together; season with salt and pepper. Add remaining oil, zucchini, asparagus, pasta, and bacon. Let stand for 1 hour before serving.

Pasta Salad with Spring Vegetables

Serves 6

8 ounces pasta twists
1/4 cup vinegar
Salt and pepper to taste
Pinch of curry powder
1 small onion, grated
1 clove garlic, peeled and
   crushed
1/4 cup oil
1 small cucumber, peeled and
   sliced
1 green pepper, seeded and
   sliced
2 tomatoes, cut into eighths
1 kohlrabi, peeled and cut
   into thin strips
1/2 pound cooked beef sausage,
   diced
1/2 cup chopped parsley
Watercress, for garnish

1. Cook pasta in boiling, salted water until just tender, following package directions; drain.
2. Mix vinegar, salt, pepper, and curry together. Add grated onion, crushed garlic, and oil. Combine pasta, cucumber, green pepper, tomatoes, kohlrabi, and sausage in salad bowl. Add oil-vinegar mixture; toss well. Sprinkle with chopped parsley.
3. Serve salad garnished with watercress sprigs.

Rigatoni Salad

Serves 4

8 ounces rigatoni
1/4 cup chopped fresh dill or
   1 teaspoon dried dill
Juice of 1/2 lemon
1 tablespoon apple juice
1 cucumber, peeled and diced
1/2 cup crumbled Pecorino cheese
   or grated Parmesan cheese
5 fresh mint leaves, chopped
1 cup plain yogurt
1 tablespoon mayonnaise
2 tablespoons sesame seeds

1. Cook rigatoni in boiling, salted water until just tender, following package directions; drain.

2. Combine dill, lemon juice, and apple juice. Mix pasta, cucumber, cheese, and mint together; toss with lemon juice mixture and let stand for 30 minutes.

3. Cook sesame seeds in dry frying pan until golden brown, stirring occasionally. Sprinkle on top of salad just before serving.

Vegetable Noodle Salad

Serves 4

1/2 pound elbow macaroni
1/2 pound green beans, cut into small pieces
1/2 pound carrots, peeled and diced
3 tablespoons mayonnaise
1 cup sour cream
3 tablespoons fruit-based vinegar
Salt and pepper to taste
Pinch of sugar
1/2 cup chopped parsley
1 cup cooked peas
3 tomatoes, cut into eighths
2 small zucchini, sliced
1/4 cup chopped fresh chives, optional

1. Cook pasta in boiling, salted water until just tender, following package directions; drain.

2. Place green beans and carrots in saucepan in 1 cup boiling salted water and cook for 15 minutes; drain.

3. Blend mayonnaise, sour cream, vinegar, salt, pepper, sugar, and parsley together. Combine noodles, green beans, carrots, peas, tomatoes, and zucchini; toss with mayonnaise dressing. Cover and refrigerate for 30 minutes. Sprinkle with chopped chives before serving, if desired.

Pasta Salad with Green Beans

Serves 4

8 ounces penne
1 1/4 cups string beans, cut into 1 1/2-inch pieces
1 onion, finely chopped
2 tablespoons mayonnaise
1 cup sour cream
2 tablespoons vinegar
1/2 cup chopped parsley
1/4 pound cooked beef sausage, sliced
10 pimento-stuffed green olives, sliced
Salt and pepper to taste

1. Cook pasta in boiling, salted water until tender, following package directions; drain.

2. Boil green beans in salted water for 15 minutes; drain, reserving 3 tablespoons of cooking liquid. Set beans aside to cool.

3. Mix onion, mayonnaise, sour cream, vinegar, reserved cooking liquid, and parsley together. Combine pasta, green beans, sausage, and olives, then toss with sour cream mixture. Season with salt and pepper, and serve.

Vegetarian Pasta Salad

Serves 4

2 1/2 quarts water
1 teaspoon salt
8 ounces green tagliatelle or other green pasta
3/4 cup gorgonzola cheese, crushed
3 tablespoons vinegar

1 1/4 cups heavy whipping cream
Salt and pepper to taste
2 shallots, peeled and chopped
1/2 cup chopped parsley
1/2 cup chopped fresh chives or 2 tablespoons dried chives
2 green peppers, seeded and cut into strips
1 hard-boiled egg, shelled and sliced

1. Cook tagliatelle in boiling, salted water until just tender, following package directions; drain.

2. Mix crushed gorgonzola with vinegar, cream, salt, pepper, shallots, parsley, and chives. Combine pasta and green peppers; toss with cheese sauce. Top with egg slices, and serve.

California Pasta Salad with Chicken

Serves 4

8 ounces mostaccioli
1/2 roasted chicken, skinned, boned, and cut into small pieces
3/4 cup Gouda cheese, diced
1 small endive, torn into pieces
1 cup seedless red grapes, halved
3/4 cup plain yogurt
1 1/4 cups heavy whipping cream
1/2 cup chopped fresh basil or 1 teaspoon dried basil
1/2 cup chopped fresh chives or 2 tablespoons dried chives
Salt and pepper to taste
Pinch of paprika
Juice of 1/2 lemon

1. Cook pasta in boiling, salted water until tender, following package directions; drain.

2. Combine chicken, cheese, endive, pasta, and grapes together in mixing bowl. Mix yogurt, cream, and chopped herbs together. Add salt, pepper, paprika, and lemon juice, mixing well. Pour yogurt dressing over pasta mixture and mix well. Cover and refrigerate for 45 minutes, then serve.

Chicken-Spaghetti Salad

Serves 4

8 ounces spaghetti, broken into
  pieces
3 carrots, peeled and cut into
  thin strips
3 tablespoons vinegar
Pinch of sugar
Pinch of pepper
1/2 teaspoon soy sauce
3 tablespoons sesame oil
1/2 roast chicken, skinned,
  boned, and cut into 1-inch
  pieces
1 cup Chinese cabbage, cut
  into thin strips
1 stalk celery, cut into very
  thin strips
1 cup cucumber, peeled, seeded,
  and cut into small pieces
2 tablespoons chives

1. Cook spaghetti pieces in boiling,
salted water until just tender,
following package directions; drain.
2. Blanch carrot strips for 2 minutes
in boiling water; drain and let cool.
3. Mix vinegar, sugar, pepper, soy
sauce, and oil together. Add pasta,
chicken, and vegetables. Sprinkle
with chives, and serve.

Exotic Pasta Salad

Serves 4

4 boneless chicken breasts
1 teaspoon coriander
2 teaspoons curry powder
Salt and pepper to taste
6 tablespoons oil
1/4 cup Marsala wine
1/2 cup almonds
2 bananas
1 tablespoon lemon juice
8 ounces tagliatelle
1/4 cup light soy sauce
2 tablespoons raisins

1. Place chicken breasts in large
bowl and coat with 1/2 teaspoon
coriander, 1/2 teaspoon curry powder,
salt, and pepper. Heat 2 tablespoons

oil in saucepan. Add chicken and
brown on all sides. Pour in wine and
simmer for 5 minutes. Remove
chicken and let cool; reserve pan
liquid.
2. Pour boiling water to cover over
almonds, then drain. Peel almonds,
then cook in 2 tablespoons oil until
golden brown. Peel and slice bananas, and sprinkle with lemon juice.
3. Cook tagliatelle in boiling, salted
water following package directions;
drain.
4. Mix soy sauce with remaining
coriander, curry powder, and oil in
bowl. Add chicken, reserved pan
liquid, bananas, almonds, and
raisins; toss well. Combine chicken
mixture with pasta. Refrigerate for 2
hours, then season to taste and
serve.

Whole-Wheat Pasta Salad with Chicken

Serves 8

1 cup chickpeas
1 quart cold water
2 teaspoons vegetable broth
1 teaspoon salt
8 ounces whole-wheat pasta
  twists or rigatoni
1 1/4 cups heavy whipping cream
1 teaspoon honey
3 tablespoons lemon juice
Salt and pepper to taste
2 tablespoons chopped parsley
2 ripe avocados, pitted and diced
1/2 cup finely sliced mushrooms
1/2 cup grated carrots
1 roasted chicken, skinned,
  boned, and cut into pieces

1. Soak chickpeas overnight in cold
water.
2. The next day, place chickpeas and
soaking liquid in large saucepan with
vegetable broth. Simmer for 40
minutes; drain.
3. Cook pasta in boiling, salted
water until just tender, following
package directions; drain.
4. Mix cream, honey, 2 tablespoons
lemon juice, salt, pepper, and

parsley together in large bowl. Stir
in vegetables and chicken. Mix well,
then let salad stand for 15 minutes.
Before serving, add remaining lemon
juice and salt and pepper to taste.

Pasta Chicken Salad

Serves 4 to 6

1/2 cup small pasta shells
2 1/2 cups diced cooked chicken
3/4 cup canned pineapple chunks,
  drained
1/2 cup chopped celery
1 tablespoon capers
1/3 cup apple cider vinegar
2 tablespoons sugar
Salt and pepper to taste
Lettuce
2 tablespoons slivered, toasted
  almonds

1. Cook pasta in boiling, salted
water until just tender, following
package directions; drain and rinse
with cold water.
2. Mix pasta, chicken, pineapple,
celery, and capers together.
3. Place vinegar and sugar in small
saucepan and heat gently until sugar
dissolves. Season with salt and
pepper, then add to chicken mixture;
toss well.
4. Line a platter with lettuce. Spoon
chicken mixture on top, sprinkle
with almonds, and serve.

Cousin Emma's Spaghetti Salad

Serves 6

8 ounces spaghetti, broken into
  pieces
3 cups diced cooked chicken
1/2 cup bottled Italian dressing
1/2 cup mayonnaise
3 tablespoons lemon juice
1 tablespoon prepared mustard
1 medium onion, chopped
3/4 cup pitted black olives, sliced
1 cup diced celery
1 tablespoon chopped pimento
Salt and pepper to taste

1. Cook spaghetti in boiling, salted water until just tender, following package directions; drain.
2. Mix chicken and Italian dressing with hot spaghetti; cool.
3. Blend mayonnaise, lemon juice, and mustard together. Stir in chopped onion, olives, celery, and pimento; add mixture to spaghetti. Season with salt and pepper. Mix well, then refrigerate until well chilled. Serve cold.

Chicken Salad with Cellophane Noodles

Serves 4

2 whole chicken breasts, fried or stewed
2 tablespoons hot water
1 teaspoon dry mustard
1 tablespoon sesame seeds
1/3 teaspoon salt
2 teaspoons sugar
1 cup chopped watercress, optional
4 scallions, chopped
8 ounces transparent (cellophane) noodles, fried
1/3 head lettuce, shredded
Italian salad dressing to taste

1. Remove skin and bones from chicken breasts; cut chicken meat into small pieces and set aside.
2. Combine hot water and mustard to form paste. Toss chicken with paste. Add sesame seeds, salt, and sugar; toss again. Add watercress, if desired, scallions, noodles, and lettuce.
3. To serve, add salad dressing and toss to mix well.

Vermicelli Salad with Crabmeat

Serves 4

8 ounces vermicelli
8 black Chinese dried mushrooms
1 pound crabmeat
4 scallions, sliced
1 cup water chestnuts, drained and cut into thin strips
1 cup bamboo shoots, drained and cut into thin strips
2 tablespoons soy sauce
2 tablespoons sweet and sour sauce
3 drops hot chili sauce
3 tablespoons oil
3 tablespoons lemon juice

1. Cook vermicelli in boiling, salted water until just tender, following package directions; drain.
2. Place mushrooms in bowl and cover with boiling water; let soak for 30 minutes. Drain and cut into strips.
3. Combine pasta, mushrooms, crabmeat, scallions, water chestnuts, bamboo shoots, soy sauce, sweet and sour sauce, chili sauce, and oil; mix well.
4. Sprinkle salad with lemon juice, and serve.

Pasta Salad with Tuna and Shrimp

Serves 4

8 ounces pasta bow ties
1 cooking apple, peeled, cored, and quartered
2 tablespoons lemon juice
Salt and pepper to taste
1 tablespoon walnut or peanut oil
1/2 teaspoon curry powder
1 tablespoon pineapple juice
1 tablespoon mustard
1 (7-ounce) can tuna fish in oil, drained, reserve oil
1/4 pound cooked shrimp, shelled and deveined
1/2 cup pineapple pieces

1. Cook pasta in boiling, salted water until just tender, following package directions; drain.
2. Cut apple quarters into thin slices and sprinkle with a little lemon juice. Combine remaining lemon juice, salt, pepper, oil, curry powder, pineapple juice, mustard, and reserved tuna fish oil; toss pasta with mixture.
3. Flake tuna fish and add to pasta salad together with shrimp, apple slices, and pineapple pieces. Mix well, and serve.

Macaroni Shrimp Salad

Serves 6

4 (4 1/2- or 5-ounce) cans shrimp, drained
2 cups cooked macaroni
1 cup chopped cauliflower
1 cup sliced celery
1/4 cup chopped parsley
1 1/4 cup chopped sweet pickles
1/2 cup mayonnaise
3 tablespoons French dressing
1 tablespoon lemon juice
1 teaspoon grated onion
1 teaspoon celery seed
1 teaspoon salt
1/4 teaspoon pepper
Lettuce
1 hard-boiled egg, shelled and sliced

1. Cover shrimp with ice water and let stand for 5 minutes; drain. Cut large shrimp in half.
2. Combine macaroni, cauliflower, celery, parsley, pickles, and shrimp.
3. Mix mayonnaise, French dressing, lemon juice, onion, and seasonings together well. Add to shrimp mixture; toss lightly. Refrigerate until well chilled. Serve on lettuce, garnished with egg slices.

Shrimp Salad Deluxe

Serves 6 to 8

8 ounces large pasta shells
1 pound cooked shrimp,
  shelled and deveined
1 cup finely chopped celery
Salt and pepper to taste
Pinch of seafood seasoning
2 cups seedless green grapes,
  halved
¹/₃ cup mayonnaise
1 tablespoon lemon juice

1. Cook pasta in boiling, salted water following package directions; drain and rinse with cold water.
2. Mix remaining ingredients and pasta together; toss well. Refrigerate until well chilled, and serve.

Rigatoni Shrimp Salad

Serves 4

8 ounces rigatoni
¹/₂ pound cooked shrimp,
  shelled and deveined
1 avocado, pitted and sliced
2 tablespoons lemon juice
2 tablespoons mayonnaise
1¹/₄ cups plain yogurt
3 tablespoons heavy whipping
  cream
2 tablespoons cognac
Salt and pepper to taste
Pinch of cayenne pepper
¹/₂ cup chopped fresh dill or 1
  tablespoon dried dill
1 honeydew melon, peeled,
  seeded, and cubed
1 cup sliced celery
Fresh dill sprigs, for garnish

1. Cook rigatoni in boiling, salted water until just tender, following package directions; drain.
2. Sprinkle shrimp and avocado slices with lemon juice.
3. Mix mayonnaise, yogurt, cream, cognac, salt, pepper, and cayenne pepper together. Add dill, pasta, shrimp, melon, avocado, and celery; toss well. Garnish with sprigs of fresh dill, and serve.

Pasta Salad with Mussels

Serves 4

4 pounds mussels
8 tablespoons olive oil
2 cloves garlic, peeled and
  chopped
1 large tomato, diced
¹/₂ cup chopped fresh basil leaves
  or 1 teaspoon dried basil
6 whole peppercorns
Pinch of sugar
2 cups dry white wine
8 ounces pasta shells
¹/₄ cup vinegar
¹/₂ cup finely chopped parsley
salt to taste
Pinch of cayenne pepper
1 green pepper, seeded and
  chopped

1. Brush mussels clean under cold running water and remove beards; discard any mussels with open shells.
2. Heat 2 tablespoons oil in large pot. Add garlic and saute for 1 minute. Add tomato, half the basil, peppercorns, sugar, and wine. Add mussels, cover, and cook over high heat for 8 minutes. Remove mussels from pot, discarding any that have not opened. Reserve cooking liquid. Remove mussels from shells; discard shells.
3. Cook pasta in boiling, salted water until just tender, following package directions; drain.
4. Combine 3 tablespoons reserved cooking liquid, vinegar, oil, remaining basil, and parsley together. Season with salt and cayenne pepper. Add pasta, green peppers, and mussels. Toss well, and serve.

Seafood Pasta Salad

Serves 8

4 pounds mussels
2 cloves garlic, peeled and
  crushed
4 sprigs parsley
2 cups dry white wine
¹/₂ pound shelled peas
¹/₂ cup vegetable broth
¹/₂ cup plus 2 tablespoons
  olive oil
Juice of 2 lemons
1 (7-ounce) can tuna fish,
  drained and flaked
¹/₂ pound small cooked shrimp,
  shelled and deveined
6 tomatoes, skinned and
  diced
2 tablespoons capers
1 pound pasta twists
Salt and pepper to taste

1. Brush mussels clean under cold running water and remove beards; discard any that are opened. Place mussels, garlic, parsley, and wine in large pot, cover, and cook over high heat for 8 minutes. Remove mussels from pot, discarding any that have not opened. Remove mussels from shells.
2. Boil peas in vegetable broth for 10 minutes; drain.
3. Combine ¹/₂ cup oil, lemon juice, tuna, mussels, shrimp, peas, tomatoes, and capers. Refrigerate for 30 minutes.
4. Cook pasta in boiling, salted water until just tender, following package directions; drain. Toss remaining 2 tablespoons oil with drained pasta.
5. Toss pasta with seafood mixture. Season with salt and pepper, and serve.

Seafarer's Delight

Serves 8 to 10

1 pound small pasta shells
1 (12-ounce) can artichoke
  hearts, drained and halved
1 red pepper, seeded and diced
1/2 pound cooked large shrimp,
  peeled, deveined, and diced
1/2 pound cooked bay scallops
1 (10-ounce) can pitted black
  olives, sliced
2/3 cup olive oil
1/3 cup red wine vinegar
1 1/2 cloves garlic, peeled and
  crushed
Salt and pepper to taste
1/2 teaspoon basil
1/2 cup grated Parmesan cheese

1. Cook pasta in boiling, salted water until just tender, following package directions; drain and let cool.
2. Combine artichoke hearts, red pepper, shrimp, scallops, olives, and pasta. Refrigerate until chilled.
3. Place oil, vinegar, garlic, salt, pepper, basil, and grated Parmesan in food processor or blender; process until well blended. Toss with pasta mixture, and serve.

Tuna Pasta Salad

Serves 4

8 ounces pasta of your choice
1 small onion, finely chopped
2 stalks celery, finely chopped
1 (7-ounce) can tuna fish,
  drained and flaked
1 green pepper, seeded and finely
  chopped
2 tablespoons sweet pickle relish
Mayonnaise to taste
Lettuce
1 tomato, sliced
1 cucumber, sliced

1. Cook pasta in boiling, salted water following package directions; drain well.
2. Mix onion, celery, tuna, green pepper, and pickle relish together.

Add to pasta with enough mayonnaise to bind salad together. Refrigerate for several hours, or overnight.
3. Serve salad on a bed of lettuce, garnished with sliced tomatoes and cucumbers.

Seashell Salad Nicoise

Serves 8

8 ounces pasta shells
2 stalks celery, minced
1 large onion, minced
3/4 cup chopped red pepper
4 pitted black olives, sliced,
  reserve can liquid
1/2 teaspoon oregano
1 anchovy fillet, minced,
  optional
1 tablespoon olive oil
Salt and pepper to taste
2 to 3 tablespoons red wine
  vinegar
1 1/2 cups partially cooked sliced
  green beans
1 (13-ounce) can water-packed
  solid white tuna, undrained
Lettuce leaves
4 medium tomatoes, cut into
  wedges

1. Cook pasta in boiling, salted water until just tender, following package directions; drain.
2. Mix pasta with celery, onion, red pepper, olives, oregano, anchovies if desired, olive oil, and 1/4 cup liquid from olives. Season with salt and pepper. Add vinegar 1 tablespoon at a time to taste. Refrigerate for 3 hours.
3. At serving time, stir green beans into salad. Drain liquid from canned tuna into salad; toss well. Arrange bed of lettuce on serving platter. Pile salad mixture on top. Top with flaked tuna and tomato wedges.

Salmon and Pasta Salad

Serves 2 to 4

2 1/2 to 3 cups large pasta
  shells
1/2 (7 3/4-ounce) can salmon,
  drained and flaked
6 cherry tomatoes, halved
1 carrot, thinly sliced
2 tablespoons minced parsley
Italian dressing to taste
Salt and pepper to taste

1. Cook pasta in boiling, salted water until just tender, following package directions; drain and let cool.
2. Combine pasta, salmon, tomatoes, and carrot in salad bowl. Toss with parsley and salad dressing. Season with salt and pepper. Refrigerate until ready to serve.

Pasta Salad with Oranges

Serves 4

8 ounces pasta bow ties
1 red apple, peeled, cored,
  and sliced
3 tablespoons lemon juice
1 1/4 cups plain yogurt
1 cup sour cream
1 tablespoon mayonnaise
3 tablespoons orange juice
Salt and pepper to taste
Pinch of sugar
1 cucumber, peeled and sliced
2 onions, cut into thin rings
2 oranges, peeled and divided
  into sections, seeds and
  membranes discarded

1. Cook pasta in boiling, salted water until just tender, following package directions; drain.
2. Sprinkle apple slices with lemon juice.
3. Mix yogurt, cream, mayonnaise, orange juice, salt, pepper, and sugar together. Add pasta, cucumber, onions, oranges, and apples. Toss well, and serve.

Whole-Wheat Pasta and Fruit Salad

Serves 8

10 cardamom seeds
2/3 pound whole-wheat pasta twists
2 ounces roasted sesame seeds
2/3 cup heavy whipping cream
1/4 cup lemon juice
2 tablespoons soy sauce
2 tablespoons sesame oil
2 to 3 teaspoons curry powder
1/2 teaspoon Indian saffron, optional
1/2 teaspoon pepper
1 pineapple, peeled, cored, and diced
6 bananas, peeled and sliced
3 tablespoons chopped chives

1. Make an incision in cardamom seeds. Place cardamom in large saucepan of boiling, salted water; add pasta and cook until tender, following package directions; drain and let cool.
2. Place sesame seeds in single layer on baking sheet and toast in 350 degree oven for 20 minutes.
3. Blend cream, lemon juice, soy sauce, oil, curry powder, saffron if desired, and pepper together. Combine pasta, dressing, pineapple, bananas, sesame seeds, and chives. Refrigerate for 15 minutes, or until ready to serve.

Beef Noodle Salad

Serves 8

1 pound fresh Chinese noodles
5 tablespoons sesame oil
3 tablespoons vinegar
Salt and pepper to taste
2 tablespoons soy sauce
1 teaspoon sugar
1/2 pound cooked beef, cut into 1/4-inch cubes
2 cups soybeans
1/2 cup sliced radishes
4 scallions, thinly sliced

1. Cook noodles in boiling, salted water until just tender, following package directions; drain.
2. Mix oil, vinegar, salt, pepper, soy sauce, and sugar together; mix with noodles. Add beef and soybeans to noodles. Sprinkle radishes and scallions on top, and serve.

Pasta Salad with Salami and Cheese

Serves 8

1 pound pasta shells
6 tablespoons red wine vinegar
Salt and pepper to taste
1/2 teaspoon paprika
5 tablespoons extra-virgin olive oil
2/3 pound Swiss cheese, cut into strips
1/2 pound salami, cut into thin strips
2 red peppers, seeded and diced
1/2 cup sliced radishes

1. Cook pasta in boiling, salted water until just tender, following package directions; drain and set aside to cool.
2. Blend vinegar, salt, pepper, paprika, and oil together. Combine cooled noodles, cheese, salami, diced pepper, radishes, and dressing. Cover and refrigerate until ready to serve.

Ham and Cheese Pasta Salad

Serves 4

1 1/2 cups pasta shells
2 cups diced cooked ham
1 cup diced Cheddar cheese
1/2 cup diced celery
1/2 cup corn oil
2 tablespoons lemon juice
1 teaspoon Dijon mustard
1/4 cup plain yogurt
1/4 cup chopped scallions
1/2 teaspoon tarragon
Salt and pepper to taste
1 cup frozen peas, thawed
1/4 cup minced parsley

1. Cook pasta in boiling, salted water until just tender, following package directions; drain.
2. Toss ham, cheese, celery, and pasta together in bowl. Blend oil, lemon juice, mustard, yogurt, scallions, tarragon, salt, and pepper together in blender or food processor; pour over pasta mixture. Cover and refrigerate for at least 1 hour.
3. Just before serving, mix peas and parsley into salad.

Macaroni-Ham Salad

Serves 4

2 cups cold cooked macaroni
1 cup diced cooked ham
1 (10-ounce) can condensed cream of chicken soup
1/4 cup diced celery
2 tablespoons chopped onion
1/4 cup chopped green pepper
2 drops Tabasco sauce
1/2 teaspoon Dijon mustard
Salt and pepper to taste
1 tomato, cut into wedges

1. Toss macaroni and ham together in salad bowl.
2. Mix soup, celery, onion, green pepper, Tabasco, mustard, salt, and pepper together. Add to macaroni and toss well. Cover and refrigerate until well chilled. Garnish with tomato wedges, and serve.

Gorgonzola and Ham Salad

Serves 4

8 ounces spaghetti
3 to 4 tablespoons vinegar
Pinch of salt
Pinch of sugar
Pinch of pepper
¼ cup virgin olive oil
1¼ cups gorgonzola cheese
6 ounces smoked ham, cut into thin strips
10 pitted black olives, halved
½ cup fresh basil leaves
¼ cup chopped pistachio nuts

1. Cook pasta in boiling, salted water until just tender, following package directions; drain and set aside to cool.
2. Mix vinegar, pinch of salt, sugar, pepper, and oil together in bowl.
3. Mix pasta with cheese, ham, olives, and basil. Pour dressing on top and toss well; let stand for 30 minutes. Sprinkle with pistachio nuts, and serve.

Spaghetti Salad with Roast Beef

Serves 8

1 pound spaghetti
1 large cucumber, peeled and diced
Salt and pepper to taste
8 tablespoons balsamic vinegar
⅛ teaspoon paprika
3 drops Tabasco sauce
½ cup olive oil
2 small onions, chopped
1 pound small tomatoes, peeled and cut into thirds
½ cup sliced radishes
½ pound cooked pork roast, cut into strips
1 pound cooked roast beef, cut into strips

1. Cook spaghetti in boiling, salted water until just tender, following package directions; drain.
2. Sprinkle diced cucumber with salt, pepper, and 1 tablespoon vinegar.
3. Blend remaining 7 tablespoons vinegar, salt, pepper, paprika, Tabasco sauce, olive oil, and onions together. Drain any liquid from cucumber; combine cucumber, pasta, tomatoes, radishes, pork, and roast beef. Add dressing and toss well. Cover and refrigerate for 15 minutes before serving.

Italian Pasta Salad

Serves 8

1 pound mixed white and green pasta twists
1 pound cooked veal roast, diced
2 tablespoons capers
2 tablespoons pine nuts
2 pounds tomatoes, skinned and diced
½ cup mayonnaise
1 teaspoon basil
2 tablespoons red wine vinegar
⅔ cup yogurt
Salt and pepper to taste

1. Cook pasta in boiling, salted water until just tender, following package directions; drain.
2. Combine veal with capers, pine nuts, tomatoes, and pasta. Mix mayonnaise, basil, vinegar, yogurt, salt, and pepper together. Toss pasta salad with dressing. Cover and refrigerate until ready to serve.

Elbow Macaroni Salad

Serves 8

1 pound elbow macaroni
5 carrots, peeled
1 pound cooked peas
1 pound cooked ham, fat removed, diced
1 pineapple, peeled, cored, and diced; reserve any juice
3 onions, chopped
2 cups mayonnaise
6 tablespoons lemon juice
Salt and pepper to taste

A few dashes Worcestershire sauce
¼ cup chopped chives

1. Cook macaroni in boiling, salted water following package directions; drain.
2. Cook carrots in saucepan with 1 cup salted water for 15 minutes. Remove from pan and slice.
3. Combine peas, ham, pineapple, onions, carrots, and pasta. Blend mayonnaise, pineapple juice, lemon juice, salt, pepper, and Worcestershire together. Toss pasta salad with dressing. Cover and refrigerate for 1 hour. Sprinkle with chives, and serve.

Beef, Macaroni, and Vegetable Salad

Serves 8 to 10

1 pound elbow macaroni
2 (10-ounce) packages frozen Brussels sprouts
2 cups cooked corned beef strips
1 large onion, chopped
⅓ cup sliced pimentos
1 cup mayonnaise
1 to 2 tablespoons prepared white horseradish
2 tablespoons sugar
⅓ cup vinegar
Lettuce

1. Cook macaroni in boiling, salted water until just tender, following package directions; drain.
2. Cook Brussels sprouts according to package directions; drain.
3. Combine macaroni, Brussels sprouts, corned beef, onion, and pimentos; toss lightly. Refrigerate until chilled.
4. Mix mayonnaise, horseradish, sugar, and vinegar together; chill.
5. To serve, arrange macaroni mixture on bed of crisp lettuce, and top with salad dressing.

Macaroni Salad

Serves 6

1 pound elbow macaroni
1/2 cup finely chopped onion
1/2 cup finely chopped celery
1/2 cup finely chopped green
  pepper
Mayonnaise
Salt and pepper to taste

1. Cook macaroni in boiling, salted water following package directions; drain.
2. Place macaroni in large bowl; add chopped vegetables. Add enough mayonnaise to bind salad; season with salt and pepper. Refrigerate until chilled, then serve.

Surprise Macaroni Salad

Serves 6

1 cup elbow macaroni
1/3 cup mayonnaise
1 tablespoon lemon juice
1 cup finely grated raw turnip
2 tablespoons chopped
  scallion
1/2 cup finely diced celery
Salt and pepper to taste
Lettuce

1. Cook macaroni in boiling, salted water until just tender, following package directions; drain and rinse with cold water.
2. In large bowl, combine macaroni, mayonnaise, lemon juice, grated turnip, scallion, celery, salt, and pepper. Mix well, then cover and refrigerate until thoroughly chilled.
3. Line platter with lettuce leaves. Spoon macaroni salad on top, and serve.

Pasta Salad Saporita

Serves 6 to 8

1/2 pound elbow macaroni
2 stalks celery, minced
1 large onion, minced
3/4 cup chopped red or green
  pepper
1/4 cup chopped parsley
2 tablespoons pickle relish
4 pitted black olives, sliced
1/2 teaspoon basil
1 tablespoon capers, reserve
  jar liquid
1 tablespoon olive oil
Salt and pepper to taste
2 to 3 tablespoons red wine
  vinegar
1 tomato, cut into wedges

1. Cook pasta in boiling, salted water until just tender, following package directions; drain and rinse in cold water.
2. Combine pasta and all remaining ingredients except vinegar. Stir in 1/4 cup liquid from capers jar. Add vinegar 1 tablespoon at a time to taste. Cover and refrigerate for 3 to 4 hours.
3. To serve, garnish with tomato wedges.

Cold Macaroni and Bean Salad

Serves 6

2 cups cooked macaroni
1 (16-ounce) can red kidney
  beans, drained
1 green pepper, seeded and
  chopped
1/2 cup finely chopped onion
1/2 cup finely chopped celery
1/4 cup salad oil
1/4 cup wine vinegar
1 clove garlic, peeled and
  minced
1/2 teaspoon basil
1/2 teaspoon oregano
Salt and pepper to taste
3/4 cup mayonnaise
2 hard-boiled eggs, shelled
  and sliced

1. Combine macaroni, kidney beans, green pepper, onion, and celery in mixing bowl.
2. Blend oil, vinegar, garlic, basil, oregano, salt, and pepper together well. Pour dressing over salad; mix well. Cover and refrigerate for at least 3 hours.
3. Before serving, add mayonnaise and mix well. Garnish with egg slices.

Cold Pasta Salad

Serves 6

8 ounces cold cooked pasta
  shells
1 tomato, diced
2 scallions, diced
1 cucumber, peeled, seeded,
  and diced
1 red onion, diced
1 Spanish onion, diced
2 green or red peppers,
  seeded and diced
2 cooked red potatoes, diced
1/2 cup diced, cold cooked
  broccoli
1/2 cup diced, cold cooked
  green beans
1/2 teaspoon basil
1/4 cup minced parsley
1/4 cup balsamic vinegar
1/8 teaspoon Dijon mustard
Pinch of oregano
1/2 teaspoon pepper
1 tablespoon frozen apple juice
  concentrate

1. Toss cold pasta with vegetables in salad bowl.
2. Blend basil, parsley, vinegar, mustard, oregano, pepper, and apple juice concentrate together well. Pour dressing over salad, and serve.

Cream Cheese Pasta Salad

Serves 6

4 ounces pasta bow ties
2 (6-ounce) jars marinated artichoke hearts, drained, reserve marinade
4 ounces cream cheese
6 tablespoons milk
Pinch of cayenne pepper
¼ cup diced cooked ham
¼ cup frozen peas, thawed
¼ pound fontina cheese, diced

1. Cook pasta in boiling, salted water until just tender, following package directions; drain.
2. Combine artichokes and their marinating liquid with pasta; set aside to cool.
3. Blend cream cheese, milk, and cayenne pepper together until smooth. Combine cream cheese mixture, pasta-artichoke mixture, ham, and peas; toss well. Refrigerate for 1 hour, or until chilled.
4. To serve, add fontina cheese to salad and mix gently.

Hot Macaroni Salad

Serves 5 to 6

8 ounces macaroni
6 slices bacon, diced
2 tablespoons vinegar
1 tablespoon finely chopped onion
Salt and pepper to taste
⅓ cup mayonnaise
½ cup sliced radishes
¼ cup chopped green pepper
¼ cup chopped parsley

1. Cook macaroni in boiling, salted water until just tender, following package directions; drain.
2. Cook bacon in frying pan until crisp; drain on paper towels. Discard all but 1 tablespoon bacon fat from pan. Add vinegar, onion, salt, and pepper to pan and heat to boiling point. Remove from heat.
3. Combine macaroni and all remaining ingredients in vinegar mixture. Serve hot.

Macaroni and Sausage Salad

Serves 4

8 ounces macaroni
¼ cup oil
1½ tablespoons vinegar
½ teaspoon salt
1 teaspoon thyme
¼ pound smoked sausage, cubed
1 cup cheese of your choice, cubed
½ cucumber, peeled and cubed
Lettuce
1 tomato, cut into wedges

1. Cook macaroni in boiling, salted water until just tender, following package directions; drain.
2. Combine oil, vinegar, salt, and thyme. Pour dressing over hot macaroni. Let cool.
3. Mix sausage, cheese, and cucumber with cold macaroni. Serve on a bed of lettuce, garnished with tomato wedges.

Macaroni Cheese Salad

Serves 6

2 cups macaroni
2 tablespoons butter
1 cup diced Cheddar cheese
1 cup sliced dill gherkins
½ cup very finely chopped onion
2 cups frozen peas
½ cup mayonnaise
Salt and pepper to taste
Shredded lettuce

1. Cook macaroni in boiling, salted water until just tender, following package directions; drain. Add butter and toss lightly. Add cheese, pickles, and onion to macaroni.
2. Cook peas according to package directions; drain and let cool. Add peas to pasta mixture.
3. Stir mayonnaise into pasta mixture, making sure the macaroni is well mixed with mayonnaise. Season with salt and pepper. Refrigerate until well chilled. Serve on a bed of shredded lettuce.

Pasta Slaw

Serves 4 to 5

¼ cup mayonnaise
1 tablespoon sour cream
1 tablespoon vinegar
2 teaspoons sugar
1 cup cooked pasta of your choice
1 cup finely shredded white cabbage
3 tablespoons grated carrot
3 tablespoons diced green pepper

1. Combine mayonnaise, sour cream, vinegar, and sugar.
2. Mix pasta and vegetables with mayonnaise dressing; toss lightly, making sure all ingredients are coated with dressing. Refrigerate until ready to serve.

Cheese and Macaroni Salad Ring

Serves 8

1 cup elbow macaroni
¼ cup French dressing
2 cups cottage cheese
¼ cup diced pimento
¼ cup diced green pepper
2 tablespoons very finely
  chopped onion
2 tablespoons chopped parsley
Lettuce
Sliced green olives, to garnish

1. Cook macaroni in boiling, salted water until tender, following package directions; drain. Add French dressing to warm macaroni and mix well. Refrigerate until chilled.
2. Add cottage cheese, pimento, green pepper, onion, and parsley to macaroni. Press into quart ring mold and refrigerate for several hours.
3. To serve, arrange lettuce on platter. Loosen macaroni mixture from side of mold with knife; turn out onto lettuce. Garnish with olives.

Tomato Jellied Pasta Ring

Serves 4 to 6

4 ounces elbow macaroni
4 cups tomato juice
2 teaspoons salt
¼ teaspoon pepper
¼ teaspoon basil
1 onion, finely chopped
2 envelopes unflavored gelatin
¼ cup cold water
2 teaspoons prepared white
  horseradish
2 tablespoons sugar
2 tablespoons lemon juice
1 tomato, sliced
Pitted black olives

1. Cook macaroni in boiling, salted water until tender, following package directions; drain and cool.
2. Combine tomato juice, 2 teaspoons salt, pepper, basil, and onion in saucepan; bring to a boil. Reduce heat and simmer for 10 minutes; strain.
3. Soak gelatin in cold water for 5 minutes. Add gelatin to hot, strained tomato juice; stir until dissolved. Add horseradish, sugar, and lemon juice. Refrigerate until mixture thickens, then stir in macaroni.
4. Pour mixture into lightly oiled, 9-inch ring mold; refrigerate until set. Unmold onto serving platter and garnish with tomato slices and black olives.

Macaroni Supper Salad

Serves 4

2 cups cooked macaroni
1½ cups diced cooked ham
1 (10-ounce) can cream of
  mushroom soup
2 tablespoons finely chopped
  celery
2 tablespoons finely chopped
  onion
2 tablespoons finely chopped
  green pepper
½ teaspoon Dijon mustard
2 drops Tabasco sauce
Salt and pepper to taste
¼ teaspoon basil
2 tomatoes, cut into wedges

1. Combine macaroni and ham. Mix soup, celery, onion, green pepper, mustard, Tabasco sauce, salt, pepper, and basil together. Add macaroni-ham mixture, tossing well. Refrigerate until well chilled.
2. Serve garnished with tomato wedges.

Ditalini Salad with Salami

Serves 4

1 cup cooked ditalini or other
  short macaroni
½ cup chopped green pepper
¼ cup chopped celery
½ cup salami strips
2 sweet pickles, finely chopped
½ cup frozen peas

½ cup mayonnaise
3 tablespoons milk
1 tablespoon lemon juice
Salt and pepper to taste
Pinch of cayenne pepper
2 hard-boiled eggs, shelled
  and quartered
2 medium tomatoes,
  quartered
2 tablespoons chopped parsley

1. Combine macaroni, green pepper, celery, salami, and pickles in mixing bowl.
2. Cook peas according to package directions, undercooking them slightly; drain and cool. Add peas to macaroni mixture.
3. Combine mayonnaise, milk, and lemon juice. Season with salt, pepper, and cayenne pepper. Pour mayonnaise over macaroni mixture; mix gently. Refrigerate until well chilled.
4. To serve, garnish macaroni salad with eggs and tomatoes. Sprinkle with parsley.

Carrot and Pasta Salad

Serves 4

8 ounces pasta of your choice
¼ cup raisins
2 tablespoons sherry wine
  vinegar
½ pound carrots, peeled and
  coarsely grated
⅓ cup peanut oil
Salt and pepper to taste
¼ cup chopped parsley
1 tablespoon chopped fresh
  basil

1. Cook pasta in boiling, salted water until just tender, following package directions; drain and cool.
2. Toss raisins with vinegar. Add pasta, carrots, oil, salt, and pepper; toss well. Cover and refrigerate for at least 3 hours. Remove from refrigerator 30 minutes before ready to serve.
3. Just before serving, add parsley and basil.

Homemade Egg Noodles

Serves 6 to 8

1¹/₃ cups flour
¹/₂ teaspoon salt
2 eggs
2 teaspoons olive oil
2 teaspoons water
¹/₂ cup butter, cut into small
  pieces
Freshly ground pepper to taste
1 cup freshly grated Parmesan
  cheese

1. Combine flour and salt in mixing bowl; form a well in center. Beat eggs, oil, and water together; pour into well. Mix thoroughly, adding a little more water if necessary to form stiff dough. Turn dough out onto lightly floured surface. Knead for about 15 minutes, to form smooth, elastic dough. Cover and let rest for 30 minutes.
2. Divide dough into 4 equal parts. Lightly flour a smooth surface and roll dough a quarter at a time until it is as thin as you can roll it. Ideally it should be 1/16th of an inch thick. Cut into strips. Spread out or hang on a line for 30 minutes to dry.
3. Bring 4 to 5 quarts of salted water to a boil. Float 1 tablespoon of oil on surface of water. Add pasta a few pieces at a time and stir. Cook until pasta floats to surface of water. Test for doneness; it should be firm, and not mushy. Drain well. Toss with butter, pepper, and grated Parmesan cheese or with sauce of your choice.

Green Noodles

Serves 6

1¹/₃ cups flour
1¹/₂ teaspoons salt
¹/₃ cup frozen chopped spinach
2 eggs
2 teaspoons olive oil
4 cups water
1 tablespoon oil
Melted butter
Freshly grated Parmesan cheese

1. Combine flour and ¹/₂ teaspoon salt in mixing bowl; form a well in center of flour mixture.
2. Cook spinach according to package directions; drain and press dry in sieve.
3. Combine eggs, olive oil, and spinach; blend until smooth. Add to dry ingredients, stirring to form very stiff dough. Add small amount of water if necessary. Knead dough until smooth and elastic. Cover and let rest for 30 minutes.
4. Divide dough into 4 equal parts; roll out until paper-thin on floured surface. Cut into strips and let dry on lightly floured surface for 1 hour.
5. Place water and 1 teaspoon salt in large saucepan and bring to a boil. Float oil on surface of water and boil pasta for 5 to 7 minutes, until just tender; drain.
6. Toss noodles with melted butter and Parmesan cheese; serve at once.

Ricotta Cheese Twirls

Serves 4 to 6

6 ounces rainbow pasta twists
³/₄ cup ricotta cheese
¹/₄ cup grated Parmesan cheese
¹/₄ cup chopped parsley
Pepper to taste
1 tablespoon butter

1. Cook pasta in boiling, salted water following package directions; drain.
2. Mix ricotta, Parmesan, parsley, and pepper together. Melt butter in frying pan. Add pasta and briefly cook over low heat. Add cheese mixture, stirring until well mixed. Continue cooking over low heat until heated thoroughly. Transfer to serving bowl, and serve warm.

Fettuccine with Garlic Butter

Serves 4

8 ounces fettuccine
¹/₄ cup butter
2 tablespoons pine nuts
2 cloves garlic, peeled and
  crushed
Pinch of Italian herb seasoning
¹/₄ cup grated Parmesan cheese

1. Cook fettuccine in boiling, salted water until just tender, following package directions; drain.
2. Melt 1 teaspoon butter in small frying pan and brown pine nuts lightly. Remove from pan and set aside.
3. In small bowl, blend garlic with remaining butter and herb seasoning. Mix pasta well with garlic butter and place in heated serving dish. Sprinkle pine nuts and grated cheese over pasta, and serve immediately.

Creamy Noodles with Nuts

Serves 4

8 ounces tagliatelle
1³/₄ cups shelled walnuts
2 cloves garlic, peeled and thinly sliced
¹/₄ cup butter
1¹/₄ cups sour cream

1. Cook pasta in boiling, salted water until just tender, following package directions; drain.
2. Grind ³/₄ cup walnuts in food mill or food processor. In large frying pan, saute ground walnuts and garlic in butter for 1 minute over medium-high heat. Add pasta to nut and garlic mixture, tossing well.
3. Place pasta in warmed serving bowl; sprinkle with remaining walnuts.
4. Heat sour cream in saucepan over low heat, stirring constantly; do not boil. Serve pasta with heated sour cream separately.

Fettucelle with Herb Sauce

Serves 4

8 ounces fettucelle
¹/₄ cup chopped parsley
¹/₄ cup fresh basil leaves
1 clove garlic, peeled and minced
¹/₄ cup extra-virgin olive oil
¹/₂ cup ricotta cheese
Freshly ground black pepper

1. Cook fettucelle in boiling, salted water following package directions; drain.
2. Place parsley, basil, and garlic in blender or food processor; blend until paste forms. Gradually add oil and ricotta; blend until smooth. Season with pepper.
3. Toss fettucelle and herb sauce together. Serve at once.

Herbed Penne

Serves 8

2 teaspoons olive oil
3 teaspoons chopped onion
1 clove garlic, peeled and minced
1 (3-ounce) can tomato paste
¹/₄ teaspoon cayenne pepper
¹/₂ teaspoon oregano
¹/₂ teaspoon marjoram
1 tablespoon chopped parsley
1 cup water
1 pound penne

1. Heat oil in saucepan. Add onion and saute until translucent. Add garlic and saute for 1 minute longer. Add tomato paste to pan 2 tablespoons at a time, stirring constantly. Add cayenne pepper, oregano, marjoram, parsley, and water. Mix well, then simmer while pasta cooks.
2. Cook penne in boiling, salted water until just tender, following package directions; drain.
3. Toss pasta and sauce together; serve at once.

Dilly Pasta Shells

Serves 4

8 ounces small pasta shells
1 cup cottage cheese
1 tablespoon milk
1 tablespoon chopped fresh dill
1 teaspoon lemon juice
Dash of Tabasco sauce

1. Cook pasta shells in boiling, salted water following package directions; drain.
2. Combine cottage cheese, milk, dill, lemon juice, and Tabasco in saucepan. Cook gently, stirring, until well heated. Toss with pasta, and serve.

Spicy Sesame Noodles

Serves 4

¹/₂ cup coarse-ground peanut butter
1 dry red jalapeno pepper, crushed
Salt to taste
3 large cloves garlic, peeled and minced
¹/₄ cup brown sesame oil
8 ounces spaghetti
2 tablespoons toasted sesame seeds

1. Place peanut butter in top of double boiler and cook until softened. Add jalapeno, salt, garlic, and oil; mix well. Cover and refrigerate for at least 3 hours.
2. Before serving, cook spaghetti in boiling, salted water following package directions; drain.
3. Reheat sauce in top of double boiler. Toss spaghetti and sauce together. Sprinkle with toasted sesame seeds, and serve at once.

Noodles Amandine

Serves 4

8 ounces egg noodles
6 tablespoons butter
1 cup slivered almonds
2 tablespoons flour
1 cup light cream
1 cup milk
Salt and pepper to taste
¹/₄ cup grated Parmesan cheese

1. Cook noodles in boiling, salted water following package directions; drain.
2. Melt 2 tablespoons butter in frying pan. Add almonds and saute over low heat until golden brown. Remove from pan and set aside.
3. Melt remaining butter in saucepan. Add flour and cook, stirring constantly, over low heat until well blended. Gradually add cream and milk. Cook, stirring constantly, until sauce thickens. Season with salt and pepper.

4. Combine noodles, sauce, and half the almonds; mix well. Sprinkle with remaining almonds and grated cheese, and serve.

Penne with Asparagus Tips

Serves 4

3 tablespoons olive oil
1 large clove garlic, peeled and halved lengthwise
3 anchovies, finely chopped
1 (14-ounce) canned peeled tomatoes, drained and coarsely chopped
4 cups fresh asparagus tips
4 ounces penne
Salt and pepper to taste

1. Heat olive oil in saucepan. Add garlic, anchovies, tomatoes, and asparagus; cover and cook over medium heat for 15 minutes.
2. Meanwhile, cook penne in boiling, salted water following package directions; drain and keep warm in covered, heated serving dish.
3. Season vegetables with salt and pepper; mix with pasta in serving dish. Cover dish for 3 minutes for flavors to blend, then serve.

Elbow Macaroni with Broccoli

Serves 4

2 quarts water
1 teaspoon salt
4½ cups broccoli florets
1 cup elbow macaroni
3 tablespoons olive oil
3 cloves garlic, peeled and finely chopped
3 anchovies, chopped
Pinch of cayenne pepper

1. Place water and salt in large saucepan and bring to a boil. Add broccoli and cook, covered, over medium heat for 15 minutes; drain, reserving cooking liquid. Set broccoli aside and keep warm.

2. Bring reserved broccoli cooking liquid to a boil. Add macaroni and boil for 8 minutes, or until just tender, stirring frequently; drain.
3. Meanwhile, heat olive oil in small saucepan. Add garlic, anchovies, and cayenne pepper; cook over low heat for 15 minutes, stirring frequently.
4. Place macaroni in heated serving dish. Mix with broccoli and anchovy sauce; let stand for 5 minutes to allow flavors to blend. Mix once more, then serve.

Pasta Shells with Broccoli

Serves 4

1 bunch fresh broccoli, cut into florets
8 ounces small pasta shells
3 tablespoons butter
¼ cup olive oil
2 cloves garlic, peeled
Salt and pepper to taste

1. Cook broccoli in boiling water until crisp-tender, about 10 minutes; drain.
2. Cook pasta in boiling, salted water following package directions; drain.
3. Heat butter and olive oil in large frying pan. Add broccoli and garlic; saute for 4 or 5 minutes, stirring constantly. Add pasta, salt, and pepper. Toss well, and serve at once.

Brussels Sprouts with Cheese-Noodle Ring

Serves 6

Cheese-Noodle Ring

1 pound broad egg noodles
3 tablespoons butter
2 cups grated Cheddar cheese
2 teaspoons Worcestershire sauce

Brussels Sprouts

4 cups fresh Brussels sprouts
1¼ teaspoons salt
2 tablespoons butter
⅛ teaspoon pepper

1. Preheat oven to 350 degrees.
2. To make cheese ring, cook noodles in boiling, salted water following package directions; drain. Add butter; toss until butter is melted. Pour into well-greased ring mold. Place mold in pan of hot water. Bake for 25 minutes. Unmold onto serving platter.
3. Melt cheese in top of double boiler; stir in Worcestershire sauce. Pour over noodle ring.
4. Place Brussels sprouts in saucepan containing 1 inch boiling water. Add salt and boil for 5 minutes. Cover and simmer for 10 minutes, or until sprouts are crisp-tender; drain. Add butter and pepper; toss lightly until butter is melted.
5. Place most of Brussels sprouts in center of cheese-noodle ring. Place remaining sprouts around outside of ring, and serve.

Hungarian Noodles and Cabbage

Serves 4

3 tablespoons butter
3 cups finely shredded white cabbage
1 teaspoon sugar
Salt and pepper to taste
8 ounces broad egg noodles

1. Melt butter in heavy skillet. Add cabbage, sugar, salt, and pepper. Cook, stirring constantly, over medium heat until lightly browned.
2. Cook noodles in boiling, salted water until just tender, following package directions; drain.
3. Combine noodles and cabbage mixture; toss well and serve.

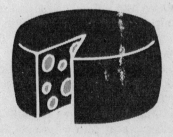

White Linguine

Serves 8

1 pound linguine
1 head cauliflower, divided into florets
1/2 cup butter
4 cloves garlic, peeled and crushed
2 tablespoons minced garlic from a jar
Salt and pepper to taste
Oregano to taste

1. Cook linguine in boiling, salted water following package directions; drain.
2. Boil cauliflower in water to cover for 12 minutes, or until tender; mash with fork.
3. Melt butter in large frying pan. Add garlic cloves and cauliflower; saute until lightly browned. Add linguine and remaining ingredients; mix well and serve.

Cauliflower with Noodles

Serves 4

2 tablespoons oil
1 small head cauliflower, divided into small florets
1/2 pound thinly sliced beef
Salt to taste
1 small onion, chopped
2 tablespoons soy sauce
1 cup beef broth
1 teaspoon cornstarch
1/2 teaspoon cold water
1/2 pound egg noodles

1. Heat 1 tablespoon oil in heavy skillet. Add cauliflower and beef slices; cook until lightly browned. Season with salt. Add onion and soy sauce; cook for 5 minutes. Stir in beef broth and simmer for 35 minutes.
2. Blend cornstarch with cold water; add to cauliflower mixture, stirring until thick and bubbly.
3. Cook egg noodles in boiling, salted water following package directions; drain. Heat remaining tablespoon oil in frying pan, add noodles, and fry until golden. Drain noodles, then mix with cauliflower. Heat thoroughly and serve.

Rotini with Carrots and Lemon Flavoring

Serves 4

8 ounces rotini
1 tablespoon butter
2 carrots, peeled and cut into very thin strips
1 teaspoon grated lemon rind
1/4 cup dry white wine
2 tablespoons lemon juice
1/2 cup heavy whipping cream
1/4 cup grated Parmesan cheese

1. Cook rotini in boiling, salted water following package directions; drain.
2. Melt butter in saucepan. Add carrots and lemon rind; saute for 2 minutes, stirring constantly. Stir in wine and simmer for 1 minute. Add lemon juice and simmer for 3 minutes longer, stirring occasionally. Add cream and bring to a boil, stirring constantly.
3. Toss carrots and lemon sauce with hot pasta. Add grated cheese and mix well. Serve at once.

Pasta with Celery

Serves 4

2 tablespoons walnut or peanut oil
1 onion, finely chopped
1 clove garlic, peeled and finely chopped
2 1/4 cups thinly sliced celery
1/2 cup vegetable broth
1/2 cup dry white wine
8 ounces pasta of your choice
3 tablespoons sesame seeds
2 teaspoons arrowroot or cornstarch
3 tablespoons heavy whipping cream
Salt and pepper to taste

1. Heat oil in saucepan. Add onion and garlic; saute until translucent. Add celery, vegetable broth, and wine; simmer for 10 minutes.
2. Cook pasta in boiling, salted water until just tender, following package directions; drain.
3. Toast sesame seeds in dry pan until golden. Remove from pan and set aside.
4. Blend arrowroot or cornstarch with cream until smooth. Add to saucepan with celery, stirring until sauce thickens. Simmer for 5 minutes more; season with salt and pepper. Add sesame seeds.
5. Place pasta in heated serving dish. Add celery mixture, toss well, and serve.

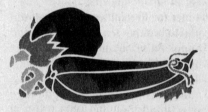

Shells with Zucchini

Serves 4

6 ounces pasta shells
3 tablespoons olive oil
3 cloves garlic, peeled and finely chopped
1 zucchini, sliced
1 teaspoon chopped fresh oregano or 1/2 teaspoon dried oregano
Salt and pepper to taste
2 tablespoons chopped parsley

1. Cook pasta in boiling, salted water until just tender, following package directions; drain.
2. Heat oil in frying pan. Add garlic and saute for 1 minute. Add zucchini and saute until golden brown. Season with oregano, salt, and pepper.
3. Mix pasta shells with vegetables. If pasta is no longer hot, cook with vegetables over medium-low heat until thoroughly heated. Sprinkle with parsley, then serve.

Zucchini and Fettuccine

Serves 4 to 6

2 medium zucchini, cut into
   julienne strips
1/4 cup olive oil
1 tablespoon butter
3 large cloves garlic, peeled and
   minced
3 tablespoons chopped fresh
   basil or 2 teaspoons dried
   basil
12 ounces fettuccine
1/2 cup grated Parmesan cheese

1. Steam zucchini in small amount
of water over high heat for 3
minutes; drain and set aside.
2. Combine oil, butter, garlic, and
basil in small saucepan. Cover and
simmer for 15 minutes; do not allow
garlic to brown.
3. Cook fettuccine in boiling, salted
water until just tender, following
package directions; drain.
4. Toss fettucine with zucchini,
garlic-basil sauce, and grated
cheese. Serve at once.

Rotelle with Zucchini Sauce

Serves 6 to 8

8 ounces rotelle
1 tablespoon oil
1 clove garlic, peeled and minced
1 cup minced onion
4 cups diced zucchini
1/2 cup sliced mushrooms
1 (15-ounce) can tomato sauce
Salt and pepper to taste
1/2 teaspoon oregano

1. Cook rotelle in boiling, salted
water following package directions;
drain.
2. Heat oil in frying pan. Add garlic,
onion, zucchini, and mushrooms;
saute until tender. Add tomato
sauce, salt, pepper, and oregano.
Simmer for 3 minutes.
3. Place hot pasta in serving dish.
Pour zucchini sauce on top, toss
well, and serve.

Vermicelli with Stir-Fried Vegetables

Serves 4

2 tablespoons sesame oil
2 cloves garlic, peeled and
   minced
1/2 pound carrots, cut into very
   thin strips
1 green pepper, seeded and cut
   into very thin strips
1/2 pound mushrooms, sliced
1/2 small cucumber, peeled and
   cut into very thin strips
1 teaspoon salt
2 tablespoons chutney
3-inch piece fresh ginger,
   peeled and sliced
8 ounces vermicelli, broken
   in half

1. Heat oil in wok or frying pan. Add
garlic, carrots, green pepper,
mushrooms, and cucumber; stir-fry
for 5 minutes. Season with salt. Stir
in chutney and ginger.
2. Cook vermicelli in boiling, salted
water following package directions;
drain. Toss vermicelli and vegetables
together, and serve at once.

Pasta with Vegetable Sauce

Serves 4

2 tablespoons butter
1 large onion, chopped
2 green peppers, seeded and
   sliced
1 clove garlic, peeled and
   crushed
1/2 cup peeled, cubed cucumber
4 tomatoes, peeled and chopped
Salt and pepper to taste
1 small bay leaf
1 small can anchovies, drained
   and chopped
About 15 pitted black olives,
   sliced
8 ounces spaghetti

1. Melt butter in saucepan. Add
onion, peppers, and garlic; saute for
3 minutes. Add cucumber and
tomatoes. Simmer for 3 or 4
minutes. Add salt, pepper, and bay
leaf; cover and simmer for 15
minutes. Add anchovies and simmer
for 3 or 4 more minutes. Add olives.
2. While vegetables are cooking,
cook spaghetti in boiling, salted
water until just tender, following
package directions; drain.
3. Toss spaghetti with vegetable
sauce, and serve.

Spinach and Noodle Ring

Serves 6

8 ounces broad egg noodles
1/4 cup butter
1 large onion, chopped
2 (10-ounce) packages frozen
   spinach
3 eggs, slightly beaten
1 cup plain yogurt
Salt and pepper to taste
Pinch of nutmeg

1. Cook noodles in boiling, salted
water following package directions;
drain.
2. Preheat oven to 350 degrees.
3. Melt butter in small frying pan.
Add onion and saute until translucent. Transfer onion to mixing
bowl and add noodles, spinach,
eggs, yogurt, salt, pepper, and
nutmeg; mix well.
4. Place mixture into greased, 6-cup
ring mold. Place mold in pan with 1
inch hot water, then bake for 45
minutes. Remove from oven and
loosen edges of mold with spatula.
Unmold onto serving platter, and
serve immediately.

Homemade Tagliatelle with Spinach

Serves 4

1³/₄ cups flour
2 eggs
¹/₂ teaspoon salt
3 cups fresh spinach, washed and torn into pieces
1 tablespoon oil
2 tablespoons butter
2 cloves garlic, peeled and halved
2 teaspoons salt
Pinch of nutmeg
Pepper to taste
3 quarts water
¹/₄ cup freshly grated Parmesan cheese

1. Mix flour, eggs, and ¹/₂ teaspoon salt together to form firm but pliable dough. Shape dough into ball and let rest under inverted bowl for 1 hour.
2. Wash spinach but do not dry; place spinach in saucepan, cover, and simmer for 5 or 6 minutes. Remove from pan and chop finely.
3. Heat oil and 1 tablespoon butter in small saucepan. Add garlic and saute until browned. Remove from pan. Place spinach, 1 teaspoon salt, nutmeg, and pepper in same saucepan and cook, covered, over very low heat for 5 minutes.
4. Roll dough out thinly on floured work surface; roll up dough, then cut into ribbon-width strips. Spread strips out on work surface to dry briefly.
5. Place water and 1 teaspoon salt in large saucepan and bring to a boil. Boil pasta for 5 minutes, or until just cooked; drain and toss with remaining butter.
6. Place pasta in heated serving dish. Spoon spinach over pasta and sprinkle with Parmesan cheese.

Macaroni with Spinach

Serves 12

5 tablespoons oil
1 pound macaroni
1 large onion, minced
1 clove garlic, peeled and finely minced
2 tomatoes, finely chopped
1 (10-ounce) package frozen chopped spinach
4 cups boiling chicken broth
2 teaspoons salt
¹/₂ teaspoon pepper
¹/₂ cup grated Parmesan or Romano cheese

1. Heat oil in large, deep pan. Fry macaroni in 2 tablespoons oil until golden brown; drain.
2. In same pan, heat remaining 2 tablespoons oil; add onion and garlic, and saute until translucent. Add tomatoes, then simmer for 10 minutes, crushing tomatoes as they cook.
3. While tomatoes are cooking, cook spinach following package directions; drain well. Add spinach to tomatoes, then add macaroni. Barely cover with boiling broth; season with salt and pepper. Cover and simmer for 25 minutes, or until liquid is absorbed. Remove to large platter, sprinkle with grated cheese, and serve.

Mrs. M's Spinach and Noodles

Serves 6

8 ounces thin egg noodles
4 eggs, separated
¹/₄ cup chopped scallions
1¹/₂ cups cooked chopped spinach
1 teaspoon salt

1. Cook noodles in boiling, salted water following package directions; drain.
2. Preheat oven to 350 degrees.
3. Beat egg yolks. Combine with scallions, spinach, noodles, and salt.

Beat egg whites until stiff; fold into noodle mixture. Pour into buttered, 1¹/₂-quart baking dish and bake for 30 minutes. Remove from oven, and serve.

Shells and Greens

Serves 5 to 6

1 pound small pasta shells
2 tablespoons olive oil
1 onion, chopped
2 cloves garlic, peeled and minced
2 cups chopped greens, such as collard, kale, or spinach
³/₄ cup shredded fontina cheese
Pinch of cayenne pepper

1. Cook pasta in boiling, salted water following package directions; drain.
2. Heat olive oil in large saucepan. Add onion and garlic; saute until translucent. Add greens and saute until wilted. Add cheese and cook, stirring, until cheese melts. Season with cayenne pepper.
3. Toss hot pasta with greens mixture, and serve immediately.

Ukrainian Mushroom Dumplings

Serves 8

Dough
2 cups flour
1 teaspoon salt
1 egg
¹/₂ cup water

Mushroom Filling
1 small onion, finely chopped
3 tablespoons butter
2 cups chopped mushrooms
Salt and pepper to taste
2 tablespoons bread crumbs
4 quarts water
2 teaspoons salt
¹/₄ pound melted butter

1. Mix flour with salt. Add egg and just enough water to make medium-soft dough. Knead dough briefly, then divide into 2 parts. Cover and set aside for 10 minutes.
2. Roll dough out on floured work surface until very thin. Cut into 1½-inch squares.
3. Melt butter in frying pan. Add onion and saute until translucent. Add mushrooms and saute for 10 minutes more. Season with salt and pepper. Add bread crumbs, mixing well. Remove from heat and set aside to cool.
4. Spoon mushroom filling in center of each dough square, leaving space around the edges. Fold up square and press edges together well.
5. Place water and salt in large saucepan and bring to a boil. Add dumplings, a few at a time, and boil for 3 to 4 minutes, stirring gently occasionally. Remove with slotted spoon and place in colander to drain. Toss with melted butter, and serve.

Piquant Vermicelli

Serves 6

8 ounces vermicelli
¼ cup butter
¼ pound mushrooms, thinly sliced
1 teaspoon marjoram
2 tablespoons chopped parsley
Salt and pepper to taste

1. Cook vermicelli in boiling, salted water following package directions; drain. Place in serving bowl and keep warm.
2. Melt butter in small saucepan. Add mushrooms; cook over low heat, stirring constantly, for 3 minutes. Spoon mushrooms over vermicelli. Add marjoram, parsley, salt, and pepper; toss until well mixed. Serve at once.

Mushroom Fettuccine

Serves 4

1 (10½-ounce) can condensed cream of mushroom soup
¾ cup milk
½ cup grated Parmesan cheese
3 cups hot cooked fettuccine
¼ cup butter

1. Stir soup in large saucepan until smooth; blend in milk and cheese. Heat, stirring occasionally.
2. Toss hot pasta with butter; toss with soup mixture. Sprinkle with Parmesan cheese, and serve.

Chinese-Style Mushrooms and Noodles

Serves 8

8 ounces fine egg noodles
2 tablespoons oil
1 cup bamboo shoots
1 cup sliced almonds
1 cup sliced mushrooms
½ cup chicken broth
3 tablespoons soy sauce
Salt to taste

1. Cook noodles in boiling, salted water following package directions; drain.
2. Heat oil in wok or frying pan; stir-fry noodles for 3 minutes. Add bamboo shoots, almonds, and mushrooms; mix well. Stir in broth, soy sauce, and salt. Cover and simmer until liquid is almost gone. Remove from heat, and serve.

Pasta with Mushrooms

Serves 4

2 tablespoons butter
2½ cups chopped mushrooms
Salt and pepper to taste
2 teaspoons paprika
3 tablespoons tomato paste
1 cup heavy whipping cream
8 ounces elbow macaroni
½ cup chopped parsley
Grated Parmesan cheese

1. Melt butter in saucepan. Add mushrooms and saute for 3 minutes. Season with salt, pepper, and paprika. Blend tomato paste and cream together, then add to mushrooms. Simmer mushrooms until pasta is cooked.
2. Cook macaroni in boiling, salted water following package directions; drain.
3. Place macaroni in heated serving dish. Add mushrooms and toss well. Sprinkle with parsley and serve with grated Parmesan cheese.

Twists with Sesame Sauce

Serves 4

8 ounces whole-wheat pasta twists
¼ cup walnut or peanut oil
2 large onions, diced
3 cloves garlic, peeled and diced
1 cup sour cream
2 tablespoons chopped fresh basil or 1 teaspoon dried basil
5 tablespoons sesame seeds

1. Cook pasta in boiling, salted water until just tender, following package directions; drain.
2. Heat oil in saucepan. Add onions and garlic; saute until translucent. Stir in sour cream and heat gently, stirring constantly. Add basil and sesame seeds.
3. Place pasta in heated serving dish. Add sauce and toss well. Serve at once.

Noodles with Mushroom Sauce

Serves 4

8 ounces egg noodles or
  tagliatelle
1 (14-ounce) can chopped
  tomatoes, drained
1 (10-ounce) can cream of
  mushroom soup
2 tablespoons tomato sauce
Salt and pepper to taste
2 tablespoons finely chopped
  parsley
1 tablespoon finely chopped
  fresh dill or 1 teaspoon
  dried dill
1 tablespoon flour
1/3 cup water, milk, or cream
4 thin lemon slices
1/2 pound mushrooms, sliced
2 tablespoons butter
Parsley, for garnish

1. Cook noodles in boiling, salted water following package directions; drain.
2. Combine tomatoes, undiluted soup, and tomato sauce in saucepan. Season with salt and pepper; add parsley and dill. Bring to a boil.
3. Blend flour and water, milk, or cream together. Add to tomato mixture. Bring to a boil again, stirring constantly. Add lemon slices and simmer for 5 minutes.
4. Brown mushrooms well in butter; add to sauce. Place noodles in heated serving dish. Mix with sauce, sprinkle with parsley, and serve.

Mushrooms in Wine

Serves 4

4 ounces egg noodles
1 pound mushrooms,
  chopped
3 tablespoons oil
1/2 teaspoon salt
Pepper to taste
1/2 cup dry red wine

1. Cook noodles in boiling, salted water following package directions; drain.
2. Brown mushrooms in hot oil; season with salt and pepper. Add wine; cover and simmer for 5 minutes.
3. Toss noodles with mushroom mixture, and serve.

Linguine with Fresh Tomatoes

Serves 4

1/2 pound linguine
2 tablespoons butter
1 pound ripe tomatoes, skinned
  and cut into 1/2-inch cubes
Salt and pepper to taste

1. Cook linguine in boiling, salted water following package directions; drain.
2. Melt 1 tablespoon butter in saucepan; add tomatoes, salt, and pepper. Cook over medium heat for 2 minutes, stirring occasionally.
3. Place pasta in heated serving dish. Spoon tomatoes on top, and serve.

Tagliatelle with Tomatoes and Mushrooms

Serves 4

2 tablespoons butter
1 large onion, chopped
2 3/4 cups sliced mushrooms,
  sprinkled with lemon juice
2 cloves garlic, peeled and finely
  chopped

Salt and pepper to taste
Pinch of sugar
6 ounces tagliatelle
1/4 cup chopped fresh sage
Grated Parmesan cheese

1. Heat butter in frying pan. Add onion and saute until translucent. Add mushrooms and garlic; cook over low heat for 10 minutes, stirring occasionally. Stir tomatoes into mushroom mixture; season with salt, pepper, and sugar.
2. Cook tagliatelle in boiling, salted water until just tender, following package directions; drain.
3. Mix pasta with vegetables. Sprinkle with sage and grated Parmesan cheese, and serve.

Green Ribbon Noodles with Tomatoes

Serves 8

12 ounces green noodles
1/2 cup olive oil
4 cups chopped, skinned
  tomatoes
1 teaspoon salt
1/8 teaspoon sugar
1/8 teaspoon pepper
1 teaspoon basil
Freshly grated Parmesan cheese

1. Cook noodles in boiling, salted water following package directions; drain.
2. Heat oil in frying pan. Add tomatoes, salt, sugar, pepper, and basil. Simmer for 5 minutes, or until tomatoes are tender; stir occasionally.
3. Arrange noodles in heated serving dish. Spoon sauce over noodles. Serve at once with freshly grated Parmesan cheese.

Fettuccine with Lecso

Serves 4

3 tablespoons sunflower oil
2 ounces lean bacon, diced
2 large onions, finely chopped
2 cups yellow pepper strips
1¼ cups diced tomatoes
1 green chili pepper, cut into
  narrow rings
8 ounces fettuccine
¼ cup grated Parmesan cheese

1. Heat oil in frying pan. Add bacon and cook until crisp. Remove from pan and drain. Remove all but 2 tablespoons fat from pan. Add onions and saute until translucent. Add peppers, tomatoes, and chili. Cook over low heat for 15 minutes. Remove from pan and toss with bacon.
2. Cook fettuccine in boiling, salted water until just tender, following package directions; drain.
3. Place pasta in heated serving dish. Add vegetables and toss well. Sprinkle with Parmesan cheese, and serve.

Spaetzle Noodles

Serves 4

3 cups flour
1 teaspoon salt
¼ teaspoon nutmeg
4 eggs, beaten
½ cup water
¼ cup butter

1. Sift flour, salt, and nutmeg together in bowl; form a well in center. Pour eggs and ¼ cup water into well, then mix with wooden spoon. Add just enough water to make dough slightly sticky, but keep it elastic and stiff.

2. Using a spaetzle machine or colander with medium holes, press noodles into large pot full of boiling salted water. Cook noodles in water about 5 minutes, or until they rise to surface. Lift noodles out and drain on paper towels.
3. Melt butter in frying pan. Add noodles and cook over low heat until lightly browned. Remove from pan, and serve.

Spaetzle with Emmenthaler Cheese

Serves 4

2½ to 2¾ cups flour
½ cup water
2 eggs
2½ teaspoons salt
4 quarts water
4 tablespoons butter
2 large onions, cut into thin
  rings
¾ cup grated Emmenthaler
  cheese

1. Sift flour into mixing bowl. Add ½ cup water, eggs, and ½ teaspoon salt; mix to form soft, but not runny, dough. Add more water if dough is too thick; add a little more flour if dough is too runny.
2. Bring water and remaining salt to a boil in large saucepan. Work small pieces of dough back and forth on dampened work surface, stretching and pulling; cut dough into narrow strips with long knife. Place dough strips in boiling water. (The spaetzle may also be pushed through a coarse sieve or special spaetzle machine into the water.) When spaetzle float to the surface, they are done. Remove from water with slotted spoon; keep warm.
3. Melt butter in large frying pan. Add onion rings and cook until golden. Remove from pan and drain.
4. Place spaetzle in heated serving dish. Pile cheese on top, and garnish with onion rings.

Pasta Squares

Serves 4

¼ cup fine semolina
5 tablespoons milk
2¼ cups flour
2 eggs
3 teaspoons salt
¼ cup olive oil
2 cloves garlic, peeled and diced
1 large onion, diced
½ cup thinly sliced celery
2 tomatoes, peeled and chopped
Salt and pepper to taste
Pinch of sugar
4 quarts water
2 tablespoons chopped parsley
1 cup freshly grated Parmesan
  cheese

1. Mix semolina with milk and let soak for 1 hour. Work flour, semolina, eggs, and 1 teaspoon salt together to form firm but pliable dough. Let dough rest under a hot bowl for 1 hour. Roll dough out to thickness of a knife; cut into 1½-inch squares and let dry for 15 minutes.
2. Heat oil in saucepan. Add garlic, onion, and celery; saute for 5 minutes, stirring constantly. Add tomatoes, salt and pepper to taste, and sugar; simmer, stirring occasionally, while pasta cooks.
3. Place water and 2 teaspoons salt in large saucepan; bring to a boil. Boil pasta squares for 5 minutes, stirring occasionally; drain.
4. Place pasta in pan with sauce; simmer for 3 minutes. Sprinkle with parsley and grated cheese, and serve.

Noodles Romanoff

Serves 4 to 6

8 ounces thin egg noodles
1 cup cottage cheese
1 cup sour cream
1 small onion, chopped
1 teaspoon Worcestershire
 sauce
Dash of Tabasco sauce
Pinch of paprika
1/2 cup grated sharp Cheddar
 cheese

1. Cook noodles in boiling, salted water following package directions; drain.
2. Preheat oven to 350 degrees.
3. Combine noodles with cottage cheese, sour cream, onion, Worcestershire sauce, Tabasco, and paprika. Put in greased casserole dish. Sprinkle with cheese and bake for 40 minutes. Remove from oven, and serve.

Japanese Chilled Noodles

Serves 4

1 pound whole-wheat vermicelli
2 cups chicken broth
1/2 cup light soy sauce
1/4 cup sake or dry sherry
1 tablespoon sugar
4 cherry tomatoes, quartered
1 scallion, finely shredded

1. Cook vermicelli in boiling, salted water following package directions; drain and rinse with cold water. Place in large, shallow glass serving dish and refrigerate for at least 1 hour.
2. Combine chicken broth, soy sauce, sake, and sugar in saucepan. Bring to a boil, stirring constantly. Reduce heat and simmer for 2 minutes. Remove from heat; let cool. Divide sauce into individual bowls and refrigerate for at least 1 hour.
3. When ready to serve, toss vermicelli with sauce and garnish with tomatoes and scallions.

Fried Rice Noodles

Serves 6 to 8

1/4 cup oil
4 small onions, sliced
2 cloves garlic, peeled and finely
 chopped
4 fresh red chilies, seeded and
 chopped
1/4 pound barbecued pork, thinly
 sliced
1/2 pound small uncooked shrimp,
 shelled and deveined
2 Chinese sausages, cut into
 thin, diagonal slices
1 cup fresh bean sprouts
2 pounds fresh rice noodles, cut
 into 1/2-inch pieces
1/4 cup soy sauce
1 tablespoon oyster sauce
Salt and pepper to taste
3 eggs, beaten
4 scallions, chopped

1. Heat half the oil in wok or frying pan. Cook onions, garlic, and chilies over medium heat until soft. Add pork, shrimp, and sausage; stir-fry for 2 or 3 minutes, until shrimp turn pink. Add bean sprouts and mix well. Remove from pan.
2. Add remaining oil to pan. When oil is very hot, stir-fry rice noodles until well heated. Add soy sauce, oyster sauce, salt, and pepper. Pour in egg, stirring constantly until egg is set and firm.
3. Return meat and shrimp mixture to pan; toss well. Cook until all ingredients are thoroughly heated. Garnish with scallions, and serve at once.

Macaroni and Cheese

Serves 6

1/4 cup butter
1/4 cup flour
1/2 teaspoon salt
2 cups milk
1/4 teaspoon dry mustard
1 1/2 cups grated sharp Cheddar
 cheese
3 cups cooked macaroni

1. Melt butter in saucepan. Add flour and salt, stirring constantly. Gradually add milk and continue stirring until sauce boils. Reduce heat. Simmer for 3 minutes, stirring constantly, until sauce thickens.
2. Add mustard and cheese to saucepan. Stir constantly, and cook over low heat until cheese melts.
3. Add macaroni to cheese sauce and mix well. Cook over low heat until thoroughly heated. Transfer to serving dish, and serve.

Macaroni Mousse

Serves 6

1 cup macaroni
1 1/2 cups milk
1 1/2 cups fresh bread crumbs
1/4 cup butter, melted
1 tablespoon grated onion
1/2 cup sliced mushrooms
1 teaspoon Worcestershire
 sauce
1/4 teaspoon prepared mustard
1 cup grated Swiss cheese
3 eggs, separated
Salt and pepper to taste

1. Preheat oven to 350 degrees.
2. Cook macaroni in boiling, salted water until just tender, following package directions; drain.
3. Combine milk, bread crumbs, butter, onion, mushrooms, Worcestershire sauce, mustard, cheese, and slightly beaten egg yolks. Mix in macaroni. Season with salt and pepper.
4. Beat egg whites until stiff; fold into macaroni mixture. Pour into greased casserole, cover, and bake for 30 minutes. Remove cover and return to oven until top browns. Serve hot.

Macaroni Bitters

Serves 6

1 pound elbow macaroni
¼ pound butter
½ cup chopped red onion
½ cup chopped green pepper
Salt and pepper to taste
1 tablespoon bitters
1 cup ricotta or cottage
  cheese
1 cup mixed grated Parmesan
  and Romano cheeses

1. Cook macaroni in boiling, salted water until just tender, following package directions; drain.
2. Melt 2 tablespoons butter in frying pan. Add onion and green pepper; saute until onion is translucent. Remove from pan and set aside.
3. Melt remaining butter in small saucepan. Add salt, pepper, and aromatic bitters.
4. Mix hot macaroni with onion, green pepper, and seasoned butter. Add ricotta or cottage cheese; mix well. Fold in grated cheese. Cook over very low heat, stirring constantly, until hot. Serve immediately.

Greek-Style Macaroni

Serves 4

6 ounces elbow macaroni
¼ cup butter
1 cup grated Kasseri cheese

1. Cook macaroni in boiling, salted water until tender, following package directions; drain.
2. Melt butter in small skillet and cook until golden, but not burnt. Remove from heat.
3. Place ⅓ of cheese in bottom of large bowl; cover with half the macaroni. Make another layer with ⅓ the cheese; add the remaining macaroni and finally the remaining cheese. Pour butter on top, and serve.

Elbow Macaroni Goldenrod

Serves 6

8 ounces elbow macaroni
2 tablespoons butter
2 tablespoons flour
2½ cups milk
Salt and pepper to taste
1 pimento, chopped
2 tablespoons minced parsley
3 hard-boiled eggs, shelled,
  yolks removed and egg
  whites chopped
Parsley, for garnish

1. Cook macaroni in boiling, salted water following package directions; drain.
2. Melt butter in saucepan; stir in flour. Gradually add milk, stirring constantly over low heat until sauce is thick and smooth. Season with salt and pepper. Add pimento, parsley, and chopped egg whites.
3. Combine sauce with macaroni. Arrange on large platter and sprinkle with egg yolks pressed through a sieve. Garnish with parsley, and serve.

Lumberjack Mac

Serves 6

8 ounces macaroni
2 cups grated medium-sharp
  American cheese
2 tablespoons Worcestershire
  sauce
¼ cup chili sauce
¾ cup melted butter

1. Cook macaroni in boiling, salted water following package directions; drain.

2. Spread macaroni on heated platter. Sprinkle with grated cheese, Worcestershire sauce, and chili sauce. Pour melted butter on top and toss with 2 forks until sauce is creamy. Serve at once.

Stilton Noodles

Serves 4

8 ounces egg noodles
1 cup crumbled Stilton cheese
1 cup sour cream
1 egg, lightly beaten
½ teaspoon salt
Pepper to taste
¼ cup butter, melted

1. Cook noodles in boiling, salted water following package directions; drain.
2. Preheat oven to 350 degrees.
3. Toss cooked noodles with remaining ingredients; mix well. Place in well-buttered, 1½-quart casserole dish. Bake for 1 hour, or until bubbly. Remove from oven, and serve.

Buttered Noodles

Serves 4

4 cups water
½ teaspoon salt
2 cups medium egg noodles
¼ cup butter, melted

1. Place water and salt in large saucepan and bring to a boil. Boil noodles for 15 minutes, stirring occasionally; drain.
2. Pour noodles into serving dish and coat with butter. Serve immediately.

Hungarian Noodles with Walnuts

Serves 4 to 5

1¹/₃ cups flour
³/₄ teaspoon salt
2 eggs
2 teaspoons oil
2 teaspoons water
1 cup finely chopped walnuts
¹/₃ cup confectioners' sugar
1 teaspoon grated lemon rind
3 tablespoons melted butter

1. Combine flour and salt in mixing bowl; form a well in center. Beat eggs, oil, and water together; pour into well. Stir with fork from outside of mixture to center. Add small amount of water if necessary to form very stiff dough.
2. Turn out onto lightly floured surface; knead about 15 minutes, until smooth and elastic. Cover and let rest for 30 minutes.
3. Divide dough into 4 equal parts; roll out 1 piece at a time as thinly as possible. Roll up; cut into ¹/₂-inch strips. Unroll strips and allow to dry for several hours on lightly floured towel.
4. Bring 4 quarts salted water to boil in Dutch oven. Add noodles; stir occasionally to keep from sticking to bottom of pot. Cook approximately 10 minutes; when done, noodles should be firm but not mushy. Drain well.
5. Combine walnuts, sugar, and lemon rind; mix well. Toss noodles with butter, then sprinkle with nut mixture and serve.

Noodles with Cheese and Bacon

Serves 4

6 ounces broad egg noodles
3 slices bacon, diced
2 tablespoons finely minced onion
¹/₂ cup creamed cottage cheese or farmer's cheese
¹/₄ cup sour cream
Salt and pepper to taste

1. Cook noodles in boiling, salted water following package directions; drain.
2. Cook bacon in frying pan until lightly browned. Add onion and continue cooking until bacon is crisp. Remove bacon and onion with slotted spoon and set aside. Discard all but 2 tablespoons bacon fat. Add noodles to reserved bacon fat; mix well.
3. Combine cheese, sour cream, salt, and pepper. Add cheese mixture, bacon, and onion to noodles. Toss to combine thoroughly, and serve.

Scalloped Noodles

Serves 4

8 ounces egg noodles
¹/₄ cup butter
1 cup bread crumbs
¹/₄ cup light cream
¹/₄ cup cracker crumbs

1. Cook noodles in boiling, salted water following package directions; drain.
2. Preheat oven to 350 degrees.
3. Melt butter in saucepan. Add bread crumbs and cook, stirring, until browned. Toss noodles with browned bread crumbs.
4. Dust bottom of buttered casserole dish with half the cracker crumbs. Cover with noodles and sprinkle with remaining cracker crumbs. Dot with butter. Bake for 1 hour, then remove from oven and serve.

Poppy Seed Noodles

Serves 4

8 ounces egg noodles
1 tablespoon butter
2 teaspoons poppy seeds

1. Cook egg noodles in boiling, salted water following package directions; drain.
2. Toss hot noodles with butter and poppy seeds. Serve at once.

Deep-Fried Crispy Noodles

Serves 4

8 ounces thin egg noodles
Vegetable oil

1. Place noodles in large saucepan in enough water to cover; bring to a boil. Cook, stirring occasionally, for 5 minutes; drain.
2. Fill deep-fat fryer half full with oil; heat to 350 degrees. Place noodles in basket and drop into oil; cook for 2 minutes. Remove from oil; drain well on paper towels.
3. Heat oil to 375 degrees. Return noodles to deep-fat fryer; cook until golden brown and crisp. Drain on paper towels, separating noodles. Place on serving dish, and serve.

Kasha Noodles

Serves 6

8 ounces egg noodles
²/₃ cup olive oil
¹/₂ pound mushrooms, sliced
1 cup chopped onion
2 cups cooked kasha
1 teaspoon salt

1. Cook noodles in boiling water following package directions; drain.
2. In large skillet, heat oil. Add mushrooms and onion; cook until both are tender. Add kasha and salt, and cook until thoroughly heated.
3. Add hot noodles to kasha mixture; toss well and serve.

Aunt Emma's Noodles and Cottage Cheese

Serves 4

8 ounces egg noodles
1 cup creamed cottage
   cheese
1 cup sour cream
$^{1}/_{4}$ cup chives
$^{3}/_{4}$ teaspoon salt

1. Cook noodles in boiling, salted water following package directions; drain.
2. While noodles are cooking, combine cottage cheese, sour cream, chives, and salt in saucepan. Cook until well heated but not boiling. Add hot noodles, toss, and serve.
3. To bake in oven, combine cheese mixture and noodles in greased baking dish; bake in 375 degree oven for 20 minutes.

Cheese Noodles

Serves 6

8 ounces medium egg noodles
2 tablespoons wheat germ
1 cup creamed cottage cheese,
   at room temperature
Pepper to taste

1. Cook noodles in boiling, salted water following package directions; drain and return to clean, dry saucepan.
2. Stir wheat germ and cottage cheese into noodles; heat over very low heat. Add pepper, and serve.

Ida's Sour Cream Noodles

Serves 4 to 6

8 ounces broad egg noodles
1 cup ricotta cheese or
   cottage cheese
1 cup sour cream
1 egg, slightly beaten
$^{1}/_{2}$ teaspoon salt
$^{1}/_{8}$ teaspoon pepper
$^{1}/_{2}$ cup sugar
$^{1}/_{4}$ cup melted butter

1. Preheat oven to 300 degrees.
2. Cook noodles in boiling, salted water following package directions; drain.
3. Combine noodles with remaining ingredients. Place in well-greased baking dish and bake for $1^{1}/_{2}$ hours. Remove from oven, and serve.

Noodle Souffle

Serves 4

$^{1}/_{2}$ cup thin egg noodles
$^{1}/_{2}$ pound salted butter
$^{1}/_{2}$ pound cottage cheese,
   mashed
1 cup sour cream
1 scant cup sugar
4 eggs, separated
1 teaspoon vanilla
4 to 5 graham crackers,
   crushed

1. Preheat oven to 350 degrees.
2. Cook noodles in boiling, salted water following package directions; drain.
3. Combine noodles, butter, cottage cheese, sour cream, sugar, and egg yolks. Beat egg whites until stiff; fold vanilla and egg whites into noodles.
4. Place noodle mixture in large greased pan. Sprinkle with graham crackers. Bake for 1 hour. Remove from oven and serve immediately.

Fried Noodles and Cottage Cheese

Serves 12

1 pound broad egg noodles
1 cup cottage cheese
Pinch of salt
1 tablespoon sugar
3 eggs, beaten
8 tablespoons butter

1. Cook noodles in boiling, salted water following package directions; drain well.
2. Combine noodles, cottage cheese, salt, and sugar. Mix eggs into noodle mixture.
3. Melt butter in heavy skillet. Add noodle mixture, a small amount at a time, and fry until brown. Remove from pan, and serve.

Rice and Noodle Casserole

Serves 12

1 cup margarine
8 ounces very thin noodles
2 cups uncooked instant rice
2 (10-ounce) cans condensed
   onion soup
2 (10-ounce) cans condensed
   chicken broth
1 tablespoon soy sauce
1 cup water
1 (8-ounce) can water chestnuts,
   drained and sliced

1. Preheat oven to 350 degrees.
2. Melt margarine in large skillet. Add uncooked noodles and cook, stirring constantly, until lightly browned; watch closely, since noodles burn fast. Add remaining ingredients to noodles; mix well.
3. Turn noodle-rice mixture into 3-quart casserole dish. Let set for 15 minutes before putting in oven; it will be very loose. Bake for 45 minutes, or until browned. Spoon out to serve. The recipe may be cut in half, if desired.

Rice and Vermicelli

Serves 4

1 cup long-grain rice
1/2 cup vermicelli, broken into
   pieces
3 tablespoons butter
2 cups chicken broth
1 teaspoon chives

1. Combine rice and vermicelli. Melt butter in 2-quart saucepan; saute rice and noodles until golden brown.
2. Add chicken broth and chives to saucepan. Cover tightly and cook over very low heat for 20 to 25 minutes, or until all liquid is absorbed. Fluff with a fork, and serve.

Noodle Ring

Serves 6 to 8

8 ounces egg noodles
1 tablespoon butter, softened
3 eggs
3/4 cup milk
1/2 teaspoon seasoned salt

1. Preheat oven to 350 degrees.
2. Cook noodles in boiling, salted water following package directions; drain. Add butter to hot noodles.
3. Beat eggs, milk, and salt together; mix with noodles. Pour noodle mixture into greased, 1-quart ring mold. Place mold in pan containing 1 inch hot water. Bake for 40 minutes.
4. Remove from oven and loosen edges of mold with spatula. Invert over serving platter, shaking gently to loosen.
5. Fill center of ring with vegetables, chicken, or meat, and serve.

Soft-Fried Noodles with Mushrooms

Serves 8 to 10

5-ounce package thin egg
   noodles
2 tablespoons safflower oil
1 cup bamboo shoots
1 cup sliced fresh mushrooms
1 cup sliced almonds
1/2 cup chicken broth
3 tablespoons soy sauce
1 teaspoon salt

1. Cook noodles in boiling, salted water following package directions; drain.
2. Heat oil in wok or frying pan over low heat. Add noodles; stir-fry for 4 minutes. Add bamboo shoots, mushrooms, and almonds; mix well. Stir in broth, soy sauce, and salt; reduce heat to very low. Cover and simmer for 20 minutes, or until liquid is almost absorbed. Transfer to heated serving dish; serve with additional soy sauce, if desired.

Noodle Pancakes

Serves 4 to 6

8 ounces egg noodles
2 eggs
Pinch of salt
1/4 cup melted butter
1/4 cup butter

1. Cook noodles in boiling, salted water following package directions; drain.
2. Beat eggs with salt in large mixing bowl. Add melted butter and noodles; toss until well mixed.
3. Melt second 1/4 cup butter in skillet. Drop tablespoonfuls of noodle mixture into pan. Brown on both sides. Remove from pan, and serve.

Spaghetti Pancake

Serves 4

2 eggs
2 tablespoons finely minced
   onion
1/2 teaspoon oregano
1/2 teaspoon salt
1/8 teaspoon pepper
3 1/2 cups cold cooked
   spaghetti
3 tablespoons butter
2 tablespoons grated Parmesan
   cheese

1. Beat eggs, onion, oregano, salt, and pepper together in medium-size mixing bowl. Add spaghetti; toss well to coat.
2. Heat 2 tablespoons butter in medium skillet over moderate heat until foam subsides. Add spaghetti mixture and sprinkle with cheese. Cook until bottom is lightly browned. Turn out onto a plate.
3. Heat remaining tablespoon of butter in pan. Slide spaghetti pancake back into pan, uncooked side down. Cook until lightly browned. Cut into 4 pieces, and serve. This is delicious served with fried Italian sausage, peppers, and onions.

Pasta Twists with Sour Cream Sauce

Serves 4

8 ounces pasta twists
1/4 cup chopped onion
1 tablespoon butter
1 (10-ounce) can condensed
   cream of celery soup
1/2 cup sour cream
1/2 teaspoon dill

1. Cook pasta in boiling, salted water following package directions; drain.
2. Saute onion in butter until translucent. Add soup, sour cream, and dill. Cook, stirring constantly, until well heated. Pour over cooked pasta, toss, and serve.

Spaghetti Ring

Serves 12

1 pound spaghetti
¹/₂ cup butter
1 green pepper, seeded and
  finely chopped
1 pimento, chopped
1 medium onion, chopped
1¹/₂ cups milk
1 cup fresh bread crumbs
¹/₂ pound cheese of your choice,
  chopped
5 eggs, beaten

1. Cook spaghetti in boiling, salted water following package directions; drain.
2. Melt butter in saucepan. Add green pepper, pimento, and onion; saute for 5 minutes. Add milk, bread crumbs, and cheese; cook, stirring constantly, until creamy. Add spaghetti and eggs; mix well.
3. Preheat oven to 350 degrees.
4. Place spaghetti mixture in buttered ring mold; set mold in pan of water and bake for 1 hour. Remove from oven; loosen edges with spatula and unmold onto serving platter. Fill center of ring with vegetables, and serve.

Fettuccine with Peaches

Serves 4

8 ounces fettuccine
¹/₂ cup heavy whipping cream
1 egg yolk
2 ripe but firm peaches, peeled
  and sliced
¹/₂ cup grated Romano cheese
1 tablespoon finely chopped
  parsley
Nutmeg, optional

1. Cook fettuccine in boiling, salted water until just tender, following package directions; drain.
2. Lightly beat cream with egg yolk. Place peaches, cream-egg yolk mixture, and cheese in saucepan; heat gently, stirring constantly, until well mixed.

3. Place fettuccine in heated serving dish. Add peach mixture and toss gently. Sprinkle with parsley and nutmeg, if desired.

Noodle Kugel

Serves 6

8 ounces medium egg noodles
4 ounces cream cheese
¹/₄ pound butter
1 cup sour cream
Seasoned salt and pepper
  to taste
¹/₄ cup sugar
4 eggs, beaten
Cornflake crumbs, to
  sprinkle

1. Preheat oven to 350 degrees.
2. Cook noodles in boiling, salted water following package directions; drain. Add cream cheese to hot noodles and toss until well mixed. Add 7 tablespoons butter, sour cream, seasonings, and sugar. Mix in eggs.
3. Place noodle mixture in greased 8- or 9-inch square pan. Sprinkle top with cornflake crumbs and dot with remaining butter. Bake for 1¹/₂ to 2 hours. Remove from oven, and serve.

Noodle Kugel with Fruit

Serves 6 to 8

8 ounces broad egg noodles
1 cup crushed pineapple
1 apple, peeled, cored, and
  grated
1 cup cottage cheese
6 tablespoons butter, melted
2 eggs, beaten
2 tablespoons lemon juice
1 cup white raisins
¹/₂ cup sugar
1¹/₂ teaspoons cinnamon,
  optional
1 cup sour cream
1 teaspoon salt

1. Preheat oven to 350 degrees.
2. Cook noodles in boiling, salted water following package directions; drain.
2. Combine noodles with remaining ingredients. Place in well-greased, shallow, heavy baking dish. Bake for 45 minutes. Remove from oven, and serve.

Upside-Down Noodle Kugel

Serves 8

¹/₄ cup margarine, softened
¹/₂ cup light brown sugar
8 slices canned pineapple,
  well drained and halved
2 eggs
¹/₄ cup oil
¹/₄ cup sugar
¹/₂ teaspoon salt
¹/₂ teaspoon cinnamon
1 tablespoon lemon juice
¹/₂ teaspoon grated lemon rind
8 ounces egg noodles
¹/₂ cup finely chopped dried
  fruits, such as apricots,
  prunes, and dates
¹/₂ cup raisins
¹/₂ cup chopped nuts

1. Preheat oven to 350 degrees. Coat 9-inch square pan with margarine; sprinkle with brown sugar. Place pineapple slices on top of sugar.
2. Beat eggs, oil, sugar, salt, cinnamon, lemon juice, and lemon rind together in large bowl.
3. Cook noodles in boiling, salted water following package directions; drain, then stir into egg mixture. Add remaining ingredients and toss well. Spoon into prepared pan.
4. Bake 40 to 50 minutes until set and golden brown. Remove from oven and let stand for 5 minutes. Loosen with spatula and invert over serving dish.

Sticky Bun Kugel

Serves 12

1 pound medium egg noodles
14 tablespoons butter
1 cup brown sugar
4 eggs, beaten
1 teaspoon cinnamon
1/2 cup sugar
1/2 cup pecan halves

1. Cook noodles in boiling, salted water following package directions; drain and cool.
2. Melt 8 tablespoons butter in saucepan; add brown sugar and cook until browned. Mash sugar mixture along sides of bundt pan and refrigerate for 30 minutes.
3. Meanwhile, mix eggs, 6 tablespoons butter, cinnamon, and sugar together. Add to cooled noodles, mixing well.
4. Preheat oven to 350 degrees.
5. Remove pan from refrigerator and press nuts into sides of pan. Spoon noodle mixture into pan and bake for 1 hour. To serve, loosen edges with knife and invert onto serving platter.

Cherry Noodle Kugel

Serves 6 to 8

8 ounces broad egg noodles
8 ounces cream cheese
1 cup sour cream
1/4 cup plus 2 tablespoons sugar
1 (1-pound 5-ounce can)
** cherry pie filling**
3/4 teaspoon cinnamon
1/2 cup chopped walnuts

1. Cook noodles in boiling, salted water following package directions; drain well.
2. Mix cream cheese, sour cream, and 1/4 cup sugar together; toss with noodles.
3. Preheat oven to 350 degrees.
4. Mix cherry pie filling with 1/2 teaspoon cinnamon and nuts. Place half

the noodle mixture in greased, 8 x 12 x 2-inch baking dish. Spread with cherry mixture. Top with remaining noodles.
5. Mix remaining 2 tablespoons sugar with 1/4 teaspoon cinnamon; sprinkle on top of noodles. Bake for 30 minutes. Remove from oven, and serve.

Old-Fashioned Noodle Pudding

Serves 7

5 tablespoons butter
2 1/2 cups cooking apples, peeled and cut into 1/2-inch slices
7 tablespoons sugar
1/3 cup packed dark brown sugar
1 3/4 teaspoons cinnamon
2 tablespoons finely chopped walnuts
2 1/2 cups just-cooked broad egg noodles
1/2 cup sour cream
1 1/4 cups creamed cottage cheese, sieved
1/2 teaspoon salt
2 eggs, well beaten

1. Melt 3 tablespoons butter in heavy frying pan. Add sliced apples; sprinkle with 3 tablespoons sugar and stir until apples are completely coated with butter. Cover and cook over low heat for 8 minutes.
2. Preheat oven to 325 degrees.
3. Mix brown sugar, 1/4 teaspoon cinnamon, and nuts together well. Spread mixture evenly over bottom of well-greased 8 x 8 x 2-inch pan.
4. Add 2 tablespoons butter to noodles, tossing until well mixed. Add sour cream, cottage cheese, salt, eggs, and cooked apples and their liquid. Mix 2 tablespoons sugar with 1 teaspoon cinnamon, and add to noodle mixture. Blend well.
5. Put noodle mixture over brown sugar layer in pan. Bake for 50 minutes. Sprinkle a mixture of 2 tablespoons sugar and 1/2 teaspoon cinnamon on top of noodle pudding, and serve at once.

Apricot Noodle Pudding

Serves 9

8 ounces medium egg noodles
3 tablespoons butter
2 eggs
1 cup creamed cottage cheese
1 cup sugar
1 cup sour cream
Salt and pepper to taste
1/4 teaspoon cinnamon
3/4 cup diced dried apricots
1/2 cup chopped walnuts

1. Cook noodles in boiling, salted water following package directions; drain. Add 1 tablespoon butter to hot noodles.
2. Preheat oven to 350 degrees.
3. Combine eggs, cottage cheese, sugar, sour cream, salt, pepper, and cinnamon in blender or food processor until smooth and creamy. Fold in apricots and nuts. Toss with noodles.
4. Place remaining butter in 9-inch square baking dish; place in oven until butter is bubbly. Add noodle mixture to dish and bake for 1 hour, or until brown crust forms on bottom and edges. Remove from oven and cool slightly before serving.

Cream Cheese Noodle Pudding

Serves 6

8 ounces broad egg noodles
1/2 cup butter, melted and cooled
8 ounces cream cheese
3/4 cup sugar
4 eggs
1 teaspoon vanilla
2 cups milk
1/2 cup cornflake crumbs
2 tablespoons sugar mixed with 1/2 teaspoon cinnamon

1. Cook noodles in boiling, salted water following package directions; drain.
2. Mix melted butter and cream cheese together. Add sugar, eggs, vanilla, and milk; mix until smooth. Add cooked noodles and refrigerate overnight.
3. Preheat oven to 350 degrees.
4. Brush large casserole dish or pan with melted butter. Place noodle mixture in dish and sprinkle first with cornflake crumbs, then with cinnamon sugar. Bake for 1 1/4 hours. Remove from oven, and serve.

Fruited Noodle Pudding

Serves 8 to 10

8 ounces egg noodles
3 large eggs
1/2 cup oil
1 (12-ounce) jar orange marmalade
1/2 cup raisins
1 (1-pound, 4-ounce) can apple slices

1. Cook noodles in boiling, salted water following package directions; drain.
2. Beat eggs until foamy; add oil and marmalade. Add noodles, mixing lightly to blend.
3. Preheat oven to 400 degrees.
4. Mix raisins and apples together. Fold fruit mixture into noodles. Turn entire mixture into well-greased, 9-inch bread pan. Bake for 45 minutes, or until nicely browned on top. Remove from oven and cool for 10 minutes. Slice, and serve.

Noodles with Prunes

Serves 4

1 pound pitted prunes
1/2 cup sugar
8 ounces broad egg noodles
1/4 cup butter
Cinnamon to taste
1 cup bread crumbs

1. Soak prunes in cold water to cover overnight. Place prunes and soaking liquid in saucepan. Cook over medium heat until prunes are soft. Add sugar and simmer for 5 minutes. Drain prunes, reserving liquid, and set aside.
2. Cook noodles in boiling, salted water following package directions; drain.
3. Preheat oven to 350 degrees.
4. Layer 1/4 of noodles, bits of butter, and then 1/2 of prunes in well-greased baking dish. Sprinkle with cinnamon. Repeat layers; top with remaining noodles. Pour over some reserved prune cooking liquid. Sprinkle with crumbs and dot with remaining butter. Bake until browned. Remove from oven, and serve.

Apples and Noodles

Serves 4

8 ounces egg noodles
1/4 cup butter
4 cooking apples, peeled, cored, and sliced
2 tablespoons sugar
Salt to taste
Cinnamon to taste

1. Cook noodles in boiling, salted water following package directions; drain.
2. Melt butter in large skillet. Add half the noodles, then the apples. Sprinkle with sugar, salt, and cinnamon. Cover with remaining noodles. Cover and cook for 10 minutes. Remove cover and cook until apples are tender and noodles browned.

Polish Noodles

Serves 4

2 cups cooked egg noodles
1 tablespoon melted butter
1 tablespoon vanilla
Grated rind of 1 lemon
1 cup canned poppy seed pastry filling

1. Toss noodles with melted butter.
2. Mix vanilla, lemon rind, and poppy seed filling together. Add to noodles and toss well. Place in saucepan and cook over low heat until thoroughly heated. Transfer to serving dish, and serve warm.

Viennese Noodles

Serves 6

8 ounces broad egg noodles
1/4 cup butter
1/2 cup chopped almonds or Brazil nuts
2 teaspoons poppy seeds

1. Cook noodles in boiling, salted water following package directions; drain.
2. Melt 1 tablespoon butter in saucepan. Add nuts and cook, stirring, over low heat until lightly browned. Add remaining butter, noodles, and poppy seeds; stir lightly until thoroughly heated. Place in heated serving dish, and serve.

Frozen Blintz Casserole

Serves 8

6 tablespoons margarine
12 frozen cheese blintzes
4 eggs
1/4 cup orange juice
1 cup sour cream
1 teaspoon vanilla

1. Preheat oven to 350 degrees.
2. Melt margarine in 9 x 13-inch pan. Place frozen blintzes in pan. Blend remaining ingredients together and pour over blintzes. Bake for 45 to 50 minutes. Remove from oven and serve.

Cheese Blintzes

Serves 8

1 teaspoon salt
1 teaspoon oil
1¼ cups milk
2 eggs
1 cup flour
8 ounces dry cottage cheese
¼ cup sugar
¼ teaspoon cinnamon
Oil for deep-frying

1. Mix salt, oil, milk, and 1 egg together well in mixing bowl. Slowly add flour; mix to form smooth batter.
2. Oil a 6-inch crepe pan lightly; heat until hot. Pour in 2 tablespoons batter; tilt pan until batter is evenly spread. Cook over low heat until set; remove from pan. Continue process until all batter is used.
3. To make filling, combine cottage cheese, remaining egg, sugar, pinch of salt, and cinnamon. Place 1 or 2 tablespoons filling in center of each blintz. Roll up blintzes.
4. Heat oil in deep skillet to 375 degrees. Fry blintzes, a few at a time, until golden brown; drain and serve topped with sour cream, blueberries, or strawberries. If you prefer, blintzes can be baked on a well-greased baking sheet in a 400 degree oven until golden; brush with melted butter before baking.

Peach Blintzes

Serves 8

¼ teaspoon salt
1 tablespoon oil
⅓ cup milk
½ cup sour cream
1 teaspoon sugar
2 eggs
⅔ cup flour
2 cups diced canned peaches, well drained
Melted butter

1. Mix salt, oil, milk, sour cream, sugar, and eggs together. Gradually add flour, mixing well to form smooth batter.
2. Lightly oil a 6-inch crepe pan. Add 2 or 3 tablespoons batter in hot pan; tilt pan to spread batter evenly. Cook over low heat until batter is set; remove from pan. Repeat process until all batter is used.
3. Place some diced peaches in center of each blintz; roll up.
4. Preheat oven to 400 degrees.
5. Place blintzes in single layer of well-greased, foil-lined baking sheet. Brush with melted butter. Bake until golden brown; remove from oven and serve with sour cream.

Pasta Amsterdam

Serves 4

1¼ cups rigatoni or pasta twists
4 hard-boiled eggs, shelled and quartered
6 small tomatoes, sliced
2 small cucumbers, sliced
1 red pepper, seeded and cut into thin strips
½ pound corned beef, sliced
2 tablespoons vinegar
3 tablespoons oil
Salt and pepper to taste
Pinch of sugar
Pinch of garlic powder
½ cup chopped parsley

1. Cook pasta in boiling, salted water until just tender, following package directions; drain.
2. Mix pasta, eggs, vegetables, and corned beef together in bowl.
3. Combine vinegar, oil, salt, pepper, sugar, and garlic powder to form dressing. Add dressing to pasta salad and toss well. Cover and let sit at room temperature for 30 minutes. Sprinkle parsley on top, and serve.

Vietnamese Beef Olives with Glass Noodles

Serves 4

2 cloves garlic, peeled and crushed
2 tablespoons cornstarch
¹/₂ cup plus 2 tablespoons soy sauce
¹/₂ cup plus 2 tablespoons sherry
Pinch of salt
Pinch of pepper
Pinch of five spices powder
3 tablespoons oil
1 pound club steak, cut into 16 pieces
4 scallions, thinly sliced
4 cups cold water
8 ounces transparent (cellophane) noodles
Juice of 1 lemon
16 lettuce leaves
16 slices cucumber

1. Combine garlic, cornstarch, 2 tablespoons soy sauce, 2 tablespoons sherry, salt, pepper, 5 spices powder, and 2 tablespoons oil. Coat meat slices on both sides with mixture; marinate for 1 hour.
2. Cover meat slices with scallions and roll up; arrange meat rolls on wooden skewers, putting 4 rolls on each skewer.
3. Pour cold water over transparent noodles; let soak for 10 minutes; drain water into saucepan. Bring water to a boil; cook noodles for 1 minute, then drain. Heat remaining oil in saucepan. Add noodles and keep warm over very low heat.
4. Grill or broil skewered meat for 5 to 7 minutes, turning frequently.
5. Mix lemon juice with ¹/₂ cup soy sauce and ¹/₂ cup sherry; divide among 4 small bowls.
6. To serve, arrange 4 lettuce leaves, 4 cucumber slices, and noodles on 4 plates. Place skewered meat on top of lettuce. To eat, wrap 1 meat roll, 1 cucumber slice, and ¹/₄ of noodles in each lettuce leave; dip into sauce.

Beef Sukiyaki

Serves 4

1¹/₂ to 2 pounds beef tenderloin, cut when partially frozen into paper-thin slices
2 tablespoons bacon drippings
8 ounces transparent (cellophane) noodles
8 dried black mushrooms
4 small onions, thinly sliced
4 leeks, thinly sliced
¹/₄ head white cabbage, cut into bite-size pieces
¹/₂ pound fresh spinach, stems removed from leaves
1 (1-pound) can bamboo shoots, drained
1 (8-ounce) can bean sprouts, drained
1 cup soy sauce
6 tablespoons sake or sherry
2 teaspoons sugar
1 cup rice

1. Arrange meat slices on round platter, slightly overlapping. Place 2 tablespoons bacon drippings into middle, cover with aluminum foil, and refrigerate.
2. Place noodles and mushrooms in separate bowls. Cover both with boiling water; soak for 20 minutes. Drain and repeat procedure 2 more times. Drain; arrange in separate bowls.
3. Place onions and leeks in separate bowls. Place cabbage, spinach, bamboo shoots, and bean sprouts in separate bowls also.
4. To prepare sauce, bring soy sauce, sake or sherry, and sugar to a boil in saucepan. Pour in bowl.
5. Cook rice according to package directions; keep warm.
6. Place electric wok or frying pan in middle of your table. Spoon rice into 4 individual bowls. Arrange meat platter, vegetables, and noodles around wok.
7. Place ¹/₄ of bacon drippings into wok and heat; add ¹/₄ of meat slices and brown quickly. Push aside and pour some sauce over meat. Add ¹/₄ of each vegetable and noodles; simmer for 3 minutes, stirring constantly.
8. Each guest is given part of cooked ingredients and starts eating while second portion is being prepared.

Rice Noodles with Beef and Broccoli

Serves 4

1/4 pound filet steak, cut into paper-thin slices while partially frozen
1 teaspoon soy sauce
1 teaspoon dry sherry
1 teaspoon vegetable oil
1 teaspoon cornstarch
1/2 teaspoon sugar
Pinch of white pepper
1 2/3 cups fresh rice noodles
1/4 cup cooking oil
1/2 cup broccoli florets
2 scallions, thinly sliced
1 teaspoon grated fresh ginger or 1/4 teaspoon powdered ginger
Sauce
1/4 cup chicken stock
2 to 3 teaspoons Chinese oyster sauce
1 teaspoon dark soy sauce
1 teaspoon dry sherry
1/4 teaspoon sugar
2 teaspoons cornstarch

1. Place steak slices in bowl with soy sauce, sherry, oil, cornstarch, sugar, and pepper. Mix well and marinate for 20 minutes.
2. Pour boiling water over noodles and stir gently to separate; drain.
3. Heat cooking oil in wok or frying pan. Stir-fry steak over high heat until lightly browned; remove from pan. Add broccoli, scallions, and ginger to pan; stir-fry for 2 minutes; remove from pan. Add noodles to wok and stir-fry until lightly browned, about 4 minutes. Transfer to serving plate.
4. In small bowl, mix together all sauce ingredients except cornstarch. Mix cornstarch with a small amount of sauce to form paste; stir into sauce.
5. Return vegetables to pan and pour in sauce. Bring to a boil, stirring constantly. Return meat to pan and reheat. Pour mixture over noodles, and serve at once.

Sofrito

Serves 6

1 cup flour
1 1/2 teaspoons salt
1/2 teaspoon freshly ground pepper
2 1/2 pounds chuck steak, cubed
3 tablespoons olive oil
1 tablespoon butter
2 to 4 cloves garlic, peeled and crushed
3 tablespoons red wine vinegar
3 tablespoons red wine
1 teaspoon sugar
2 tablespoons chopped parsley
1 cup water or beef stock
8 ounces tagliatelle

1. Mix flour, salt, and pepper together in plastic or paper bag; add meat and shake briskly until meat is evenly coated. Remove meat from bag and shake off any excess flour.
2. Heat olive oil and butter in Dutch oven. Brown meat in several batches until evenly browned. Add garlic and saute briefly. Return all meat to pan, add vinegar and wine, and bring to boiling point. Reduce heat and simmer for 3 minutes. Add sugar, parsley, and water or stock; cover and simmer for 1 1/4 hours, or until meat is completely tender and can be cut with fork.
3. Cook pasta in boiling, salted water following package directions; drain.
4. Place pasta in heated serving dish. Spoon beef mixture on top, and serve.

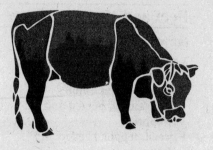

Pasta Beef Burgundy

Serves 4 to 6

3 tablespoons vegetable oil
12 small white onions
2 pounds lean stewing beef, cubed
1 tablespoon flour
2 cups dry red wine
1 cup beef bouillon
1 clove garlic, peeled and minced
1 tablespoon tomato paste
1/4 teaspoon thyme
1 bay leaf
1/2 teaspoon parsley
1 teaspoon salt
1/2 teaspoon pepper
1/2 pound mushrooms, quartered
10 ounces rigatoni
Parsley, for garnish

1. Heat oil in large frying pan. Saute onion lightly and remove from pan. Add beef cubes and saute until browned. Sprinkle cubes with flour and toss to coat meat. Cook for 2 minutes, stirring frequently. Add wine, bouillon, garlic, tomato paste, and seasonings. Stir well, cover, and cook over very low heat for 3 hours, or until meat is tender; add more bouillon if needed.
2. Add onions for last hour of cooking time; add mushrooms the last 15 minutes.
3. Cook rigatoni in boiling, salted water until just tender, following package directions; drain.
4. Place rigatoni in deep serving dish. Pour beef burgundy on top and toss until well mixed. Serve garnished with parsley.

Beef and Macaroni Stew

Serves 4

1 tablespoon butter
1 pound ground beef
1/2 cup chopped onion
1 clove garlic, peeled and chopped
1 green pepper, seeded and chopped
1 (28-ounce) can tomatoes, drained
1 cup macaroni, broken into small pieces
2 tablespoons chopped parsley
1/2 teaspoon thyme
2 teaspoons salt
1/4 teaspoon pepper
1/2 to 3/4 cup beef stock or water

1. Melt butter in large saucepan. Add meat and cook for 10 minutes, until browned, separating with fork as it cooks. Add onion, garlic, green pepper, tomatoes, macaroni, 1 tablespoon parsley, thyme, salt, and pepper. Add stock or water; mix well.
2. Cover and cook for 20 minutes, or until macaroni is tender. Stir occasionally. Sprinkle with remaining parsley and serve.

Greek Macaroni-Meat Bake

Serves 8

3 tablespoons butter
1/2 cup chopped onion
1 clove garlic, peeled and minced
1 pound ground beef
3/4 teaspoon salt
1/8 teaspoon pepper
3/4 teaspoon cinnamon
1/4 teaspoon sugar
1/4 cup tomato paste
8 ounces cooked macaroni
1/4 cup grated Romano cheese
1 egg

Custard Topping

1/4 cup butter
1/4 cup flour
2 cups milk, warmed
2 eggs, beaten

1. Melt butter in large, heavy skillet. Add onion and garlic; saute until very tender. Add ground beef and cook until browned, separating with fork as it cooks. Cover and simmer for 20 minutes. Add salt, pepper, cinnamon, sugar, and tomato paste. Cook for 10 minutes. Combine meat mixture, cooked macaroni, and Romano cheese; stir well. Add egg, stirring until well mixed.
2. Preheat oven to 375 degrees.
3. Turn ground beef mixture into greased 13 x 9 x 2-inch baking dish. Pack tightly and smooth surface.
4. Make custard topping: Melt butter in saucepan. Add flour, stirring until bubbly. Remove from heat. Slowly add warmed milk, stirring constantly. Return mixture to heat and cook, stirring constantly, until sauce thickens. Slowly add hot mixture to eggs while continuing to stir. Pour mixture back into saucepan and cook over low heat, stirring constantly, until mixture becomes thick. If the mixture becomes lumpy, puree it in a blender or food processor, then return it to saucepan.
5. Spread custard topping over ground beef mixture. Dust with additional Romano cheese and cinnamon. Bake for 30 minutes, or until custard is set. Let stand for several minutes, then cut into 8 squares and serve.

Yankee Doodle Macaroni

Serves 6

5 tablespoons butter
2 cups finely chopped onion
2 cloves garlic, peeled and finely chopped
1/2 cup sliced mushrooms
1 pound ground beef
1 (28-ounce) can whole tomatoes, undrained
1 tablespoon chopped parsley
Salt and pepper to taste
8 ounces macaroni
Grated Parmesan cheese

1. Heat 3 tablespoons butter in saucepan. Add onions, garlic, and mushrooms; saute until onion becomes pale yellow in color. Add meat; cook until browned. Add tomatoes, parsley, salt, and pepper. Cover and simmer for 45 minutes.
2. Cook macaroni in boiling, salted water following package directions; drain. Toss in 2 tablespoons butter.
3. To serve, place macaroni on heated platter, pour meat sauce on top, and sprinkle with grated cheese.

Pasta Chili

Serves 4

8 ounces whole-wheat pasta twists
1 tablespoon oil
1 onion, chopped
1 clove garlic, peeled and minced
1 pound lean chopped beef
2 teaspoons or more chili powder
1 cup marinara sauce
1/2 teaspoon basil
1/2 teaspoon oregano
1/2 cup chopped green pepper
1 cup grated Cheddar cheese

1. Cook pasta in boiling, salted water following package directions; drain.
2. Heat oil in large frying pan. Add onion and garlic; saute until translucent. Add beef. Cook until browned. Stir in chili powder, marinara sauce, basil, oregano, and green pepper; simmer for 10 minutes, stirring occasionally.
3. Add pasta to beef mixture; stir well and heat thoroughly. Remove pan from heat. Sprinkle cheese over meat-pasta mixture. Cover and let stand for 5 minutes, or until cheese is melted. Serve at once.

Macaroni and Beef Pastry

Serves 4 to 6

2 tablespoons butter
¹/₂ cup finely chopped onion
1 pound lean ground beef
1 tablespoon tomato paste
Salt and pepper to taste
8 ounces macaroni
2 cups milk
2 eggs
Pinch of nutmeg
Pinch of allspice
2 cups cottage cheese
2 ounces feta cheese
4 sheets phyllo pastry
About ¹/₄ cup melted butter

1. Melt butter in frying pan. Add onion and saute until translucent. Add ground beef and cook until browned, separating with fork as it cooks. Add tomato paste, salt, and pepper; mix well. Simmer until liquid is almost completely absorbed. Remove from heat.
2. Cook macaroni in boiling, salted water following package directions; drain.
3. Combine milk, eggs, nutmeg, allspice, cottage cheese and feta cheese; mix well.
4. Preheat oven to 375 degrees.
5. Layer half the macaroni in bottom of greased baking dish. Cover with layer of meat, then with remaining macaroni. Pour milk mixture on top. Brush each phyllo sheet with melted butter. Cover top of baking pan with phyllo sheets; poke several times with fork to make air holes. Sprinkle with water and bake for 30 minutes, or until golden brown. Remove from oven, and serve.

Quick Macaroni Scramble

Serves 4

1 cup macaroni
1 tablespoon oil
¹/₂ cup chopped onion
1 clove garlic, peeled and minced
1 pound ground beef
¹/₄ cup chopped parsley
Salt and pepper to taste
¹/₂ teaspoon basil
1 (19-ounce) can chunky vegetable soup

1. Cook macaroni in boiling, salted water following package directions; drain.
2. Heat oil in heavy skillet; saute onion and garlic until translucent. Add ground beef and cook until browned, separating with fork as it cooks. Add parsley, salt, pepper, and basil.
3. Add vegetable soup to meat mixture, stirring until well mixed. Cook over medium heat until hot. Add macaroni and continue to cook until heated thoroughly. Transfer to serving dish, and serve piping hot.

Quick and Easy Noodle Dinner

Serves 2

¹/₂ pound ground beef
1 tablespoon dried onion flakes
1 (10-ounce) can cream of chicken soup
¹/₂ cup milk
¹/₂ teaspoon sage
1 cup egg noodles or rotini

1. Brown ground beef in heavy skillet. Add dried onion, soup, milk, sage, and uncooked noodles; mix well. Cover and cook over low heat for 30 minutes, or until noodles are tender. Serve immediately.

Pastitsio

Serves 4

³/₄ cup butter
1 onion, finely chopped
1 clove garlic, peeled and finely chopped
1¹/₂ pounds ground beef
1 bay leaf
Salt and pepper to taste
¹/₄ teaspoon cinnamon
1¹/₂ cups water
¹/₄ cup tomato paste
8 ounces elbow macaroni
¹/₂ cup grated Parmesan cheese
4 cups milk, warmed
6 tablespoons flour
4 egg yolks, beaten
3 egg whites
¹/₂ cup bread crumbs

1. Melt 1 tablespoon butter in large frying pan. Add onion and garlic; saute until translucent. Add ground beef and cook until browned, separating with fork as it cooks. Add bay leaf, salt, pepper, cinnamon, and ¹/₂ cup water. Simmer for 10 minutes; skim off fat.
2. Cook macaroni in boiling, salted water until just tender, following package directions; drain and toss with 4 tablespoons butter and ¹/₂ cup grated Parmesan cheese.
3. Melt 6 tablespoons butter in saucepan. Add flour, stirring until well mixed. Gradually add milk; cook, stirring constantly, until sauce boils. Remove from heat. Add 2 tablespoons hot sauce to egg yolks; stir egg yolk mixture into remaining sauce. Bring to a boil again, then remove from heat.
4. Preheat oven to 350 degrees.
5. Sprinkle bottom of buttered, 8 x 14-inch baking pan with bread crumbs and half the grated cheese. Spread macaroni in layer on top. Pour ¹/₄ of cream sauce over macaroni. Layer meat mixture over sauce, then coat with unbeaten egg whites. Top with remaining cream sauce, sprinkle with remaining Parmesan cheese, and dot with remaining butter. Bake for 1 hour, until golden brown. Remove from oven, and serve.

Noodle Ring with Meat Sauce

Serves 4

2 tablespoons oil
1 onion, chopped
1 clove garlic, peeled and crushed
1 cup ground beef
1 tablespoon tomato sauce
1 cooking apple, peeled, cored, and chopped
Salt and pepper to taste
¼ teaspoon sugar
¼ teaspoon basil
1 (8-ounce) can tomatoes, undrained
12 ounces egg noodles
Chopped parsley

1. Heat oil in saucepan. Add onion and garlic; saute until onion begins to brown. Add meat; cook, stirring, over medium heat for 5 minutes. Add tomato sauce, apple, salt, pepper, sugar, basil, and tomatoes. Cover and simmer for 40 minutes.
2. While sauce is cooking, cook noodles in boiling, salted water following package directions; drain. Pack noodles into well-greased ring mold; keep hot.
3. When ready to serve, turn noodle ring onto hot dish; pile meat sauce in middle. Sprinkle with chopped parsley, and serve.

Hamburger and Sauerkraut Pierogis

Serves 4

2 cups flour
1 large egg or 2 small eggs
½ teaspoon salt
⅓ to ½ cup water
½ pound ground beef
¼ cup minced onions
½ cup sauerkraut
¼ cup butter, melted

1. Mix flour, eggs, and salt together. Stir in just enough water to form stiff dough. Divide dough in half; roll out each portion until paper-thin.

Cut circles in dough with biscuit cutter. Allow to set.
2. Brown ground beef in frying pan, separating with fork as it cooks. Add onion; saute for 5 minutes. Pour off excess fat. Add sauerkraut; mix well.
3. Place 1 teaspoon ground beef filling on half the dough circle. Moisten edges with water. Fold over unfilled side and seal edges.
4. Cook pierogis in large saucepan of boiling, salted water for 3 to 5 minutes. Using slotted spoon, lift gently out of water and place in single layer on serving dish. Pour melted butter on top, and serve immediately.

Beef Round over Noodles

Serves 4 to 6

2 tablespoons peanut or corn oil
1 teaspoon soy sauce
½ teaspoon sugar
2 teaspoons sherry
3 cups peeled and thinly sliced onions
2 teaspoons cornstarch
1 tablespoon soy sauce
1½ pounds beef round roast, cut into 1-inch pieces
1 tablespoon Worcestershire sauce
1 teaspoon garlic salt or 1 clove garlic, peeled and minced
½ cup sliced mushrooms, optional
8 ounces thin egg noodles

1. Heat oil in large frying pan with 1 teaspoon soy sauce, sugar, and 1 teaspoon sherry. Add onions and saute until translucent.
2. Mix cornstarch, 1 tablespoon soy sauce, and 1 teaspoon sherry in bowl. Dredge meat in mixture, making sure every piece is coated.

Add meat to onions and cook until browned. Stir in Worcestershire sauce and garlic. Cover and simmer for 1 hour, stirring occasionally. Add mushrooms, if desired, for last 10 minutes of cooking time.
3. Cook noodles in boiling, salted water following package directions; drain.
4. Place noodles in serving dish. Spoon beef mixture on top, and serve.

Berghoff Ragout

Serves 8

14 tablespoons butter
3½ pounds boneless round steak, cut into thin strips
1 cup chopped onion
1½ cups chopped green pepper
1 pound sliced mushrooms
½ cup flour
2 cups beef broth
1 cup dry white wine
1 teaspoon salt
1 teaspoon Worcestershire sauce
3 drops Tabasco sauce
8 ounces egg noodles

1. Melt 8 tablespoons butter in large frying pan. Brown meat over medium-high heat; remove from pan. Add onion to pan and saute for 2 minutes. Add green pepper and mushrooms; saute for 3 minutes more.
2. Melt 4 tablespoons butter in saucepan. Add flour, stirring until well blended. Slowly add beef broth; cook, stirring constantly, until sauce thickens. Stir in wine, salt, Worcestershire sauce, and Tabasco. Add meat and vegetables. Cover and simmer for 1 hour, or until meat is tender.
3. Cook noodles in boiling, salted water following package directions; drain and toss with 2 tablespoons butter.
4. Place noodles in heated serving dish. Pile meat mixture on top, and serve.

Beef Lo Mein

Serves 4

8 ounces lo mein noodles
1 tablespoon sesame oil
1 cup peanut oil
¹/₂ pound flank steak, cut diagonally into thin strips
4 cloves garlic, peeled and minced
3 cups bean sprouts, rinsed and drained
¹/₂ cup shredded bamboo shoots
¹/₂ cup shredded Chinese cabbage
3 tablespoons soy sauce
3 tablespoons dry sherry
1 tablespoon miso (soybean paste)
1 teaspoon sugar

1. Cook noodles in boiling, salted water until just tender, following package directions; drain well and toss with sesame oil.
2. Heat peanut oil in wok or frying pan. Add beef and cook, stirring, over high heat for 1 minute; remove from pan and set aside. Drain off all but 2 tablespoons oil from pan.
3. Add garlic and vegetables to pan; stir-fry for 1 minute. Add soy sauce, miso, and sugar; stir-fry for 15 seconds. Add meat and noodles to pan; stir-fry until meat is cooked and mixture is thoroughly heated. Serve at once.

Zesty Short-Rib Stew

Serves 6

2 tablespoons salad oil
5 pounds beef short ribs, cut into 2-rib portions
1 medium onion, quartered
1 (16- to 18-ounce) bottle barbecue sauce
1 cup water
5 medium carrots, cut in half crosswise
2 (10-ounce) packages frozen Brussels sprouts
4 ounces broad egg noodles

1. Heat oil in 8-quart Dutch oven. Add short ribs and cook a few at a time over medium-high heat until well browned on all sides; remove from pan.
2. Add onion to drippings in Dutch oven and cook over medium heat about 5 minutes, or until tender, stirring occasionally. Drain excess fat. Return ribs to Dutch oven. Stir in barbecue sauce and water; heat to boiling. Reduce heat and simmer for 1¹/₂ hours, stirring occasionally.
3. Add carrots to Dutch oven. Cover and simmer for 30 minutes. Add Brussels sprouts and bring to a boil over medium heat. Add noodles, cover, and simmer for 15 minutes, or until noodles are tender. Skim fat from liquid, and serve.

Beef Goulash

Serves 4

3 tablespoons vegetable oil
1 pound round steak, cubed
3 medium onions, chopped
¹/₂ teaspoon salt
¹/₄ teaspoon pepper
¹/₂ teaspoon garlic salt
1 teaspoon paprika
¹/₄ teaspoon sugar
2 cups hot water
1 tablespoon flour
¹/₄ cup cold water
¹/₂ cup heavy whipping cream
8 ounces egg noodles

1. Heat oil in Dutch oven. Add meat cubes and cook for 10 minutes, or until well browned. Stir in onions; cook until soft. Stir in salt, pepper, garlic salt, paprika, and sugar; blend well. Pour in hot water, cover, and simmer for 1¹/₂ hours.

2. Place flour and cold water in small jar or container; shake to blend, being sure to break up all lumps. Add flour mixture to meat, about 7 minutes before end of cooking time. Stir constantly until sauce is thick and bubbly. Remove from heat; stir in cream.
3. Cook noodles in boiling, salted water following package directions; drain.
4. Place noodles in heated serving bowl. Top with beef goulash, and serve.

Beef Stew Twists

Serves 4

2 tablespoons butter
1 onion, chopped
1¹/₄ pounds beef cubes
Salt and pepper to taste
1 bay leaf
1¹/₂ teaspoons red wine vinegar
2 cups beef broth
8 ounces pasta twists
2 tablespoons flour
2 tablespoons softened butter
¹/₂ cup plain yogurt

1. Preheat oven to 350 degrees.
2. Melt 2 tablespoons butter in Dutch oven. Add onion and saute until translucent. Add beef cubes and brown on all sides. Add salt, pepper, bay leaf, wine vinegar, and beef broth. Cover tightly and bake for 2 hours.
3. Cook pasta twists in boiling, salted water following package directions; drain.
4. Remove pan from oven; remove bay leaf. Blend flour with 2 tablespoons softened butter; stir into beef mixture. Simmer on stove top for 2 minutes, stirring constantly, until sauce thickens. Add yogurt and cooked pasta; mix well. Adjust seasoning, if needed, and serve.

Sauerbraten with Noodles

Serves 8

1 cup red wine vinegar
1 cup red wine
2 cups water
2 medium onions, thinly sliced
1 stalk celery, cut into 1-inch pieces
2 cups carrots, shredded
2 whole allspice
4 whole cloves
1 tablespoon salt
1/8 teaspoon pepper
1 (4-pound) boned rump roast
1/4 cup flour
2 tablespoons oil
2 tablespoons sugar
1/2 cup crushed gingersnaps (about 6 cookies)
1 pound egg noodles

1. In large bowl, combine wine vinegar, wine, water, onions, celery, carrots, spices, salt, and pepper. Add meat, cover, and refrigerate for 2 days; turn meat several times.
2. Remove meat from marinade, reserving marinade. Pat dry and dust with 2 tablespoons flour. Heat oil in Dutch oven or large saucepan. Brown meat well on all sides. Add marinade. Cover and simmer for 2 1/2 hours, or until meat is tender. Remove meat and keep warm.
3. Strain sauce. Puree vegetables in food processor or blender and return to sauce. Blend remaining flour with 1/4 cup water until smooth. Add to sauce with sugar. Cook, stirring, until thickened. Add gingersnaps and heat thoroughly. Slice meat and reheat in sauce.
4. Cook noodles in boiling, salted water following package directions; drain. Add noodles to meat; toss well and serve.

Sauerbraten Meatballs

Serves 4

1 pound lean ground beef
1/4 cup milk
1/4 cup bread crumbs
1/8 teaspoon ground cloves
1/8 teaspoon ground allspice
1/2 teaspoon salt
Pepper to taste
2 tablespoons vegetable oil
1 cup plus 2 tablespoons water
1/2 cup vinegar
1/4 teaspoon powdered ginger
1 bay leaf
1/4 cup brown sugar
8 ounces egg noodles
2 tablespoons butter
2 tablespoons flour

1. Mix ground beef, milk, bread crumbs, cloves, allspice, salt, and pepper together. Form into meatballs. In frying pan, brown meatballs in hot oil; pour off excess fat. Add 1 cup water, vinegar, ginger, bay leaf, and brown sugar to meatballs. Cover and simmer for 30 minutes. Skim off fat. Remove meatballs from pan and keep warm.
2. Cook noodles in boiling, salted water following package directions; drain and toss with butter.
3. Mix flour and 2 tablespoons water together. Gradually stir flour paste into pan juices to make gravy.
4. Place noodles on heated serving dish. Place meatballs on top of noodles and pour gravy over all.

Pork Chops with Tortellini

Serves 4

4 loin pork chops, 1 inch thick
2 cups cheese-filled tortellini
1/4 cup butter
Salt and pepper to taste
2 teaspoons rosemary
1 teaspoon sage
Parsley, for garnish

1. Place pork chops on rack in broiler pan. Broil 8 inches from source of heat for 20 to 30 minutes, until chops are well done; turn once.
2. Cook pasta in boiling, salted water following package directions; drain.
3. Melt butter in saucepan. Add pasta, salt, pepper, rosemary, and sage; heat thoroughly, shaking pan frequently. Place pasta on heated serving platter; place pork on pasta. Garnish with parsley, and serve.

Fettuccine with Pork

Serves 4

2 tablespoons corn oil
1 1/4 pounds pork fillet, cut into 1-inch cubes
1 large onion, chopped
3 large tomatoes, peeled and chopped
2 cloves garlic, peeled and crushed
2 chili peppers, finely chopped
Salt and pepper to taste
2 teaspoons lemon juice
2 teaspoons honey
1 tablespoon Worcestershire sauce
1 cup hot vegetable broth
8 ounces fettuccine
1 cup freshly grated Cheddar cheese

1. Heat oil in large, heavy saucepan. Add pork and onion; saute until browned. Add tomatoes, garlic, and chili peppers. Stir in salt, pepper, lemon juice, honey, Worcestershire sauce, and vegetable broth. Cook over low heat for 30 minutes.
2. Cook fettuccine in boiling, salted water until just tender, following package directions; drain.
3. Place pasta in heated serving dish. Top with meat sauce, sprinkle with cheese, and serve.

Stufatu

Serves 6

1/4 cup olive oil
1 large onion, chopped
4 cloves garlic, peeled and finely
　chopped
10 ounces lean stewing beef,
　cubed
10 ounces lean pork loin,
　cubed
3 large tomatoes, peeled and
　diced
2 slices bacon, diced
1/2 cup dry white wine
1 teaspoon salt
Pepper to taste
Water
1 pound macaroni
1/4 cup freshly grated Gruyere
　cheese
2 tablespoons chopped parsley

1. Heat oil in Dutch oven. Add onion and garlic; saute until translucent. Add beef and pork cubes and cook until browned on all sides. Add tomatoes and bacon; cook for 3 minutes. Add wine, salt, pepper, and enough water to just cover meat. Cook over low heat for 2 hours.
2. Cook macaroni in boiling, salted water following package directions; drain.
3. Preheat oven to 400 degrees.
4. Place meat mixture in large, ovenproof dish. Top with macaroni and then with grated cheese. Bake until cheese is melted and golden brown. Garnish with parsley, and serve.

Penne with Savory Pork

Serves 4

1 1/2 pounds boneless pork,
　diced
2 large onions, chopped
2 tablespoons peanut oil
1 clove garlic, peeled and
　chopped
1/2 tablespoon lemon juice
3 large ripe tomatoes, peeled and
　chopped

1/4 teaspoon chili sauce
1 teaspoon sugar
1 1/2 tablespoons Worcestershire
　sauce
Salt and pepper to taste
12 ounces penne
1 cup grated Cheddar cheese
1/2 cup salted peanuts

1. Brown pork and onions together in oil. Add garlic and lemon juice; stir well. Add tomatoes, chili sauce, sugar, Worcestershire sauce, salt, and pepper. Simmer for 15 to 20 minutes, or until pork is tender and thoroughly cooked.
2. Meanwhile, cook penne in boiling, salted water following package directions; drain.
3. Just before serving, stir grated cheese and peanuts into pork mixture. Heat until cheese is melted. Place penne in heated serving dish. Top with pork mixture, toss well, and serve.

Pork, Vegetable, and Macaroni Stew

Serves 6

1 pound boneless pork shoulder,
　cut into small pieces
1 tablespoon butter
1 medium onion, sliced
3 carrots, sliced
2 1/2 cups water
1 teaspoon salt
1 cup macaroni
2 cups canned green beans,
　undrained

1. Melt butter in large frying pan. Brown pork. Add onion and carrots. Stir in water and salt; bring to a boil. Cover and boil gently for 45 minutes, until meat and carrots are tender.
2. Stir macaroni and beans into meat mixture. Cover and boil gently for 10 minutes, or until macaroni is tender; stir occasionally. Add more water during cooking if mixture becomes too dry.
3. Transfer to deep serving dish, and serve.

Pork Chow Mein

Serves 4

12 black dried mushrooms
10 ounces fresh Chinese
　noodles
1 pound pork fillet, cut into
　1/2-inch thick strips
1 to 2 tablespoons cornstarch
3 tablespoons soy sauce
4 cups oil for deep-frying
1/4 cup corn oil
2 carrots, cut into thin slices
2 scallions, thinly sliced
1 cup bean sprouts
Salt to taste
1 teaspoon cornstarch,
　optional

1. Soak dried mushrooms in boiling water for 15 minutes; drain, reserving soaking liquid.
2. Cook Chinese noodles in boiling, salted water for 6 minutes; drain, rinse with cold water, and dry on paper towels.
3. Dip pork strips in cornstarch, then roll in 1 tablespoon soy sauce.
2. Heat 4 cups oil in deep-fat fryer or wok to 350 degrees. Fry noodles a batch at a time until crispy and brown; drain on paper towels and keep warm.
3. Heat 1/4 cup corn oil in frying pan or wok. Add pork and stir-fry for 2 minutes. Add carrots, scallions, and bean sprouts; stir-fry for 3 minutes more. Add mushrooms with soaking liquid and remaining soy sauce; stir-fry for 2 minutes. Season with salt. If desired, thicken sauce with 1 teaspoon cornstarch, blended with a little soy sauce.
4. Combine noodles and pork mixture in heated serving dish; serve at once.

Pork Dumplings

Serves 4

¹/₂ pound fatty pork, cut into small pieces
2 dried black mushrooms
1 scallion, chopped
¹/₂ teaspoon grated fresh ginger or ¹/₄ teaspoon powdered ginger
2 teaspoons chopped parsley
¹/₂ egg white, beaten
³/₄ teaspoon salt
1 teaspoon sugar
1¹/₂ teaspoons light soy sauce
¹/₂ teaspoon dark soy sauce
1 tablespoon cornstarch
2 to 3 tablespoons frozen peas, thawed
1 small carrot, diced
18 wonton wrappers, thawed if frozen
Hot mustard and soy sauce, for dipping

1. Place pork in food processor or blender; grind to smooth paste. Place ground pork in mixing bowl.
2. Soak mushrooms in boiling water for 15 minutes; drain. Squeeze water from mushrooms, remove stems, and chop caps finely. Add mushrooms, scallion, ginger, parsley, egg white, salt, sugar, soy sauces, and cornstarch to pork, kneading until sticky paste forms. Cover with plastic wrap and refrigerate for 1 hour.
3. Cook peas and carrots in boiling water for 2 minutes; drain.
4. Separate wonton wrappers; trim off the 4 corners, then cover with cloth until needed.
5. To form dumplings, place 2 teaspoons of pork mixture in center of each wonton wrapper; fold all sides of wrapper up to form small sack. Press wrapping firmly around filling, leaving top of dumpling open. Place 2 peas and a carrot cube into opening on top of each dumpling and press lightly into filling.
6. Arrange dumplings into lightly greased steaming basket or on oiled wire cake rack; set on rack in wok. Add water to below level of rack to prevent boiling water from touching dumplings. Cover and bring to a boil; steam dumplings for 12 minutes, or until cooked thoroughly. Serve straight from steamer with dips of hot mustard and soy sauce.

Fried Wontons

Serves 6

1 tablespoon peanut oil
¹/₂ pound finely chopped pork
¹/₂ cup canned water chestnuts, drained and finely chopped
3 scallions, finely chopped
¹/₂ teaspoon grated fresh ginger or ¹/₄ teaspoon powdered ginger
1 tablespoon soy sauce
¹/₂ pound wonton wrappers
Oil for deep-fat frying

1. Heat oil in frying pan; add pork and cook until browned. Remove from pan.
2. Combine pork, water chestnuts, scallions, ginger, and soy sauce. Lay wonton wrappers flat and place 1 teaspoon of filling in center of each wrapper. Brush edges of wrappers with water. Fold over to form triangle; press together firmly to ensure tight seal and that no air pocket is left inside.
3. Brush folded edge of wonton with water; fold right and left point of triangle toward each other so that they meet on fold. Press to seal.
4. Heat oil to 375 degrees in deep-fat fryer or wok. Fry wontons in batches for about 2 minutes, or until crisp and golden. Drain on paper towels and keep warm while cooking remaining wontons.

Pork Chops with Noodles

Serves 6

6 thick pork chops
1 clove garlic, peeled and minced
1 teaspoon crushed caraway seeds
2 teaspoons paprika (preferably mild Hungarian paprika)
¹/₂ teaspoon salt
Pepper to taste
1 cup dry white wine
8 ounces egg noodles
2 tablespoons butter
1 cup sour cream, optional

1. Place pork chops in ovenproof casserole dish. Mix garlic, caraway seeds, paprika, salt, pepper, and wine together; pour over pork chops. Cover and refrigerate for 2 to 3 hours.
2. Preheat oven to 325 degrees.
3. Bake pork chops and marinade, uncovered, for 1 hour, or until pork is tender. Add more wine if needed.
4. Cook noodles in boiling, salted water following package directions; drain and toss in butter.
5. Place noodles on serving platter. Remove pork chops from oven and place on top of noodles. Stir sour cream into pan juices, if desired, and heat, being careful not to boil. Pour sour-cream gravy over pork chops, and serve.

Fettuccine Stroganoff

Serves 4

1/4 cup butter
1 onion, chopped
1 clove garlic, peeled and
  minced
1 1/2 pounds pork cubes
1/4 pound mushrooms, sliced
2 tablespoons flour
2 cups chicken broth
1/4 cup dry white wine
Salt and pepper to taste
1/4 teaspoon paprika
8 ounces fettuccine
1 cup sour cream

1. Melt butter in Dutch oven. Add onion and garlic; saute until translucent. Add pork cubes; brown well on all sides. Add mushrooms and saute for 2 minutes more. Stir in flour; simmer for 5 minutes.
2. Gradually add broth and wine, stirring constantly. Season with salt, pepper and paprika. Cover and simmer for 1 hour, or until pork is tender.
3. Cook fettuccine in boiling, salted water following package directions; drain.
4. Just before serving, stir sour cream into pork mixture. Place fettuccine on heated serving platter. Pour pork stroganoff mixture on top and toss gently. Serve at once.

Quick Frankfurter and Noodle Dinner

Serves 4

2 tablespoons butter
1 pound frankfurters, cut into
  thirds diagonally
1 onion, finely chopped

1/2 teaspoon basil
1 (10-ounce) can condensed
  cream of celery soup
1/2 cup milk
1/2 cup chopped tomatoes
2 cups cooked broad egg noodles
Pepper to taste
1/4 cup chopped parsley

1. Melt butter in frying pan. Add frankfurters and onion; cook until browned. Add basil, soup, milk, tomatoes, noodles, and pepper; mix well. Cook, stirring occasionally, until well heated.
2. Place in serving dish. Sprinkle with parsley, and serve.

Spaghettini with Lamb Shanks

Serves 4

1/4 cup butter, softened
4 carrots, chopped
2 celery ribs, chopped
3 pounds lamb shanks, cut into
  2-inch pieces
Salt and freshly ground pepper to
  taste
1 tablespoon flour
1 cup canned Italian-style
  tomatoes, drained
1 cup dry white wine
1 cup water
1 teaspoon chopped fresh thyme
  or 1/4 teaspoon dried thyme
1 bay leaf
1 pound spaghettini
2 strips lemon rind, chopped
1 tablespoon chopped parsley

1. Melt 2 tablespoons butter in Dutch oven. Saute vegetables until tender. Add meat and season generously with salt and pepper; cook until browned.
2. Blend remaining butter with flour; stir into meat mixture and cook until flour browns. Add tomatoes, wine, water, thyme, and bay leaf; simmer for 1 hour.

3. Remove meat from pot 15 minutes before serving time; strain sauce.
4. Cook spaghettini in boiling, salted water until just tender, following package directions; drain and toss with sauce. Place pasta on large platter. Arrange lamb shanks on top. Sprinkle with lemon rind and parsley, and serve.

Cousin Marta's Pork Fillets

Serves 4

8 ounces egg noodles
1 pound pork fillet, very thinly
  sliced
3 tablespoons butter
1 medium onion, finely
  chopped
1 to 2 cloves garlic, peeled
  and crushed
1 thick slice bacon, diced
1 small green pepper, seeded
  and diced
1 small red pepper, seeded and
  diced
1 teaspoon salt
1/4 teaspoon freshly ground
  black pepper
1 1/2 teaspoons sweet paprika
1/2 cup heavy whipping cream

1. Cook noodles in boiling, salted water following package directions; drain.
2. Flatten pork slices with heel of your hand; saute in butter until lightly browned. Remove from pan and keep warm.
3. Add onion and garlic to same pan and saute until they just begin to brown. Add diced bacon and saute until crisp. Add peppers and saute for 2 minutes, or until soft. Add salt, pepper, paprika, and cream; cook, stirring constantly, until just below boiling point. Simmer for 1 minute. Return pork to pan and heat gently in sauce for 1 to 1 1/2 minutes more.
4. Place noodles in heated serving dish; top with pork and cream sauce, and serve at once.

Ham and Pasta Shells

Serves 4

2 cups pasta shells
1 cup creamed cottage cheese
$1/4$ cup butter
1 cup diced cooked ham
Salt to taste
Pinch of cayenne pepper
$1/4$ cup chopped parsley

1. Cook pasta in boiling, salted water following package directions; drain. Toss pasta with cottage cheese.
2. Melt butter in saucepan. Add ham and cook until well heated. Add pasta mixture; season with salt and cayenne pepper.
3. Transfer mixture to heated serving dish. Sprinkle with parsley, and serve.

Viennese Ham Fleckerl

Serves 4

$2 1/4$ cups flour
5 eggs, 3 of them separated
2 pinches of salt
$1/2$ cup softened butter
Pepper to taste
Pinch of nutmeg
$1/2$ cup sour cream
$1/2$ pound diced cooked lean ham
$1/4$ cup bread crumbs
3 tablespoons grated Parmesan
    cheese

1. Mix flour, 2 eggs, and a pinch of salt together; add enough water to make firm dough. Cover and let rest for 30 minutes. Roll out dough, but not too thinly; let dry. Cut into 2-inch squares. Cook in boiling, salted water for 4 minutes; drain.
2. Mix $1/4$ cup butter with 3 egg yolks; blend in pinch of salt, pepper, nutmeg, and sour cream. Mix pasta, ham, and egg yolk mixture together. Whisk egg whites until stiff and fold into ham-pasta mixture.
3. Preheat oven to 400 degrees.
4. Sprinkle bottom of buttered baking dish with 2 tablespoons bread crumbs. Add ham-pasta mixture, smoothing top with spoon. Sprinkle with remaining bread crumbs and grated cheese. Melt remaining butter and drizzle over top. Bake for 20 minutes, until browned and thoroughly heated. Remove from oven, and serve.

Ham Pasta Toss

Serves 4

$1/2$ pound smoked ham, cut into
    strips
$1/2$ cup sliced mushrooms
1 leek, white part only, cut into
    thin strips
2 tablespoons butter
1 cup sour cream or creme
    fraiche
1 tablespoon Dijon mustard
Salt and pepper to taste
Milk, as needed
8 ounces pasta of your choice

1. Saute ham, mushrooms, and leek in butter. Add sour cream or creme fraiche and mustard. Blend well. Heat mixture thoroughly; season with salt and pepper. Add a little milk if sauce becomes too thick.
2. Cook pasta in boiling, salted water following package directions; drain. Pour ham mixture over pasta and toss well. Serve immediately.

Pasta Twists with Ham Sauce

Serves 4

2 tablespoons butter
4 shallots, peeled and finely
    chopped
1 clove garlic, peeled and finely
    chopped
$1/4$ pound cooked lean ham, cut
    into very fine strips
$1/2$ cup hot beef broth
1 cup light cream
12 ounces pasta twists
1 egg yolk
$1/2$ cup chopped fresh chives
    or 1 tablespoon dried chives

1. Melt butter in saucepan; saute shallots and garlic until translucent. Add ham and beef broth; cook until well heated. Add cream, stirring constantly, and cook over medium heat until slightly reduced. Simmer while pasta is cooked.
2. Cook pasta twists in boiling, salted water until just tender, following package directions; drain.
3. Blend egg yolk with 2 tablespoons hot cream sauce, then blend into saucepan with remaining sauce. Cook until heated thoroughly; do not boil.
4. Combine pasta and cream sauce. Place in heated serving dish, sprinkle with chives, and serve.

Sophia's Angel Hair Pasta

Serves 4

3 tablespoons butter
$1/4$ pound prosciutto, finely
    diced
1 large clove garlic, peeled
    and minced
$1/4$ pound fresh mushrooms,
    thinly sliced
$1/4$ cup dry white wine
12 ounces angel hair pasta
    (capellini)
$1/3$ cup light cream
$1/4$ cup freshly grated Parmesan
    cheese
Finely chopped parsley
Freshly ground black pepper
    to taste

1. Melt 2 tablespoons butter in saucepan. Add prosciutto, garlic, and mushrooms; saute for 1 minute. Add wine and simmer for 10 minutes.
2. Cook pasta in boiling, salted water until just tender, following package directions; drain and toss with cream and 1 tablespoon butter.
3. Gently toss ham mixture with pasta. Add cheese; toss lightly. Sprinkle with parsley and freshly ground pepper. Serve at once.

Lamb and Apple Twist

Serves 4

5 tablespoons olive oil
2 large onions, diced
3 cloves garlic, peeled and finely
   chopped
1½ pounds lamb taken from leg
   joint, cut into coarse chunks
Salt and pepper to taste
1 teaspoon curry powder
1 cup hot beef broth
1 bay leaf
2¼ cup coarsely chopped, peeled
   cooking apples
8 ounces pasta twists
1 teaspoon cornstarch
3 tablespoons chopped parsley

1. Heat 4 tablespoons olive oil in large pan and brown meat. Add onions and garlic; saute until translucent. Season meat with salt, pepper, and curry powder. Add broth and bay leaf. Cover and cook over low heat for 1½ hours. Add apples to meat 20 minutes before end of cooking time.
2. Cook pasta twists in boiling, salted water following package directions; drain.
3. Add enough water to cornstarch to make paste; add to lamb and apple mixture, stirring until sauce thickens. Place pasta in heated serving dish. Cover with lamb and apple mixture, and sprinkle with parsley. Serve immediately.

Green Noodles with Lamb Ragout

Serves 4

3 tablespoons oil
1½ pounds lamb shoulder, cut
   into chunks
1 tablespoon butter
2 cloves garlic, peeled and
   chopped
1 sprig fresh rosemary, chopped,
   or ½ teaspoon dried rosemary
1 tablespoon tomato paste
½ cup beef broth
Salt and pepper to taste
8 ounces green noodles

1. Heat oil in Dutch oven. Add lamb and brown on all sides over medium heat; pour off excess fat. Add butter, garlic, and rosemary. Combine tomato paste and beef broth; stir into lamb mixture. Season with salt and pepper. Cover and simmer for 45 to 60 minutes, or until lamb is tender.
2. Cook noodles in boiling, salted water following package directions; drain.
3. Place noodles in heated serving dish. Top with ragout, and serve.

Lamb Stew with Noodles

Serves 6

¼ cup olive oil
2 pounds boneless leg of lamb,
   cut into 1-inch cubes
1 (2-ounce) can anchovy fillets,
   drained and cut into small
   pieces
½ teaspoon basil
1 teaspoon grated lemon rind
1 clove garlic, peeled and
   crushed
2 tablespoons white wine vinegar
½ teaspoon freshly ground
   pepper
1 cup beef consomme
2 teaspoons cornstarch
2 tablespoons cold water
3 cups cooked egg noodles

1. Heat oil in heavy skillet. Add lamb; cook over medium heat until well browned. Drain off excess oil. Add anchovies, basil, lemon rind, garlic, vinegar, pepper, and consomme to lamb. Cover and simmer for 1 hour, or until lamb is tender. Add boiling water if mixture becomes too dry.
2. Combine cornstarch and 2 tablespoons cold water, stirring until well blended. Stir cornstarch mixture into stew; cook, stirring constantly, until sauce thickens. Add cooked noodles, mix well, and cook gently until heated thoroughly.
3. Transfer to serving dish, and serve.

Lasagna Pastitsio

Serves 6 to 8

1 pound lasagna noodles
1 cup butter
2 egg whites
1 cup grated Parmesan cheese
1 pound ground veal
1 onion, chopped
Salt and pepper to taste
1 pound ripe tomatoes, peeled
   and strained
Bread crumbs, for dusting
Sauce
¼ cup butter
5 tablespoons flour
4 cups milk, scalded
Salt and pepper to taste
2 egg yolks, well beaten

1. Cook lasagna noodles in boiling, salted water until barely tender following package directions; drain. Rinse with cold water and drain again. Return noodles to pot. Melt ½ cup butter and pour over lasagna noodles. Beat egg whites lightly and add to lasagna noodles. Sprinkle with 3 tablespoons cheese; mix again.
2. Melt 5 tablespoons butter in heavy skillet; add veal and onion; cook until browned, separating meat with fork as it cooks. Season with salt and pepper; add tomatoes.

Simmer until all liquid has been absorbed.

3. To make sauce, melt butter in saucepan. Add flour slowly, stirring constantly. Blend scalded milk slowly into butter and flour; stir over low heat until sauce is smooth. Remove from heat; add salt and pepper. Blend egg yolks into sauce; stir until smooth.

4. Preheat oven to 350 degrees.

5. Divide lasagna noodles, veal, and sauce into 2 portions each. Butter baking pan and sprinkle with bread crumbs. Lay half the lasagna noodles over bread crumbs; sprinkle with some grated cheese. Add half the veal mixture, spreading it evenly. Place remaining lasagna noodles over veal. Sprinkle with more cheese, add remaining meat, and remaining sauce. Sprinkle remaining cheese on top, then dust with bread crumbs. Melt remaining butter and drizzle on top. Bake for 30 minutes, or until deep golden brown. Remove from oven, and serve.

Angel Hair Pasta with Veal and Artichokes

Serves 4

1 clove garlic, peeled and halved
1 tablespoon olive oil
1 pound veal round, pounded
    until thin and cut into bite-size
    pieces
¹/₂ teaspoon salt
¹/₈ teaspoon pepper
1 cup chopped canned tomatoes
¹/₄ cup sherry
¹/₄ teaspoon oregano
1 (10-ounce) package frozen
    artichoke hearts
8 ounces angel hair pasta
    (capellini)

1. Saute garlic in hot oil in large frying pan. Discard garlic.

2. Season veal with salt and pepper. Add to oil in frying pan and cook until lightly browned. Add tomatoes, sherry, and oregano; mix well. Add artichoke hearts. Cover and simmer for 1 hour, or until meat is tender.

3. Cook pasta in boiling, salted water until just tender, following package directions; drain.

4. Place pasta on heated serving dish; spoon veal mixture and pan juices on top, and serve.

Veal Shanks with Pasta

Serves 4

3 pounds veal shanks, cut into
    thick slices with marrow intact
Salt and pepper to taste
¹/₄ cup flour
6 tablespoons butter
1 onion, chopped
1 clove garlic, peeled and minced
2 carrots, peeled and diced
2 stalks celery, chopped
¹/₂ cup dry white wine
¹/₄ cup chicken broth
1 bay leaf
¹/₄ teaspoon thyme
8 ounces pasta of your choice

Gremolata

2 tablespoons finely chopped
    parsley
1 clove garlic, peeled and finely
    minced
1 teaspoon finely grated lemon
    peel

1. Season veal with salt and pepper. Dredge in flour; shake off excess. Melt butter in deep skillet or Dutch oven. Add veal and brown well on all sides; remove from pan.

2. Add onion and garlic to same pan; saute until translucent. Add carrots, celery, wine, chicken broth, bay leaf, and thyme. Add veal shanks, standing on their sides to prevent marrow falling from bone during cooking. Bring to a boil. Cover pan tightly; reduce heat to simmer. Cook for 1 hour, or until veal is tender. Add more broth if mixture looks dry at any time.

3. Cook pasta in boiling, salted water following package directions; drain.

4. Combine gremolata ingredients, mixing well. Place pasta on heated platter. Place veal on top of pasta and cover with sauce. Sprinkle with gremolata, and serve.

Veal Piquant

Serves 2

8 tablespoons flour
¹/₂ teaspoon salt
¹/₄ teaspoon pepper
¹/₂ pound veal, cut into thin flat
    slices
3 tablespoons peanut oil
1 onion, minced
1 clove garlic, peeled and minced
1 green pepper, seeded and cut
    into 1-inch squares
2 medium red tomatoes, cut into
    wedges
6 medium mushrooms, sliced
1 cup chicken bouillon
¹/₄ cup minced scallion greens
8 ounces fettuccine

1. Combine flour, salt, and pepper in plastic bag. Add veal and shake bag vigorously to coat veal.

2. Heat oil in frying pan and add veal; brown on both sides. Add onion and saute for 2 minutes. Add garlic, green pepper, tomatoes, and mushrooms. Add broth; mix well. Cover and simmer for 30 minutes.

3. Add scallions to veal mixture. Simmer for 30 minutes more, or until veal is tender.

4. Cook fettuccine in boiling, salted water following package directions; drain and place in heated serving dish. Spoon veal mixture on top, and serve.

Linguine with Veal

Serves 4

1¼ pounds veal shoulder
2 cloves garlic, peeled and finely chopped
1 sprig fresh rosemary, finely chopped, or ½ teaspoon dried rosemary
2 tablespoons butter
2 ounces lean bacon, diced
½ cup dry white wine
1 (1-pound) can tomatoes, drained, reserve juice
Salt and pepper to taste
½ cup mushrooms
8 ounces linguine

1. Make slits in veal and fill with garlic and rosemary.
2. Melt 1½ tablespoons butter in saucepan. Cook bacon until fat melts; add veal and brown well on all sides. Add wine and broil until liquid is reduced by half, turning meat from time to time. Add tomatoes, crushing them with wooden spoon. Season with salt and pepper. Simmer for 1 hour, gradually adding reserved tomato juice. Remove meat and cut into small cubes; return to sauce.
3. Melt remaining butter in small frying pan; add mushrooms and saute until tender. Add to saucepan with veal.
4. Cook linguine in boiling, salted water following package directions; drain.
5. To serve, place pasta in heated serving dish and spoon veal mixture on top.

Veal Goulash

Serves 4

2 tablespoons butter
2 onions, sliced
1 clove garlic, peeled and crushed
1 tablespoon paprika
1 tablespoon tomato paste
1 teaspoon thyme
1 teaspoon marjoram

1½ pounds boneless veal leg or shoulder, cut into 2-inch cubes
1 red pepper, seeded and diced
1½ cups chicken stock
1 bay leaf
Salt and pepper to taste
8 ounces egg noodles
1 cup sour cream
1 tablespoon chopped parsley

1. Preheat oven to 325 degrees.
2. Melt 1 tablespoon butter in frying pan. Add onions and garlic; saute until translucent. Mix with paprika, tomato paste, thyme, and marjoram. Place in bottom of casserole dish.
3. Melt remaining butter in frying pan and brown veal lightly. Place on top of onion mixture in casserole dish. Add red pepper and enough stock to cover meat. Add bay leaf; season with salt and pepper. Cover and bake for 1 hour, or until meat is tender.
4. While casserole is cooking, cook noodles in boiling, salted water following package directions; drain.
5. To serve, toss veal mixture with noodles. Spoon sour cream on top and sprinkle with chopped parsley.

Pasta Fleckerl with Veal

Serves 4

2¼ cups flour
2 eggs
Pinch of salt
¼ pound bacon, diced
1 large onion, finely chopped
¾ pound boneless veal shoulder, ground
1 teaspoon paprika
Salt and pepper to taste
2 tomatoes, skinned and chopped
2 green peppers, seeded and cut into strips
½ cup beef broth
½ cup grated Parmesan cheese
3 tablespoons butter

1. Mix flour, eggs, and salt together in mixing bowl. Add just enough

water to form smooth, firm dough. Cover and let rest for 30 minutes.
2. Cook bacon until fat melts; add onions and cook with bacon for 5 minutes. Add veal and cook until browned; season with paprika, salt, and pepper. Stir in tomatoes and green pepper strips. Pour in broth and simmer for 15 minutes, stirring occasionally.
3. Roll out dough, not too thinly, and cut into 2-inch squares. Cook in large saucepan filled with boiling, salted water for 4 minutes; drain well.
4. Preheat oven to 350 degrees.
5. Mix veal ragout and pasta together; stir in ¼ cup grated cheese. Transfer to buttered baking dish. Dot with butter and bake for 10 minutes. Sprinkle remaining cheese on top, and serve.

Alaskan Fisherman's Stew

Serves 6

¼ cup butter
1½ cups sliced celery
½ cup chopped onion
1 clove garlic, peeled and minced
1 (28-ounce) can whole tomatoes, undrained
1 (8-ounce) can tomato sauce
2 teaspoons salt
½ teaspoon paprika
½ teaspoon chili powder
¼ teaspoon pepper
8 ounces spaghetti
2 cups boiling water
2 pounds thick fish fillets, thawed if frozen, cut into 1-inch cubes
¼ cup grated Parmesan cheese

1. Melt butter in large, heavy pan. Add celery, onion, and garlic; saute for 3 minutes. Add tomatoes, tomato sauce, and seasonings. Cover and simmer for 15 to 20 minutes.
2. Add uncooked spaghetti and boiling water to pan; mix, cover pan, and simmer for 10 minutes, or until spaghetti is almost tender.

3. Add fish, cover, and simmer for 10 minutes, or until fish flakes easily when tested with fork. Serve hot with grated cheese sprinkled over top.

Golden Gate Tuna and Noodles

Serves 6

1/2 pound mushrooms, sliced
1/2 cup sliced onion
1/2 cup thinly sliced green peppers
3 (7-ounce) cans chunk-style tuna fish packed in oil, drained, reserve liquid
2 (10-ounce) cans condensed cream of tomato soup
1/2 cup milk
1/8 teaspoon thyme
Salt to taste
1/2 cup sour cream
12 ounces medium egg noodles
1/2 cup butter
1/2 cup coarsely chopped filberts or almonds

1. In saucepan, heat reserved tuna oil and saute mushrooms, onion, and green pepper. Stir in tuna, soup, milk, thyme, and salt; cook until heated thoroughly, stirring occasionally. Stir in sour cream and simmer until heated thoroughly.
2. Meanwhile, cook noodles in boiling, salted water following package directions; drain.
3. Melt butter in small frying pan; add nuts and cook until toasted. Toss nuts with noodles. Spoon tuna sauce on top, and serve.

Thai Rice Noodles with Seafood Sauce

Serves 4

Vegetable oil for deep-frying
8 ounces rice noodles, broken into pieces
Sauce
1 tablespoon vegetable oil
1 onion, finely chopped
2 cloves garlic, peeled and finely chopped

1/2 pound shrimp, shelled and deveined
1/2 cup crabmeat
2 teaspoons brown sugar
2 tablespoons tamarind water
1 teaspoon salt
1 tablespoon soy sauce
2 cups fresh bean sprouts
2 teaspoons grated orange rind

1. Heat oil to 375 degrees in deep-fat fryer or wok. Fry rice noodles, a few at a time, for about 30 seconds per batch. The noodles will swell and float. When done, remove from fat and drain on paper towels.
2. To make sauce, heat 1 tablespoon oil in wok or frying pan. Add onion and garlic; cook, stirring, until lightly browned. Add shrimp and crab; cook until shrimp turn pink. Stir in brown sugar, tamarind water, salt, and soy sauce. Add noodles and mix well; cook until thoroughly heated.
3. Place mixture in serving dish. Surround with bean sprouts and sprinkle with orange rind.

Glass Noodles with Shrimp

Serves 4

1 cup transparent (cellophane) noodles
3 cups oil for deep-frying
3 tablespoons corn oil
1/2 pound pork fillet, cut into 1/2-inch thick strips
1 3/4 cups onion rings
3 cloves garlic, peeled and finely chopped
1 small red pepper, seeded and diced
1 1/2 cups bean sprouts
3 tablespoons soy sauce
2 tablespoons oyster sauce
Pinch of salt
2 to 3 tablespoons sugar
Juice from 1/2 lemon
1/2 pound cooked shrimp, shelled and deveined
2 tablespoons chopped parsley or 1 teaspoon chopped coriander

1. With scissors, cut noodles into 3-inch long pieces. Heat 3 cups oil to 350 degrees in deep-fat fryer or wok. Fry noodles in batches until golden; drain on paper towels.
2. Heat 3 tablespoons oil in frying pan or wok. Add pork and stir-fry for 2 minutes, turning constantly; remove from oil. Add onion, garlic, and red pepper; stir-fry for 2 minutes. Add bean sprouts, soy and oyster sauces, salt, sugar, and lemon juice. Stir-fry for 5 minutes more.
3. Combine noodles, pork, vegetables, and shrimp together and cook until thoroughly heated. Garnish with parsley or coriander, and serve.

Curried Shrimp with Vermicelli

Serves 6

6 tablespoons butter
3 tablespoons minced onion
2 cloves garlic, peeled and finely minced
6 tablespoons flour
3 teaspoons curry powder
1/2 teaspoon salt
1/8 teaspoon pepper
1 (10-ounce) can condensed consomme
3 cups milk
3 tablespoons chutney
1/3 cup lemon juice
2 pounds cooked shrimp, shelled and deveined
1 pound vermicelli

1. Melt butter in saucepan. Saute onion and garlic for several minutes. Stir in flour, curry powder, salt, and pepper. Add consomme and milk gradually. Cook, stirring constantly, until sauce thickens.
2. Add chutney, lemon juice, and shrimp to saucepan. Heat thoroughly.
3. Cook vermicelli in boiling, salted water following package directions; drain.
4. Place pasta in heated serving bowl. Pour shrimp mixture on top, and serve.

Shrimp Spaghettini

Serves 4

1 pound shrimp, shelled and deveined
Water
2 tablespoons soy sauce
Lemon juice
2 tablespoons corn oil
1 scallion, thinly sliced
2 cloves garlic, peeled and minced
1/2 cup chopped fresh basil leaves
Pinch of marjoram
8 ounces spaghettini
1/4 cup finely chopped parsley
Pinch of cayenne pepper

1. Boil shrimp in water to cover and soy sauce until shrimp turn pink, about 2 or 3 minutes. Remove shrimp from pan, reserving cooking liquid. Sprinkle shrimp with lemon juice.
2. Heat oil in large frying pan. Saute scallion and garlic for 2 minutes. Add 1 cup reserved cooking liquid, basil, and marjoram. Bring to a boil, then reduce heat and simmer for 1 minute.
3. Cook spaghettini in boiling, salted water following package directions; drain.
4. Add pasta, shrimp, parsley, and cayenne pepper to frying pan with sauce; toss until well mixed. Cook gently until heated thoroughly. Transfer to heated serving bowl, and serve.

Stir-Fried Shrimp and Crispy Noodles

Serves 4

1 green pepper, seeded and cut into 1/4-inch strips
1 cup bean sprouts
1 teaspoon grated fresh ginger or 1/4 teaspoon powdered ginger
2 cups plus 2 tablespoons vegetable oil

1/2 pound cooked shrimp, shelled and deveined
1 tablespoon dry sherry
1 tablespoon soy sauce
Salt to taste
12 ounces thin egg noodles

1. Combine green pepper, bean sprouts, and ginger; stir-fry in 2 tablespoons oil for 2 minutes. Push vegetables to sides of pan and add shrimp; stir-fry just until shrimp turn pink. Combine shrimp and vegetables; stir in sherry and soy sauce. Salt to taste. Keep warm over very low heat.
2. Cook noodles in boiling, salted water following package directions; drain and rinse thoroughly in cold water. Dry on paper towels.
3. Heat 2 cups oil in wok or deep frying pan to 375 degrees. Fry handfuls of noodles at a time for about 5 minutes or until browned, turning frequently. Drain on paper towels.
4. Place crispy noodles on serving platter. Top with shrimp mixture, and serve piping hot.

Shrimp with Feta Cheese

Serves 4

1 tablespoon lemon juice
1 1/4 pounds medium shrimp, shelled and deveined
2 tablespoons olive oil
1/4 cup chopped onion
1 clove garlic, peeled and minced
1 cup tomato sauce
1/4 cup dry white wine
1 tablespoon butter
1 tablespoon brandy or ouzo
1/4 teaspoon oregano
1 tablespoon chopped parsley
1/2 pound feta cheese, diced
8 ounces rigatoni

1. Pour lemon juice over shrimp and let stand while making sauce.
2. Heat oil in heavy skillet. Add onion and garlic; saute until translucent. Add tomato sauce and wine; simmer for 15 minutes.

3. Melt butter and saute shrimp until pink, about 3 to 4 minutes. Gently warm brandy in small saucepan. Ignite and pour over shrimp. When flame extinguishes, add oregano and parsley. Transfer shrimp to 1 1/2-quart casserole dish.
4. Preheat oven to 375 degrees.
5. Combine juices from pan in which shrimp were cooked with tomato and wine sauce; pour over shrimp. Top with feta cheese, pressing cheese into sauce. Bake for 15 minutes, or until hot and bubbly.
6. While shrimp are baking cook rigatoni in boiling, salted water following package directions; drain. Place rigatoni in serving dish. Pour shrimp mixture on top, toss lightly, and serve.

Pasta Shells Deluxe

Serves 4

1 1/2 cups broccoli florets
2 tablespoons butter
1 onion, finely chopped
1 clove garlic, peeled and finely chopped
1/2 pound mushrooms, sliced
1/2 cup heavy whipping cream
1/2 cup chopped tomato
1 teaspoon basil
1/2 teaspoon oregano
Salt and pepper to taste
1/2 pound cooked shrimp, shelled and deveined
8 ounces small pasta shells
1/4 cup grated Parmesan cheese

1. Cook broccoli in boiling water to cover for 2 minutes; drain.
2. Melt butter in saucepan. Add onion and garlic; saute until translucent. Add mushrooms and saute for 5 minutes longer. Stir in cream, blending well. Add tomato, basil, oregano, salt, and pepper; mix well.
3. Add broccoli and shrimp to sauce; simmer for 5 minutes, or until heated thoroughly. Be careful not to overcook shrimp.

4. Cook pasta shells in boiling, salted water following package directions; drain.

5. Place pasta in heated serving dish. Pour broccoli-shrimp mixture over pasta; sprinkle with grated Parmesan, and serve.

Fettuccine with Garlic Shrimp

Serves 6

$^3/_4$ cup extra-virgin olive oil
6 cloves garlic, peeled and sliced
1 fresh red chili pepper, sliced
2 pounds large shrimp, shelled and deveined
4 fresh basil leaves or 1 teaspoon dried basil
Salt to taste
1 pound fettuccine

1. Heat oil in frying pan. Add garlic and chili; saute for 1 minute. Add shrimp and cook over medium-high heat until shrimp turn pink, about 3 minutes. Add basil and salt.

2. Cook pasta in boiling, salted water following package directions; drain.

3. Place fettuccine in heated serving bowl. Pour shrimp and oil remaining in pan on top; toss and serve piping hot.

Thorny Shrimp Balls

Serves 8

24 large shrimp, shelled and deveined
3 scallions, white part only, finely minced
1 teaspoon finely minced fresh ginger
$^1/_4$ teaspoon salt
1 tablespoon mirin (sweet rice wine) or 2 teaspoons pale dry sherry
2 tablespoons miso (soy bean paste)
1 egg white, well beaten, or $^1/_3$ teaspoon cornstarch

2 (2-ounce) packages transparent (cellophane) noodles, cut into $^3/_4$-inch lengths
Oil for deep-frying
Lemon slices and soy sauce, for serving, optional

1. Mash or chop shrimp until finely minced, adding scallions and ginger at the same time. When very fine, add salt, mirin, and miso; mix well. Add egg white or cornstarch. Using either your fingers or 2 teaspoons, form shrimp mixture into small balls.

2. Place cut-up noodles on waxed paper and roll balls over noodles until they are well covered; they should look like sea urchins. Cover and keep chilled unless using immediately. Remove from refrigerator about half an hour before frying time.

3. Heat enough oil in deep-fat fryer, wok, or deep skillet to cover shrimp balls. Fry 3 or 4 at a time; the noodles will puff up immediately. Remove balls from oil before noodles brown; this will take a couple of minutes at the most. The finished shrimp balls should be white and puffy. Drain and serve, either by themselves or with lemon slices and soy sauce.

Sara's Fresh Shrimp Spaghetti

Serves 4

3 tablespoons butter
$^1/_4$ cup minced shallots
1 clove garlic, peeled and finely chopped
$1^1/_4$ cups heavy whipping cream
1 tablespoon chili sauce
$^1/_4$ cup chopped parsley
$1^1/_2$ pounds fresh shrimp in shells
Salt and pepper to taste
12 ounces spaghetti

1. Melt butter in saucepan. Add shallots and garlic; saute until translucent. Stir in cream, chili sauce, and parsley; bring to a boil, stirring constantly. Add shrimp and cook until pink and thoroughly heated. Season with salt and pepper.

2. Cook spaghetti in boiling, salted water following package directions; drain.

3. Place spaghetti on heated serving platter. Spoon shrimp and sauce on top, and serve.

Shrimp with Green Noodles

Serves 4

1 pound shrimp, shelled and deveined
1 tablespoon lemon juice
2 tablespoons butter
1 small onion, diced
2 cloves garlic, peeled and crushed
$^2/_3$ cup heavy whipping cream
$^3/_4$ cup sour cream
1 cup freshly grated Parmesan cheese
12 ounces green noodles
Salt and pepper to taste
1 teaspoon tarragon

1. Sprinkle shrimp with lemon juice. Melt butter in saucepan; saute shrimp until they turn pink. Add onion and garlic; saute briefly. Pour cream and sour cream over shrimp and bring to a boil. Add $^1/_2$ cup Parmesan cheese and simmer for 5 minutes.

2. Cook pasta in boiling, salted water until just tender, following package directions; drain.

3. Season shrimp mixture with salt, pepper, and tarragon. Place pasta in heated serving dish. Cover with shrimp mixture and top with remaining grated cheese. Serve at once.

Chicken and Sun-Dried Tomato Pasta

Serves 4

1 (7-ounce) jar oil-packed sun-
  dried tomatoes, drained,
  reserve liquid, and coarsely
  chopped
1 tablespoon olive oil
1 onion, finely chopped
3 cloves garlic, minced
2 boneless chicken breasts,
  cut into strips
1 tablespoon tomato sauce
1 teaspoon basil
Salt and freshly ground pepper
  to taste
8 ounces fettuccine
¹/₄ cup finely chopped parsley

1. Heat 1 tablespoon reserved
tomato oil and olive oil in large
frying pan. Add onion and garlic;
saute for 5 minutes. Add chicken
strips; saute until tender, about 8
minutes. Add tomato sauce and mix
well. Add basil, sun-dried tomatoes,
salt, pepper, and 2 more tablespoons reserved tomato oil.
2. Cook fettuccine in boiling, salted
water following package directions;
drain.
3. Place fettuccine in heated serving
dish; pour chicken-tomato mixture
on top and toss lightly. Sprinkle with
parsley, and serve.

Cara's Clam Spaghetti

Serves 8

¹/₂ cup salad oil
1 cup finely chopped onion
2 cloves garlic, peeled and
  minced
6 tablespoons butter
³/₄ cup dry white wine
³/₄ cup chicken broth
¹/₂ teaspoon oregano
2 (8-ounce) cans minced clams,
  drained, reserve ¹/₂ cup liquid
³/₄ cup grated Parmesan or
  Romano cheese
Pepper to taste
1 pound spaghetti

1. Heat oil in large skillet. Add onion
and garlic; saute until tender, about
3 to 5 minutes. Stir in butter, wine,
chicken broth, oregano, and
reserved clam juice. Simmer for 20
minutes. Add clams and heat until
clams are just heated. Remove from
heat and stir in grated cheese and
pepper.
2. Meanwhile, cook spaghetti in
boiling, salted water following
package directions; drain.
3. Place spaghetti in heated serving
dish; cover with clam mixture, and
serve.

Vermicelli with Fresh Clams

Serves 6 to 8

2 pounds clams in their shells
2 cloves garlic, peeled
¹/₂ cup olive oil
¹/₄ cup chopped parsley
Salt and freshly ground pepper
  to taste
1 pound vermicelli
¹/₂ cup butter, melted

1. Scrub clams and soak in cold
water for 1 hour; drain.
2. In large, heavy skillet, saute garlic
in olive oil until browned; remove
from pan and discard. Add clams,
cover, and cook over medium heat
for 5 minutes. Add parsley and
seasonings; cook 3 minutes more.
3. Meanwhile, cook vermicelli in
boiling, salted water following
package directions; drain and place
in heated serving dish.
4. Remove clams from pan. Strain
pan liquid through cheesecloth to
remove any grit. Toss vermicelli with
pan liquid. Place clams on top,
drizzle with melted butter, and serve
immediately.

Linguine Seafood Supreme

Serves 4

¹/₂ pound shrimp, shelled and
  deveined
2 cups baby clams, canned or
  fresh
3 tablespoons butter
1 small onion, finely chopped
1 clove garlic, peeled and finely
  chopped
1 tablespoon flour
2 teaspoons Dijon mustard
¹/₄ cup water
¹/₃ cup dry white wine
Salt and pepper to taste
¹/₄ cup finely chopped parsley
10 ounces linguine
Parsley sprigs, for garnish

1. Cook shrimp in boiling water until
pink, about 2 to 3 minutes; remove
from pan and set aside. Drain off
packing liquid from fresh or canned
clams and set aside.
2. Melt butter in saucepan. Saute
onion and garlic until translucent.
Add flour and mustard, stirring to
blend well. Pour in reserved clam
liquid, water, wine, salt, pepper, and
parsley. Cover and simmer for 10
minutes, stirring occasionally.
3. Cook linguine in boiling, salted
water following package directions;
drain.
4. Stir shrimp and clams into saucepan; simmer until heated thoroughly.
Pour seafood mixture over linguine
on heated serving platter, garnish
with parsley, and serve.

Seafarer's Fettuccine

Serves 8

7 tablespoons butter
2 tablespoons olive oil
5 cloves garlic, peeled and
  slivered
1 pound large shrimp, shelled
  and deveined
Salt and pepper to taste
1 (8-ounce) can minced clams,
  undrained

1 (8-ounce) can Italian-style
  tomatoes, undrained
1 teaspoon oregano
¼ cup dry white wine
1 pound fettuccine
¼ cup chopped parsley
½ cup grated Parmesan cheese

1. Heat 2 tablespoons butter, olive oil, and garlic in large skillet until it sputters. Add shrimp, salt, and pepper. Cook, stirring, for 10 minutes. Remove shrimp from pan. Add clams and can liquid to skillet along with tomatoes, oregano, and wine. Cook until sauce is slightly thickened.
2. Cook fettuccine in boiling, salted water following package directions; drain and toss with 4 tablespoons butter.
2. Return shrimp to skillet and simmer for 10 minutes. Dot with 1 tablespoon butter and sprinkle with parsley. Pour mixture over fettuccine, sprinkle with grated Parmesan cheese, and serve.

Linguine with Mushroom-Clam Sauce

Serves 6

1 pound linguine
½ cup butter
2 cloves garlic, peeled and
  minced
1 pound mushrooms, sliced
1 (10½-ounce) can minced
  clams, undrained
½ cup chopped parsley
1 teaspoon salt
¼ teaspoon pepper

1. Cook linguine in boiling, salted water following package directions; drain.
2. Melt butter in large skillet. Add garlic and mushrooms; saute until golden. Stir in clams and clam liquid, parsley, salt, and pepper; cook over medium heat until hot.
3. Combine linguine and mushroom mixture in heated serving bowl; toss well and serve.

Seafood and Tagliatelle

Serves 6

¼ cup butter
1½ cloves garlic, peeled and
  minced
2 teaspoons lemon juice
Salt and pepper to taste
½ pound small shrimp, shelled
  and deveined
1 cup minced clams,
  undrained
1 pound tagliatelle

1. Melt butter in large frying pan. Add garlic, lemon juice, salt, and pepper; simmer for 5 minutes. Add shrimp and cook until just pink. Add clams and liquid; cook over low heat for 15 minutes.
2. Meanwhile, cook pasta in boiling, salted water following package directions; drain.
3. Place pasta in heated serving bowl. Pour seafood mixture on top and toss. Serve at once.

Japanese Noodles with Horseradish

Serves 4

14 ounces Udon (Japanese
  whole-wheat pasta) or thin
  spaghetti
¼ cup oil
3 onions, finely chopped
1¼ cups sliced mushrooms
1¼ cups grated carrots
½ pound shrimp, shelled and
  deveined
¼ cup soy sauce
¼ cup sweet and sour sauce
1 large white horseradish

1. Cook pasta in boiling, salted water until just tender, following package directions; drain.

2. Heat oil in large frying pan or wok. Add onions and stir-fry for 1 minute. Add mushrooms and carrots; stir-fry for 3 minutes more. Add shrimp and stir-fry until pink. Mix in soy sauce, sweet and sour sauce, and cooked pasta. Keep warm over very low heat.
3. Grate horseradish. Place pasta mixture in heated serving bowl; serve horseradish separately.

Thin Spaghetti Orientale

Serves 4

1 boneless chicken breast,
  skinned and cut into ¼-inch
  strips
1 tablespoon dry sherry
3 tablespoons soy sauce
2 tablespoons oil
2 cups mixed vegetables, such
  as green beans, sliced
  mushroms, green pepper
  strips, and shredded carrots
½ cup chicken broth
1 tablespoon cornstarch
2 tablespoons cold water
½ pound cooked shrimp, shelled
  and deveined
8 ounces thin spaghetti

1. Marinate chicken in sherry and 2 tablespoons soy sauce for 20 minutes.
2. Heat oil in wok; stir-fry vegetables for 2 to 3 minutes. Push vegetables to the side; add chicken and stir-fry for 3 to 4 minutes, until tender. Return vegetables to center of pan and mix with chicken. Add broth. Mix cornstarch with cold water, then stir into sauce to thicken. Add shrimp. Heat until sauce boils and shrimp are well heated.
3. Cook spaghetti in boiling, salted water following package directions; drain and toss with 1 tablespoon soy sauce. Place in wok with chicken-shrimp mixture, and toss well. Transfer to serving dish, and serve at once.

Bami Goreng

Serves 4

8 ounces thin spaghetti
5 tablespoons oil
2 cloves garlic, peeled and finely chopped
$3/4$ pound boneless chicken breasts, cut into $1/2$-inch thick strips
$3/4$ cup chicken broth
2 tablespoons soy sauce
Salt and pepper to taste
1 tablespoon chopped fresh ginger or 1 teaspoon powdered ginger
4 scallions, thinly sliced
3 stalks celery, thinly sliced
1 small red pepper, seeded and diced
$1/2$ pound shrimp, shelled and deveined
$1^{1}/4$ cups Chinese cabbage leaves, shredded

1. Cook pasta in boiling, salted water following package directions; drain.
2. Heat 2 tablespoons oil in large frying pan or wok; stir-fry garlic for 30 seconds, until softened but not browned. Add chicken and stir-fry for 2 minutes. Add broth, soy sauce, salt, and pepper; simmer until reduced by a third. Remove from pan and set aside.
3. Heat remaining oil in pan. Add ginger, scallions, celery, and red pepper; stir-fry for 2 minutes. Add shrimp and Chinese cabbage; stir-fry until shrimp are pink and thoroughly heated. Add chicken mixture and pasta; cook, stirring, until well heated. Transfer to heated serving dish, and serve.

Pasta Souffle with Smoked Salmon

Serves 4

8 ounces small pasta shapes, such as bow ties or elbow macaroni
6 eggs, separated
1 cup light cream
$1/2$ cup milk
Salt and white pepper to taste
$3/4$ cup grated Gruyere
$1/2$ teaspoon paprika
6 ounces smoked salmon, diced
$1/2$ cup chopped fresh chives

1. Cook pasta in boiling, salted water until just tender, following package directions; drain. Rinse with cold water and drain again.
2. Mix egg yolks with cream, milk, salt, and pepper. Beat egg whites until stiff peaks form. Mix half the grated cheese and $1/4$ teaspoon paprika into stiff egg whites. Fold into egg yolk mixture.
3. Combine salmon, pasta, and chives. Season with salt and pepper.
4. Preheat oven to 350 degrees.
5. Butter 4 small ovenproof dishes. Place pasta mixture in dishes and pour egg mixture on top. Sprinkle with remaining cheese. Place dishes on middle shelf of oven and bake for 30 minutes, or until golden brown. Remove from oven, and serve at once.

Salmon and Mussels Giorgio

Serves 4

8 ounces thin spaghetti
$1^{1}/2$ pounds salmon fillets
Juice of $1/2$ lemon
2 tablespoons butter
2 small onions, diced
1 tablespoon flour
1 cup white wine
1 cup hot beef broth
Salt and pepper to taste
8 ounces canned mussels, drained

1 pound tomatoes, skinned and cubed
$1/4$ cup grated Parmesan cheese

1. Cook spaghetti in boiling, salted water following package directions; drain.
2. Sprinkle fish with lemon juice.
3. Melt butter in saucepan. Add onions and saute for 5 minutes. Add fish and saute on both sides until lightly browned; sprinkle with flour. Add wine and hot broth, stirring well. Simmer for 5 minutes. Season with salt and pepper. Add mussels and tomatoes; cook over low heat for 10 minutes.
4. Place spaghetti on large platter. Put fish mixture on top. Sprinkle with grated cheese, and serve.

Macaroni with Tuna Sauce

Serves 6

1 pound macaroni
5 canned sardines, drained
$1^{1}/4$ pounds ripe tomatoes, peeled and strained, or $1^{1}/2$ tablespoons tomato paste diluted with 2 cups water
1 cup oil or $3/4$ cup butter
2 cloves garlic, peeled and chopped
Salt and pepper to taste
1 bay leaf
$1/2$ cup canned tuna fish, drained and flaked
2 tablespoons chopped parsley
$1/2$ cup grated Parmesan cheese

1. Cook macaroni in boiling, salted water following package directions; drain.
2. Wash sardines thoroughly, first in cool water, then in vinegar. Remove skins and fins, if any, by rubbing gently with finger tips; remove center bone. Cut sardines into small pieces.
3. Place tomatoes or diluted tomato paste into saucepan with oil or butter. Bring to a boil; add garlic, salt, pepper, and bay leaf. Cook until sauce thickens. Remove bay leaf.

4. Add tuna fish, sardines, and parsley to sauce; simmer for 5 minutes, or until heated thoroughly. Remove from heat and add grated Parmesan cheese; stir well.

5. Place macaroni in heated serving bowl; top with tuna sauce, and serve.

Linguine with Spinach and Mussels

Serves 4

1 (10-ounce) package frozen
   creamed spinach
2 (4-ounce) cans mussels in
   water, drained, reserve liquid
12 ounces linguine
¼ cup Parmesan cheese
1 clove garlic, peeled and
   crushed
Salt and pepper to taste

1. Place frozen block of spinach and liquid from mussels in saucepan; cook over low heat for 10 minutes, or until spinach separates.

2. Chop contents of 1½ cans of mussels, reserving rest for garnish.

3. Cook linguine in boiling, salted water following package directions; drain.

4. Mix chopped mussels, spinach, cheese, garlic, salt, and pepper together in saucepan; bring to a boil. Place linguine in heated serving dish; spoon mussels mixture on top, and garnish with reserved whole mussels. Serve more grated cheese separately.

Angel Hair Pasta with Scallops

Serves 6

¼ cup olive oil
1 pound bay scallops
2 onions, sliced
1 red pepper, seeded and cut into
   very thin strips
2 ripe tomatoes, skinned and
   diced
½ cup pine nuts
1 tablespoon capers

1 pound angel hair pasta
   (capellini)
Salt and freshly ground pepper
   to taste
¼ cup finely chopped parsley

1. Heat 2 tablespoons olive oil in large frying pan. Add scallops and saute over medium-high heat until cooked, about 3 minutes; remove from pan.

2. Add 2 tablespoons more oil to same pan; saute onions, red pepper strips, and tomatoes until crisp-tender. Stir in pine nuts and capers. Remove from heat.

3. Cook pasta in boiling, salted water following package directions; drain.

4. Return scallops to vegetable mixture and heat gently. Season with salt and pepper. Place pasta on heated serving dish. Spoon scallops on top; sprinkle with parsley, and serve.

Clams Fettuccine

Serves 4

¼ cup butter
½ cup chopped onion
3 tablespoons flour
1 teaspoon sugar
1 teaspoon oregano
½ teaspoon salt
Pepper to taste
1 (1-pound) can whole tomatoes,
   undrained
1 (8-ounce) can tomato sauce
1 (8-ounce) can minced clams,
   undrained
¼ cup sliced pitted black olives
4 cups just-cooked fettuccine
¼ cup grated Parmesan cheese

1. Melt 2 tablespoons butter in saucepan. Add onion and saute until translucent.

2. Combine flour, sugar, oregano, salt, and pepper; stir into saucepan

with onion. Add tomatoes, tomato sauce, clams and can liquid, and olives. Cook, stirring constantly, until mixture thickens.

3. Combine fettuccine, 2 tablespoons butter, and cheese; toss until pasta is evenly coated with cheese. Place in deep serving dish; pour sauce on top, and serve.

Szechuan Cold Sesame Noodles

Serves 8

3 quarts water
1 tablespoon corn oil
1 pound fresh Chinese whole-
   wheat noodles
2 tablespoons plus 2 teaspoons
   oriental sesame oil
2 cups canned bean sprouts,
   drained
1 cup shredded cooked chicken
3 tablespoons sesame seeds
6 tablespoons soy sauce
1 tablespoon red wine vinegar
1 tablespoon oil, heated
1 teaspoon sugar
2 tablespoons chopped scallions
2 teaspoons grated fresh ginger
   or ¼ teaspoon powdered
   ginger
2 teaspoons finely chopped garlic
1 tablespoon unsalted peanuts,
   ground

1. Bring water and corn oil to a boil in large saucepan; separate noodles carefully, then cook following package directions. Drain; place on serving platter and toss with 1 tablespoon sesame oil until well coated. Place bean sprouts and chicken on top of noodles.

2. Grind sesame seeds in blender or food processor; blend with 2 teaspoons sesame oil to form paste. Add soy sauce, vinegar, hot oil, sugar, scallions, ginger, and garlic. Pour sauce over chicken, bean sprouts, and noodles. Sprinkle with 1 tablespoon sesame oil and peanuts. Refrigerate until well chilled. Before serving, toss until well mixed.

Pasta and Chicken Stew

Serves 4

1 (2½-pound) chicken
6 cups water
1 teaspoon salt
3 whole allspice
3 whole peppercorns
½ bay leaf
1 carrot, chopped
1 stalk celery, chopped
1 tablespoon oil
1 onion, diced
2 cloves garlic, peeled and
    diced
2 cups diced eggplant
2 cups diced zucchini
2 cups diced tomatoes
1 sprig fresh thyme or ¼
    teaspoon dried thyme
1 cup pasta bow ties

1. Place chicken, water, salt, all-spice, peppercorns, and bay leaf in large pot; bring to a boil. Cook over very low heat for 1½ hours, skimming froth as needed. Add carrot and celery to stock at end of first half hour of cooking.
2. Heat oil in large frying pan. Add onion and garlic; saute until translucent. Add eggplant, zucchini, tomatoes, and thyme; saute for 10 minutes longer.
3. Remove chicken from pot. Strain chicken stock and add 1 cup to vegetable mixture. Place remaining stock in large saucepan and bring to a boil. Add pasta and boil for 5 minutes.
4. Remove skin and bones from chicken; cut up chicken meat and add to vegetables. Pour cooked pasta and remaining stock over chicken-vegetable mixture; toss until well blended, then serve.

Paprika Noodle Bake

Serves 4 to 6

1 (5-pound) chicken, boiled
5 tablespoons butter
1 large onion, diced
4 cups cooked broad egg noodles
Paprika to taste

1. Remove skin from chicken; separate meat from bones.
2. Melt butter in large frying pan; add onion and saute until browned. Add noodles and cook over low heat for 3 minutes. Add chicken; mix well.
3. Preheat oven to 375 degrees.
4. Place chicken mixture in baking dish. Sprinkle top generously with paprika. Cover and bake for 25 minutes. Uncover and place under broiler for 2 minutes, or until top is browned. Remove from oven, and serve.

Kota Kapuma

Serves 4 to 5

1 (4- to 5-pound) chicken, cut
    into serving pieces
1¼ cups butter
3 medium onions, diced
2 cloves garlic, peeled and finely
    diced
1 (6-ounce) can tomato paste
1 (1-pound) can tomato sauce
½ to ¾ teaspoon cinnamon
1 to 2 bay leaves
Salt and pepper to taste
¾ cup white wine, optional
Pinch of sugar
Pinch of oregano
¾ cup water
8 ounces linguine
1½ cups grated kefaloteri or
    Romano cheese

1. Quickly brown chicken in 1 cup butter; remove from pan.
2. Saute onions and garlic in remaining butter until soft. Add tomato paste, tomato sauce, cinnamon, bay leaves, salt, pepper, wine if desired, sugar, oregano, and water; mix well. Bring to a slow

simmer and add chicken pieces. Simmer for 45 minutes, or until chicken is done.
3. Cook linguine in boiling, salted water following package directions; drain. Melt ¼ cup butter and let brown; pour browned butter over pasta, tossing well. Quickly add grated cheese and toss well. Cover and let cheese melt.
4. Place pasta on large platter. Place chicken pieces and sauce over pasta, and serve.

Chicken Thighs Italiano

Serves 6 to 8

8 chicken thighs
½ cup dry white wine
2 tablespoons tarragon
    vinegar
¼ cup chopped celery
1 onion, finely chopped
¼ cup chopped red pepper
1 clove garlic, peeled and
    finely chopped
¼ cup olive oil
½ teaspoon basil
¼ teaspoon oregano
¼ cup butter
1 tablespoon tomato paste
½ pound mushrooms, sliced
Salt and pepper to taste
8 ounces vermicelli

1. Place chicken in shallow glass dish. Mix wine, vinegar, celery, onion, red pepper, garlic, olive oil, basil, and oregano together; pour over chicken. Cover and refrigerate overnight. Remove chicken from marinade, reserving marinade.
2. Preheat oven to 350 degrees.
3. Melt butter in large frying pan; add chicken and brown on both sides. Transfer chicken to 2-quart baking dish.
4. Bring reserved marinade to a boil in saucepan. Reduce heat and stir in tomato paste; add mushrooms. Simmer for 1 minute. Pour sauce over chicken. Sprinkle with salt and pepper. Cover and bake for 1 hour, or until chicken is tender.

5. Cook vermicelli in boiling, salted water following package directions; drain.

6. Place pasta in heated serving dish. Place chicken thighs on top, then pour on sauce. Serve piping hot.

Pasta Marengo

Serves 4

2 tablespoons oil
4 chicken breasts
1 onion, finely chopped
1 clove garlic, peeled and finely chopped
1/2 cup dry white wine
2 cups chopped fresh tomatoes
1 cup sliced mushrooms
1/4 cup chopped parsley
1 bay leaf
Pinch of thyme
Salt and pepper to taste
8 ounces fettuccine
Parsley, for garnish

1. Heat oil in Dutch oven; add chicken and cook about 15 minutes, or until evenly browned on both sides. Remove chicken from pan.

2. Add onion and garlic to Dutch oven and saute for 5 minutes. Add wine; cook, stirring constantly, for 5 minutes. Return chicken to pan along with tomatoes, mushrooms, parsley, bay leaf, thyme, salt, and pepper. Cover and simmer for 20 minutes. Uncover and simmer for 15 minutes longer, or until sauce is thick and chicken tender.

3. While chicken is cooking, cook fettuccine in boiling, salted water following package directions; drain.

4. Serve chicken marengo on bed of pasta; garnish with parsley.

Spaghetti with Chicken Breast

Serves 4

1 tablespoon corn oil
2 onions, diced
1 1/4 pounds boneless chicken breasts, skinned and cut into small pieces
3/4 cup canned sweet corn, drained
1 cup chicken broth
Salt to taste
Pinch of paprika
12 ounces spaghetti
3 tablespoons chopped fresh chives

1. Heat oil in saucepan. Add onion and saute until golden. Add chicken and saute until golden. Stir in corn, chicken broth, salt, and paprika; cook over low heat for 15 minutes.

2. Cook spaghetti in boiling, salted water until just tender, following package directions; drain.

3. Place pasta in heated serving dish. Spoon chicken mixture on top and toss well. Sprinkle with chives, and serve.

Chicken and Homemade Noodles

Serves 5

2 cups flour
2 teaspoons salt
2 eggs
2 tablespoons melted butter
1 (3- to 4-pound) chicken
Salt and pepper to taste

1. Sift flour and salt together. Form deep well in center; add eggs and melted butter to well. Mix eggs and butter into flour until ball of dough forms. Knead gently on floured work surface; roll until paper-thin. Let dry for 1 hour. Cut dough into 2-inch wide strips. Stack strips on top of each other, then cut into paper-thin strips. Spread out noodles and let dry until hard.

2. Simmer chicken in salted water to cover until tender, about 2 hours. Remove chicken from pan; separate meat from bones.

3. Bring stock to boil. Drop noodles in boiling stock and cook, stirring occasionally, about 10 minutes, or until noodles are tender; drain, reserving stock. Serve chicken meat on top of noodles. Season stock with salt and pepper, and spoon enough over chicken and noodles to moisten. Serve with gravy.

Spaghetti with Chicken and Asiago

Serves 4 to 6

2 boneless chicken breasts, cubed
3 tablespoons olive oil
1/2 teaspoon salt
Freshly ground pepper to taste
1 (8-ounce) can baby peas, undrained
1 pound spaghetti
3 tablespoons grated Asiago
1 egg, beaten

1. Saute chicken in olive oil until golden. Season with salt and generous amount of pepper.

2. Heat peas in their own liquid in saucepan. Drain liquid from peas into chicken. Simmer for 5 minutes. Add peas to chicken mixture; season with more pepper. Simmer for 5 minutes longer.

3. Cook spaghetti in boiling, salted water until just tender, following package directions; drain. Place in heated bowl.

4. Blend cheese and egg together. Pour gradually into chicken and peas; stir until sauce is well heated. Toss half the chicken mixture with pasta. Spoon remaining chicken sauce on top, and serve.

Chicken Hedgehogs

Serves 3

$1/2$ pound boneless chicken
   breast, cubed
1 egg
3 tablespoons flour
2 teaspoons sugar
2 teaspoons light soy sauce
2 teaspoons dry sherry
$1/4$ teaspoon salt
$1^1/4$ cups rice vermicelli
Cooking oil

1. Place chicken in food processor or blender with egg, flour, sugar, soy sauce, sherry, and salt; blend until smooth paste forms. Place in bowl, cover with plastic wrap, and refrigerate for 20 minutes.
2. Form chicken mixture into 18 balls. Finely crush vermicelli. Roll each ball in noodles until well coated.
3. Heat about 1 inch of oil in deep frying pan over medium heat. Fry 6 chicken balls at a time for about 3 minutes, or until golden and cooked thoroughly. Drain well on paper towels; serve warm with soy sauce or sweet chili sauce.

Green Noodle Fricassee

Serves 4

$1^1/4$ pounds boneless chicken
   breasts
1 sprig tarragon, finely
   chopped, or 1 teaspoon dried
   tarragon
$1/8$ teaspoon white pepper
Juice of $1/2$ lemon
$1/4$ cup butter
2 shallots, peeled and chopped
$1/2$ pound shrimp, shelled
   and deveined
1 cup light cream
1 egg yolk
3 ounces dry champagne
1 teaspoon salt
Pinch of cayenne pepper

1. Sprinkle chicken breasts with tarragon, pepper, and lemon juice; cover and marinate for 10 minutes. Remove chicken from marinade, discarding marinade. Cut chicken into $1/2$-inch wide strips.
2. Heat butter in large, heavy skillet. Saute chicken strips for 4 minutes, turning frequently, until evenly browned on both sides. Add shallots and saute for 1 minute more. Add shrimp and continue to saute, stirring constantly, for 1 minute more.
3. Beat cream with egg yolk; stir into chicken mixture; cook over medium heat, stirring constantly, until heated thoroughly. Do not allow mixture to boil. Stir in champagne; season with salt and cayenne pepper. Keep warm over very low heat while noodles are cooking.
4. Cook green noodles in boiling, salted water following package directions; drain and toss with fricassee. Serve at once.

Pasta Medley

Serves 5 to 6

3 quarts water
1 teaspoon salt
$1^1/2$ cups pasta shells
1 small onion, chopped
$1/4$ cup butter
2 tablespoons flour
2 chicken bouillon cubes
   dissolved in 2 cups hot water
1 cup diced cooked chicken or
   turkey
$1/2$ cup chopped cooked bacon
1 cup cooked mixed vegetables
   of your choice

1. Place water and salt in saucepan and bring to a boil. Boil pasta, stirring occasionally, until just tender, following package directions; drain.
2. Saute onion in 2 tablespoons butter until translucent. Remove from pan and set aside.
3. Melt remaining butter in saucepan. Add flour, stirring constantly. Gradually add chicken bouillon and bring to a boil, stirring constantly. Simmer for 2 minutes.
4. Add pasta, diced turkey or chicken, bacon, and vegetables to bouillon; mix well. Simmer for 5 minutes, or until heated thoroughly, then serve.

Chicken Livers with Eggs and Noodles

Serves 4

4 eggs
$1/4$ teaspoon salt
1 tablespoon vegetable oil
$1/2$ pound mushrooms,
   sliced
2 scallions, sliced
1 pound chicken livers,
   cubed
2 tablespoons dry sherry
5 tablespoons soy sauce
8 ounces vermicelli
2 tablespoons chopped
   parsley

1. Combine eggs and salt; pour into oiled skillet. Cook without stirring over medium heat until eggs are set; cut into $1/2$-inch cubes.
2. Heat oil in wok or frying pan. Stir-fry mushrooms and scallions for 1 to 2 minutes; push vegetables to side. Add chicken livers and stir-fry for 1 to 2 minutes. Add dry sherry and 4 tablespoons soy sauce. Mix liver and vegetables together well. Add cubed eggs and cook until heated thoroughly.
3. Cook vermicelli in boiling, salted water following package directions; drain and toss with 1 tablespoon soy sauce. Place vermicelli on serving platter. Top with liver mixture and garnish with chopped parsley.

Spaghetti and Chicken Livers

Serves 6

¹/₄ cup vegetable oil
¹/₂ pound chicken livers, cut
  into small pieces
1 pound spaghetti
3 tablespoons sweet butter
³/₄ cup grated Parmesan cheese
3 eggs
³/₄ cup grated Gruyere cheese
Pepper to taste

1. Heat oil in small frying pan; add chicken livers and cook for 3 to 4 minutes, until browned.
2. Cook spaghetti in boiling, salted water following package directions; drain and toss with half the butter.
3. Preheat oven to 350 degrees.
4. Spread half the spaghetti in buttered baking pan. Sprinkle half the Parmesan cheese on top. Put livers on top of cheese, cover with remaining spaghetti, and sprinkle with remaining Parmesan cheese.
5. Beat eggs in small bowl. Add Gruyere cheese and pepper; pour over spaghetti. Melt remaining butter and drizzle over top. Bake for 20 minutes, or until golden. Remove from oven, and serve.

African Chicken Livers

Serves 4

2 tablespoons cooking oil
1 large onion, chopped
2 cloves garlic, peeled and
  chopped
1 teaspoon grated fresh
  ginger
1 pound chicken livers, cut
  into bite-sized pieces
1 tablespoon flour
2 tablespoons ground roasted
  peanuts
1 large tomato, peeled and
  chopped
³/₄ teaspoon basil
1 cup chicken stock or water
1 teaspoon ground coriander
1 teaspoon salt

1 teaspoon fresh chili, chopped
Freshly ground black pepper
8 ounces spaghettini
2 hard-boiled eggs, peeled and
  quartered

1. Heat oil in large frying pan. Saute onion, garlic, and ginger until lightly browned. Add chicken livers and saute for 2 minutes, stirring frequently. Sprinkle livers with flour and leave to brown slightly. Add peanuts, stirring well; cook for 2 minutes.
2. Add tomato and basil to liver mixture; saute for 2 minutes more. Add stock or water, coriander, salt, chili, and pepper. Cover and simmer for 5 minutes.
3. Cook spaghettini in boiling, salted water until just tender, following package directions; drain.
4. Place pasta on heated serving platter. Add chicken liver mixture and toss lightly. Garnish with egg quarters, and serve.

Sauteed Liver with Oregano

Serves 4

3 tablespoons olive oil
3 tablespoons butter
1 pound calves' liver, skinned
  and cut into thin strips
2 scallions, chopped
2 cloves garlic, peeled and
  chopped
2 teaspoons chopped fresh
  oregano or ³/₄ teaspoon
  dried oregano
³/₄ teaspoon salt
Freshly ground pepper to
  taste
¹/₄ cup dry white wine
¹/₄ cup heavy whipping cream
8 ounces linguine

1. Heat oil and butter in frying pan. Add liver and saute until it changes color. Add scallions, garlic, oregano, salt, and pepper; saute until liver is tender. Remove from heat and keep warm.

2. Add wine to pan and boil rapidly until reduced by half; add cream, stirring constantly; cook until thoroughly heated. Return liver to pan and reheat gently in sauce.
3. Cook linguine in boiling, salted water following package directions; drain.
4. Place linguine in heated serving dish. Spoon livers and sauce on top, and serve.

Turkey Potpourri

Serves 4

¹/₄ cup butter
¹/₂ pound mushrooms, sliced
¹/₄ cup chopped green pepper
1 (10-ounce) can cream of
  celery soup
1¹/₂ cups shredded Cheddar
  cheese
¹/₂ cup sour cream
2 cups cooked turkey
12 ounces egg noodles

1. Melt butter in large frying pan; saute mushrooms and green pepper until tender, about 5 minutes. Blend in soup, cheese, and sour cream. Cook until cheese melts, stirring constantly. Stir in turkey. Cook over low heat until heated thoroughly.
2. Cook noodles in boiling, salted water following package directions; drain.
3. Place noodles in serving dish. Spoon turkey mixture on top, and serve.

Hungarian Turkey Ragout

Serves 4

2 tablespoons oil
1¼ pounds boneless turkey breast, cut into thin slices
1 tablespoon butter
1 onion, finely chopped
1¼ cups thinly sliced mushrooms, sprinkled with lemon juice
½ cup sour cream
1 teaspoon cornstarch
1 teaspoon paprika
½ cup dry white wine
Salt and pepper to taste
8 ounces broad egg noodles

1. Heat oil in large, heavy skillet. Brown turkey on both sides, then remove from pan. Melt butter into oil remaining in pan; saute onion until translucent. Add mushrooms, cover, and simmer for 10 minutes.
2. Mix sour cream with cornstarch and paprika. Return meat to pan, add sour cream mixture and wine to meat. Simmer for 5 minutes, or until heated thoroughly. Season with salt and pepper.
3. Cook noodles in boiling, salted water following package directions; drain. Add noodles to turkey ragout, tossing to mix well. Serve hot.

Fusilli with Creamed Turkey

Serves 4

8 ounces fusilli
2 tablespoons butter
¼ cup chopped onion
1 (10-ounce) can condensed cream of mushroom soup
½ soup-can water
½ cup shredded sharp Cheddar cheese
1 tablespoon dry sherry
Salt and pepper to taste
2 cups chopped cooked turkey
¼ cup chopped parsley

1. Cook pasta in boiling, salted water following package directions; drain.
2. Melt butter in saucepan; saute onion until translucent. Add soup, water, cheese, and sherry; mix well. Cook, stirring constantly, until cheese melts. Season with salt and pepper.
3. Add turkey, parsley, and fusilli; toss well, and serve.

Mezzani with Eggs and Red-Devil Sauce

Serves 4

2 quarts salted water
1½ tablespoons salad oil
8 ounces mezzani
1 tablespoon olive oil
1 teaspoon finely chopped parsley or fresh sage
10 hard-boiled eggs, peeled and halved lengthwise

Red-Devil Sauce

½ cup tarragon vinegar
1 teaspoon dry mustard
1 teaspoon paprika
½ teaspoon white pepper
1 clove garlic, peeled and sliced
¾ teaspoon salt
2 bay leaves
¼ teaspoon cayenne pepper
½ cup beef consomme
2 tablespoons butter
1 tablespoon Worcestershire sauce
1 (15-ounce) can tomato sauce

1. Bring salted water to a boil; add salad oil. Add mezzani slowly and cook for 14 minutes, or until tender; drain.
2. While pasta is cooking, make sauce. Combine vinegar, mustard, paprika, white pepper, garlic, salt, bay leaves, and cayenne pepper in saucepan. Boil until mixture is reduced by half. Strain through fine sieve, then return to saucepan. Add consomme, butter, Worcestershire sauce, and tomato sauce. Simmer for 8 minutes.

3. Place hot pasta in serving dish. Add olive oil and toss lightly. Sprinkle with parsley or sage. Place eggs over pasta; pour sauce over eggs, and serve hot.

Turkey-Leek Rotini

Serves 4 to 6

1 pound leeks, white part and 2 inches of green stem, quartered lengthwise then sliced
5 tablespoons butter
1 pound boneless turkey breast cutlets, cut into 1 x ¼-inch slivers
Salt and pepper to taste
Flour for dredging
2 tablespoons vegetable oil
1 pound rotini
¼ cup white port wine
¾ cup half and half
⅓ cup blue cheese, crumbled
1 cup shredded Muenster cheese
¼ cup chopped parsley

1. Cook leeks in 3 tablespoons melted butter in large skillet over medium-high heat for 5 minutes, stirring frequently. Remove leeks from pan and set aside.
2. Season turkey strips with salt and pepper. Dredge with flour; shake off excess flour.
3. Heat oil and remaining butter in skillet. Saute turkey, tossing frequently, for 5 minutes or until golden. Remove from pan and set aside with leeks.
4. Cook rotini in boiling, salted water until just tender, following package directions; drain.
5. Deglaze skillet over medium-high heat with wine, scraping pan bottom to remove browned particles. Simmer for 1 minute. Add leeks, turkey, half and half, cheeses, and parsley. Season with salt and pepper.
6. Toss rotini with sauce, and serve at once.

Oriental Vegetable and Peanut Pasta

Serves 6

1 pound vermicelli
1/2 cup finely chopped onion
1 1/2 tablespoons rice vinegar
1 tablespoon dry sherry
1 tablespoon chopped fresh
  ginger or 1 teaspoon
  powdered ginger
3 tablespoons plus 1 teaspoon
  sesame oil
1 teaspoon dry mustard
Pinch of cayenne pepper
1/2 pound tofu
1/4 cup peanut butter
3 tablespoons tamari
1 cup snow pea pods
1 cup small broccoli florets
1/2 cup button mushrooms

1. Cook vermicelli in boiling, salted water following package directions; drain.
2. Puree onion, vinegar, sherry, ginger, 1 teaspoon oil, mustard, cayenne pepper, tofu, peanut butter, and tamari together in food processor or blender. Place in saucepan and heat over low heat.
3. Heat 3 tablespoons oil in wok or frying pan; stir-fry pea pods, broccoli, and mushrooms until crisp-tender.
4. Toss pasta, puree, and vegetables together. Serve at once.

Mezzani with Fresh Tomatoes

Serves 6

12 ounces mezzani
2 tablespoons olive oil
2 tablespoons butter
1 clove garlic, peeled and
  crushed
1 large scallion, minced
5 cups chopped ripe tomatoes
Freshly ground pepper to taste
1 teaspoon basil
1 teaspoon chopped chives
1 teaspoon oregano
1/2 teaspoon sugar
1 teaspoon salt
Freshly grated Parmesan cheese

1. Cook mezzani in boiling, salted water following package directions; drain.
2. Combine olive oil and butter in saucepan; heat until butter melts. Add garlic and scallion; cook over medium heat for 5 minutes. Stir in remaining ingredients; cook, stirring, for several minutes, or until tomatoes are soft.
3. Toss mezzani with tomato sauce. Top with Parmesan cheese, and serve.

Rotini-Vegetable Mix

Serves 4

8 ounces rotini
3 tablespoons butter
2 cups diced zucchini
1 cup small broccoli florets
1/2 cup chopped onion
1/2 teaspoon basil
1/4 teaspoon marjoram
1 (10-ounce) can condensed
  Cheddar cheese soup
2 cups shredded sharp Cheddar
  cheese
1/2 teaspoon Dijon mustard
2 cups chopped tomatoes
Freshly ground pepper to taste

1. Cook rotini in boiling, salted water until just tender, following package directions; drain.

2. Melt butter in saucepan. Add zucchini, broccoli, and onion; saute until crisp-tender. Add basil, marjoram, soup, cheese, and mustard; mix well. Cook, stirring constantly, until cheese melts. Gently stir in tomatoes and pasta. Cook until heated thoroughly. Season with pepper, and serve.

Fontina Spaghetti

Serves 4

3 tablespoons butter
1 large onion, finely chopped
2 cloves garlic, peeled and finely
  chopped
1/2 cup diced celery
1/4 pound mushrooms, sliced
1 (15-ounce) can tomato sauce
1 (28-ounce) can whole
  tomatoes, drained and chopped
1 teaspoon oregano
1 bay leaf
Salt and pepper to taste
8 ounces spaghetti, halved
2 cups shredded fontina cheese
1/4 cup chopped parsley

1. Melt butter in large saucepan. Add onion and garlic; saute until translucent. Add celery and mushrooms; saute for 3 minutes more. Stir in tomato sauce, tomatoes, oregano, bay leaf, salt, and pepper; mix well. Cook over medium-high heat until mixture boils; reduce heat and simmer for 5 minutes. Remove bay leaf.
2. Return tomato sauce to boil. Add uncooked spaghetti, cover, and cook over low heat for 20 minutes, stirring occasionally.
3. Remove cover and add cheese. Cook, stirring constantly, until cheese melts. Season with more salt and pepper, if desired. Sprinkle with parsley, and serve.

Luxurious Angel Hair Pasta

Serves 6

2 cups creme fraiche or heavy
  whipping cream
$1/4$ cup brandy
1 bay leaf
1 pound angel hair pasta
  (capellini)
1 tablespoon oil
$1/4$ cup sweet butter, softened
1 pound golden caviar
Freshly ground pepper to taste

1. Place creme fraiche or cream, brandy, and bay leaf in saucepan. Cook over medium heat until mixture reaches boiling point. Reduce heat and cook over very low heat for 5 minutes. Discard bay leaf.
2. Cook pasta in boiling, salted water, to which 1 tablespoon oil has been added; cook until just tender following package directions. Drain and toss gently with butter until each strand is coated.
3. Place pasta in heated serving dish. Pour cream mixture and caviar on top; toss gently. Sprinkle with pepper, and serve at once.

Tyrolean Stuffed Pasta

Serves 4

$2^1/_2$ cups whole-wheat flour
3 eggs
2 pinches of salt
$2^1/_4$ cups spinach
$1/2$ cup butter
Pinch of white pepper
Pinch of grated nutmeg
$1/2$ cup grated Emmenthaler
  cheese
1 egg white, beaten
4 quarts salted water
6 tablespoons chopped chives

1. Mix flour, eggs and pinch of salt together. Add just enough water to make workable pasta dough. Cover and let dough rest for 1 hour.
2. Wash spinach well and place in saucepan without drying spinach off; without adding any water, cook over medium heat for 2 minutes. Drain spinach; squeeze well and chop finely.
3. Melt 2 tablespoons butter in saucepan. Add spinach, pinch of salt, pepper and nutmeg. Cook until liquid evaporates; remove from heat and let cool. Mix in $1/4$ cup grated cheese.
4. Roll dough out in 4 equal portions to $1/_{16}$-inch thickness; cut into $3^1/_2$-inch circles. With teaspoon, divide spinach among dough circles, placing it on half of each circle. Brush edges of dough with beaten egg white. Press dough edges together to form crescent shape; lay on floured cloth.
5. Place salted water in large saucepan and bring to a boil. Cook stuffed pasta for 6 minutes. Lift stuffed pasta from water with slotted spoon and toss in remaining butter. Garnish with chives and remaining grated cheese. Serve immediately.

Gardener's Delight

Serves 4

1 medium onion, finely
  chopped
1 clove garlic, peeled and
  finely chopped
3 medium ripe tomatoes, peeled
  and finely chopped
3 medium to large zucchini,
  shredded
1 carrot, peeled and shredded
1 teaspoon salt
Freshly ground pepper to taste
2 teaspoons chopped fresh basil
  or 1 teaspoon dried basil
1 teaspoon fresh chopped
  oregano or $1/2$ teaspoon dried
  oregano
$1/2$ teaspoon fresh chopped thyme
  or $1/4$ teaspoon dried thyme
2 tablespoons olive oil
1 tablespoon butter
12 ounces pasta of your choice
1 cup freshly grated Parmesan
  cheese

1. Combine vegetables in large bowl. Add salt, pepper, basil, oregano, and thyme; toss lightly.
2. Heat olive oil and butter in large skillet. Add vegetable mixture and saute quickly over medium heat. Reduce heat and simmer for 15 minutes.
3. Meanwhile, cook pasta in boiling, salted water following package directions; drain.
4. Serve sauce on hot pasta with generous spoonfuls of grated Parmesan cheese.

Ellen's Spicy Red Pasta

Serves 8 to 10

$1/3$ cup olive oil
6 cloves garlic, peeled and
  crushed
2 (1-pound) cans Italian-style
  tomatoes, drained, reserve
  liquid, and chopped
3 tablespoons red wine vinegar
3 hot cherry peppers,
  from a jar
1 teaspoon sugar
Salt and pepper to taste
2 pounds linguine
1 tablespoon chopped fresh
  basil

1. Heat olive oil in frying pan. Add garlic and saute until browned; remove garlic from pan and discard. Add chopped tomatoes; heat briefly, then remove from heat.
2. In separate pan, bring tomato liquid, vinegar, cherry peppers, and sugar to a boil. Cook until thick syrup forms; remove pepper after 10 minutes for medium-hot sauce, or at the end for very hot sauce. Combine with tomatoes and oil. Season with salt and pepper; remove from heat.
3. Cook linguine in boiling, salted water until just tender, following package directions; drain.
4. Just before serving, reheat sauce, adding chopped basil. Toss with pasta, and serve.

Fusilli with Green Pasta Sauce

Serves 8 to 10

1 cup butter
$\frac{1}{2}$ cup chopped parsley
$\frac{1}{2}$ cup chopped scallions, green parts only
1 cup heavy whipping cream
1 cup freshly grated Parmesan cheese
$\frac{1}{4}$ cup lemon juice
2 pounds fusilli
Freshly ground pepper to taste

1. Melt butter in saucepan. Add parsley and scallions; cook until just softened. Add cream. Cook, stirring constantly, until sauce bubbles; stir in grated Parmesan and lemon juice.
2. Cook pasta in boiling, salted water until just tender, following package directions; drain.
3. Place fusilli in heated serving bowl. Toss with sauce, sprinkle with pepper, and serve.

Green and Yellow Pasta

Serves 4

$\frac{1}{2}$ pound spinach pasta
$\frac{1}{2}$ pound regular pasta
2 tablespoons butter
2 cloves garlic, peeled and minced
3 cups cubed zucchini
2 cups plain yogurt, or mixture of yogurt and sour cream
3 tablespoons chopped fresh basil or parsley
Freshly grated Parmesan cheese

1. Cook pasta in boiling, salted water until just tender, following package directions; drain.
2. Meanwhile, melt butter in saucepan; saute garlic and zucchini until garlic becomes golden. Turn off heat and stir in yogurt. Toss pasta with yogurt mixture. Stir in basil or parsley. Serve, accompanied by freshly grated Parmesan cheese.

Penne with Eggplant

Serves 6

2 ($\frac{1}{2}$-pound) eggplants, sliced $\frac{1}{2}$-inch thick
Salt and pepper to taste
1 tablespoon flour
1 cup olive oil
1 ($15\frac{1}{2}$-ounce) jar meatless marinara sauce
$\frac{1}{2}$ pound Cheddar cheese, coarsely shredded
12 ounces penne

1. Sprinkle eggplant with salt and pepper; dip in flour so eggplants are lightly coated.
2. Preheat oven to 350 degrees.
3. Heat oil in 12-inch skillet. Fry eggplant slices a few at a time, until golden-brown on both sides; drain. Arrange half the eggplants in oblong, 2-quart baking dish. Spread with half the marinara sauce; top with half the cheese. Repeat layers.
4. Bake for 20 minutes, until bubbly and cheese has melted.
5. Meanwhile, cook penne in boiling, salted water following package directions; drain.
6. Serve eggplant mixture directly from baking dish, with plain penne served on the side.

Tofu Noodle Hash

Serves 4 to 5

$\frac{1}{4}$ cup oil
1 small onion, finely chopped
1 small green pepper, finely chopped
2 cloves garlic, peeled and crushed
1/2 pound tofu, crumbled
1 teaspoon dill weed
2 cups finely chopped green cabbage
$2\frac{1}{2}$ to 3 cups cooked spinach noodles
1 (1-pound) can whole tomatoes, drained
Salt and pepper to taste
1 cup grated Monterey Jack cheese

1. Heat oil in frying pan. Saute onion and green pepper until soft. Add garlic and tofu. Sprinkle with dill weed and stir in cabbage and noodles. Break up tomatoes and stir into mixture.
2. Cook until heated thoroughly, mixing all ingredients together well. Season with salt and pepper. Sprinkle with grated cheese, cover, and simmer until cheese melts. Serve immediately.

Tortellini in Gorgonzola Mayonnaise

Serves 4

1 pound tortellini of your choice
$\frac{1}{4}$ cup olive oil
Juice of $\frac{1}{2}$ lemon
$\frac{1}{2}$ red onion, sliced in rings
$\frac{1}{2}$ cup chopped red pepper
$\frac{1}{2}$ pound gorgonzola cheese
Salt and pepper to taste
$\frac{1}{2}$ cup mayonnaise
$\frac{1}{2}$ cup sour cream
Parsley, for garnish

1. Cook tortellini in boiling, salted water until just tender, following package directions; drain.
2. Combine olive oil, lemon juice, onion, and sweet pepper; toss with hot tortellini. Crumble half the cheese and mix with tortellini. Let cool. Season with salt and pepper.
3. Mash remaining cheese and combine with mayonnaise and sour cream. Toss with tortellini. Serve immediately, garnished with parsley.

Pasta by Night

Serves 4

1 tablespoon olive oil
1 clove garlic, peeled and
   minced
2 pounds pear tomatoes, peeled,
   chopped, and drained
1 cup shredded zucchini
Freshly ground black pepper
3 tablespoons non-fat powdered
   milk
1 pound angel hair pasta
   (capellini)
2 tablespoons chopped fresh
   chives

1. Heat oil to medium heat in frying pan. Add garlic, tomatoes, zucchini, and pepper; saute briefly. Slowly stir in dry milk and simmer for 10 minutes.
2. Cook pasta in boiling, salted water following package directions; drain.
3. Place pasta in heated serving bowl. Spoon sauce on top and garnish with fresh chives.

Easy Peanut Noodles

Serves 4

1 cup chicken marinade
1²/₃ cup freshly ground chunky
   peanut butter
About 1 tablespoon dry sherry
   or chicken broth, optional
12 ounces fresh Chinese
   noodles or vermicelli

1½ teaspoons sesame oil
¼ cup minced scallion greens
¼ cup minced celery leaves

1. Heat marinade in large, heavy saucepan. Add peanut butter and cook over medium-low heat, stirring constantly, until mixture becomes sauce consistency throughout. Add sherry or chicken broth if sauce appears too thick.
2. Cook noodles in boiling, salted water following package directions; drain.
3. Stir sesame oil into peanut butter. Spoon sauce over noodles; toss well. Sprinkle with scallions and celery leaves, and serve.

Beef Parma Style

Serves 4

1½ pounds beef round steak
½ cup bread crumbs
⅓ cup grated Parmesan
   cheese
1 egg
2 tablespoons water
¼ cup flour
⅓ cup oil
1 medium onion, minced
1 (6-ounce) can tomato paste
2 cups hot water
½ teaspoon marjoram
1 teaspoon salt
¼ teaspoon pepper
½ pound mozzarella cheese,
   thinly sliced
8 ounces fettuccine

1. Place meat between sheet of waxed paper and pound until quite thin. Cut into serving-size pieces.
2. Combine bread crumbs and Parmesan cheese. Beat egg and 2 tablespoons water together. Dip meat in flour, turning to coat evenly; shake off excess flour. Dip meat in egg mixture and then in crumb mixture. Pat crumbs into meat to coat well.
3. Heat oil in heavy skillet over medium heat. Brown meat on all sides. Remove from pan. Add onions and brown lightly. Add tomato paste, hot water, and seasonings; stir well. Bring to a boil and cook for 5 minutes.
4. Preheat oven to 350 degrees.
5. Place meat in shallow baking dish. Cover with sauce, reserving ¼ cup. Top with mozzarella cheese and pour reserved sauce over cheese. Cover with foil and bake for 2 hours.
6. Cook fettuccine in boiling, salted water following package directions; drain. Place pasta on serving platter. Spoon meat and sauce on top, and serve.

Agnolotti with Cream Sauce

Serves 6

Pasta Dough

2 cups flour
1 teaspoon salt
3 eggs
2 teaspoons olive oil
1 tablespoon water

Filling

2 tablespoons olive oil
$^1/_4$ cup finely chopped onion
$^1/_4$ pound ground veal
1 egg
2 cups finely chopped cooked
  chicken breast
$^1/_8$ pound finely chopped
  prosciutto
$^1/_4$ teaspoon rosemary
$^1/_8$ teaspoon nutmeg
Salt and pepper to taste

Cream Sauce

3 tablespoons butter
6 tablespoons flour
Salt and pepper to taste
1$^1/_2$ cups chicken broth
1$^1/_2$ cups light cream
$^1/_2$ cup grated Parmesan
  cheese
$^1/_8$ teaspoon nutmeg

To Cook Pasta

4 quarts water
2 teaspoons salt
1 tablespoon oil

1. To prepare pasta dough, combine flour and salt in mixing bowl. Mix eggs, oil, and water together well in separate bowl. Add to flour, mixing to form stiff dough. Turn out onto floured board; knead for 5 minutes.

Cover with plastic wrap and let rest for 30 minutes.

2. Prepare filling while dough rests. Heat oil in small, heavy skillet. Add onion and saute until tender. Add veal and cook, stirring, until meal is crumbly and lightly browned. Transfer mixture to bowl; cool slightly. Add remaining filling ingredients; mix well.

3. Divide pasta dough into 4 equal parts. Cover any dough not being used to prevent drying. Roll dough, one part at a time, on lightly floured surface to $^1/_{16}$-inch thick. Cut into 3-inch circles with round biscuit cutter or glass. Reroll scraps.

4. Place heaping $^1/_2$ teaspoon filling on each round. Dampen edge of circle with a little water. Fold into half-moon shape; seal. With folded edge toward you, bring two ends together; pinch. Finished pasta looks like small circular hats with cuffs. Place pasta on tray; cover with towel until ready to cook, or freeze for future use.

5. To prepare sauce, melt butter in medium saucepan. Add flour, salt, and pepper; mix well. Cook for 1 minute, stirring constantly, then gradually add broth. Cook, stirring constantly, until sauce thickens; remove from heat. Stir in cream, then return to heat. Cook, stirring constantly, until sauce is thick and smooth. Add cheese and nutmeg. Keep sauce warm while cooking pasta.

6. To cook pasta, place water, salt, and oil in large saucepan and bring to a boil. Boil pasta for 10 minutes; drain well. Top pasta with cream sauce, and serve immediately. Sprinkle with additional Parmesan cheese, if desired.

Cannelloni

Serves 4 to 5

2 tablespoons olive oil
1 large onion, finely chopped
2 cloves garlic, peeled and finely
  chopped
$^1/_2$ pound ground beef
Salt and pepper to taste
$^1/_2$ teaspoon oregano
$^1/_2$ teaspoon sage
2 teaspoons tomato paste
1 (16-ounce) can whole
  tomatoes, undrained
8 ounces cannelloni
1$^1/_4$ cups grated Parmesan cheese
3 tablespoons sour cream
$^1/_4$ cup butter

1. Heat oil in frying pan. Saute onion and garlic until translucent. Add ground beef and cook until browned. Remove from heat; season with salt, pepper, oregano, and sage. Stir in tomato paste and set aside to cool.

2. Preheat oven to 400 degrees.

3. Crush tomatoes and place in saucepan with tomato liquid. Cook until some of the liquid evaporates.

4. Precook cannelloni, if necessary, following package directions; drain.

5. Stir half the Parmesan cheese with sour cream; combine with meat. Fill cannelloni with mixture. Lay cannelloni in buttered baking dish. Pour tomato sauce on top; sprinkle with remaining Parmesan cheese and dot with butter. Bake for 45 minutes. Remove from oven, and serve.

Cannelloni with Cheese Sauce

Serves 4 to 5

8 ounces cannelloni

Filling

1 large onion, chopped
1 clove garlic, peeled and minced
2 tablespoons olive oil
1 (10-ounce) package frozen chopped spinach, thawed
2¹/₂ cups ground cooked ham
2 eggs, beaten
³/₄ teaspoon oregano
¹/₂ teaspoon salt
¹/₄ teaspoon pepper

Sauce

¹/₃ cup butter
¹/₃ cup flour
¹/₂ teaspoon salt
Pinch of nutmeg
Pinch of white pepper
1 cup chicken broth
1 cup light cream
¹/₂ cup grated Parmesan or Romano cheese
1 cup grated white Cheddar or Swiss cheese

1. Precook cannelloni, if necessary, following package directions; drain.
2. Preheat oven to 350 degrees.
3. To make filling, saute onion and garlic in olive oil until translucent. Press thawed spinach firmly through strainer to remove all water. Combine onion mixture, spinach, ham, eggs, and seasonings in large bowl; mix well.
4. Fill each cannelloni with 3 tablespoons filling. Place in single layer in buttered, shallow baking dish.
5. To make sauce, melt butter in medium-size saucepan. Blend in flour and seasonings. Cook, stirring constantly, until bubbly. Add chicken broth and cream, stirring well. Cook over medium heat, stirring constantly, until sauce is thick and smooth. Remove from heat and add cheeses; stir until cheese melts.
6. Pour sauce evenly over cannelloni. Bake for 30 minutes. Remove from oven, and serve.

Linguine and Chicken

Serves 6

10 tablespoons butter
¹/₂ pound mushrooms, sliced
¹/₂ cup flour
4 cups chicken broth
1¹/₂ cups milk
¹/₂ cup heavy whipping cream
Salt and pepper to taste
1 pound linguine
1 (4-pound) roasted chicken, boned, skinned, and diced
¹/₂ cup bread crumbs
¹/₂ cup grated Parmesan cheese

1. Melt 2 tablespoons butter in small frying pan. Add mushrooms and saute for 5 minutes.
2. Melt remaining butter in saucepan. Add flour, stirring until well blended. Add broth and milk; cook over low heat, stirring constantly, until sauce begins to thicken. Add cream; season with salt and pepper.
3. Preheat oven to 450 degrees.
4. Cook pasta in boiling, salted water until just tender, following package directions; drain.
5. Place pasta in well-greased casserole dish. Cover with chicken and mushrooms; pour sauce on top. Sprinkle with bread crumbs and cheese. Bake for 30 minutes, or until bread crumbs are browned and the sauce bubbles. Remove from oven, and serve.

Chicken Cacciatore

Serves 4

3 pounds chicken pieces
¹/₂ cup flour, seasoned with salt and pepper
¹/₄ cup olive oil
1 onion, thinly sliced
2 cloves garlic, peeled and finely chopped
¹/₄ pound mushrooms, sliced
1 (16-ounce) can whole tomatoes, undrained

1 (8-ounce) can tomato sauce
¹/₂ teaspoon salt
¹/₂ teaspoon oregano
1 bay leaf
8 ounces spaghetti

1. Coat chicken with seasoned flour. Heat oil in large frying pan. Add chicken and cook over medium-high heat until browned. Remove chicken from pan and set aside.
2. Place onion and garlic in same frying pan and saute until translucent. Add mushrooms and saute briefly. Add tomatoes with can liquid, tomato sauce, salt, oregano, and bay leaf. Stir and break tomatoes into pieces.
3. Return chicken to pan, cover, and simmer for 30 to 40 minutes, or until chicken is tender and well cooked.
4. Cook spaghetti in boiling, salted water following package directions; drain. To serve, place spaghetti on serving platter; arrange chicken and sauce on top.

Chicken Fricarole

Serves 8

1 (5- to 6-pound) stewing chicken, cut into serving pieces
1 stalk celery, sliced
2 tablespoons chopped parsley
1 small onion, sliced
1 bay leaf
6 peppercorns
2 teaspoons salt
¹/₂ cup chopped onions
2 tablespoons butter
1 pound medium egg noodles
2 cups asparagus tips
1 cup diced cooked ham
¹/₂ cup sliced black olives
1 (10¹/₂-ounce) can condensed cream of chicken soup
1 cup grated Parmesan cheese

1. Preheat oven to 350 degrees.
2. Place chicken in large casserole dish with celery, parsley, sliced onion, bay leaf, peppercorns, and salt. Add water to barely cover. Cover and bake for 2 hours. Pour off and reserve broth, removing peppercorns and bay leaf.
3. Saute chopped onions in butter until translucent. Remove from pan and set aside.
4. Cook noodles in boiling, salted water following package directions; drain.
5. Scatter onions, noodles, asparagus tips, ham, and olives over chicken. Combine soup with reserved chicken broth and ½ cup cheese; pour over all. Sprinkle with remaining cheese. Return to oven and continue to cook, uncovered, for 45 minutes, or until lightly browned and bubbly; stir several times during cooking time. Remove from oven, and serve.

Chicken Tetrazzini

Serves 4 to 6

1 (3- to 4-pound) stewing chicken
2 onions
2 carrots
2 sprigs parsley
½ teaspoon thyme
1 bay leaf
8 ounces spaghetti
6 tablespoons butter
Dash of garlic powder
¼ cup flour
1½ cups chicken stock
½ cup dry white wine
Salt and pepper to taste
¼ pound mushrooms, sliced
3 to 4 tablespoons heavy whipping cream
¼ cup grated Parmesan cheese
2 tablespoons bread crumbs
2 tablespoons toasted sliced almonds

1. Place chicken in large pot in water to cover. Add onions, carrots, and herbs. Bring water to a boil, then simmer for about 45 minutes, or until chicken is tender; skim as needed. Let chicken cool in stock, overnight if possible.
2. Remove skin and bones from chicken, then cook these in stock until stock is reduced to 2 to 3 cups. Cut chicken meat into long strips and set aside.
3. Cook spaghetti in boiling, salted water following package directions; drain. Toss with 1 tablespoon butter flavored with a little garlic powder. Place in ovenproof dish and keep warm.
4. To make sauce, melt 4 tablespoons butter in saucepan. Add flour, stirring until well blended. Add chicken stock. Bring to a boil, stirring constantly, and cook for 2 minutes. Add wine and simmer for 3 minutes more.
5. Preheat oven to 400 degrees.
6. Place chicken in mound on top of spaghetti. Sprinkle with salt and pepper. Saute mushrooms in 1 tablespoon butter until tender, then put on top of chicken.
7. Add cream to sauce; check seasoning. Spoon sauce over chicken. Sprinkle top with grated Parmesan and bread crumbs. Bake for 10 to 15 minutes, until top is browned and crisp. Sprinkle with almonds, and serve at once.

Fettucelle and Chicken

Serves 4 to 6

2 boneless chicken breasts, skinned and cut into ½-inch pieces
8 tablespoons butter
1 teaspoon olive oil
1½ teaspoons salt
Freshly ground pepper to taste
1 pound fettucelle

1. Heat 6 tablespoons butter and olive oil in frying pan. Add chicken and cook, stirring constantly, for 15 minutes; chicken should still be juicy. Add salt and pepper. If necessary, add more butter to keep chicken moist. Remove from pan and keep warm.
2. Cook fettucelle in boiling, salted water following package directions; drain. Toss with 2 tablespoons butter and half of chicken. Top with remaining chicken sauce, and serve.

Chicken Peperonata

Serves 4 to 6

1 (3½-pound) roasted chicken, skinned and cut into serving pieces
1 tablespoon olive oil
2 teaspoons salt
2 quarts water
8 ounces pasta shells
½ cup melted butter
⅓ cup grated Parmesan cheese
1 to 1½ cups marinara sauce, heated

1. Place oil, salt, and water in large saucepan and bring to a boil. Boil pasta for 12 minutes, or until tender; drain. Toss with butter and grated cheese.
2. Place chicken in center of large serving dish; arrange shells around chicken. Pour hot marinara sauce over chicken, and serve.

Rigatoni and Chicken Breast

Serves 4 to 6

1 pound rigatoni
¹/₄ pound butter
¹/₂ cup grated Parmesan cheese
2 egg yolks, beaten
1 cup heavy whipping cream
1 teaspoon salt
Freshly ground pepper to taste
¹/₂ boneless chicken breast,
    ground twice

1. Cook rigatoni in boiling, salted water following package directions; drain and set aside.
2. Melt butter in heavy saucepan. Add ¹/₄ cup of the Parmesan cheese, egg yolks, cream, salt, pepper, and chicken. Stir until chicken is well coated.
3. Place rigatoni in large saucepan. Stir in hot chicken mixture, mixing well. Simmer for 15 minutes, stirring occasionally. Serve in soup bowls. Sprinkle with remaining Parmesan cheese.

Spaghettini with Chicken and Peas

Serves 4 to 6

1 boneless chicken breast,
    cubed
2 tablespoons olive oil
¹/₂ teaspoon salt
Pepper to taste
1 (8-ounce) can baby peas,
    undrained
1 pound spaghettini
3 tablespoons grated Parmesan
    cheese
1 egg, beaten

1. Saute chicken in olive oil until golden. Season with salt and pepper. Remove from pan and set aside.
2. Heat peas in can liquid. Drain peas, reserving liquid. Place chicken in saucepan; cover with reserved pea liquid. Simmer for 5 minutes. Add peas and more pepper. Simmer for 5 minutes longer.

3. Cook spaghettini in boiling, salted water following package directions; drain well. Place in heated serving bowl.
4. Blend cheese and egg together; pour gradually into chicken and peas. Toss pasta with half the chicken sauce. Top with remaining chicken sauce, and serve.

Italian-Style Chicken Livers

Serves 4 to 6

2 onions, chopped
2 slices bacon, diced
2 tablespoons olive oil
1 teaspoon salt
Pepper to taste
1 (1-pound) can Italian plum
    tomatoes, drained
¹/₈ teaspoon crushed red pepper
¹/₂ pound chicken livers,
    quartered
1 tablespoon butter
1 pound linguine

1. Saute onions and bacon in olive oil until onions are soft. Add salt, pepper, and tomatoes; use wooden spoon to break up tomatoes. Simmer for 20 minutes. Stir in red pepper. Simmer until sauce begins to thicken.
2. In medium skillet, saute chicken livers in melted butter for 5 minutes, stirring to ensure even cooking. Place livers and butter in tomato sauce. Simmer while pasta cooks.
3. Cook linguine in boiling, salted water following package directions; drain. Place linguine in heated serving bowl. Cover with sauce and livers, and serve.

Fettuccine alla Gorgonzola

Serves 6

3 cups unsifted flour
6 eggs
2¹/₄ teaspoons salt
¹/₄ cup water, if needed
¹/₂ pound gorgonzola cheese
¹/₂ cup unsalted butter
2 cups heavy whipping cream
Pepper to taste
4 quarts water
Grated Parmesan cheese
Grated Romano cheese

1. Place flour in bowl and form a large well in center. Break eggs into hole. Add ¹/₄ teaspoon salt. With a fork, begin mixing eggs and flour together until stiff dough forms. Knead dough for about 20 minutes, until dough is very smooth. Place dough under a large bowl and let rest for 30 minutes.
2. Cut off a quarter of the dough and place on lightly floured work surface, leaving remaining dough under bowl. Roll until paper-thin. Roll up dough loosely and cut into strips about ¹/₄ inch wide. To dry, unroll and spread dough strips out on dry cloth or hang on a rack for at least 4 hours.
3. While dough is drying, put gorgonzola cheese, butter, cream, and pepper into large, deep skillet; cook over low heat, stirring.
4. Place water and 2 teaspoons salt in saucepan and bring to a boil. Boil fettucine about 3 minutes, or until just tender; drain and immediately add to cheese mixture. Toss very lightly and sprinkle mixture of Parmesan and Romano cheeses on top. Serve at once.

Fettuccine con Quatro Formaggio

Serves 4

1/2 pound green fettuccine
1/4 cup sweet butter
1 1/4 cups Parmesan cheese, grated
3 tablespoons shredded Gruyere cheese
2 tablespoons crumbled gorgonzola cheese
2 tablespoons diced Bel Paese cheese
Salt and pepper to taste

1. Cook fettuccine in boiling, salted water following package directions; drain.
2. Toss hot fettuccine with butter, cheeses, salt, and pepper. Serve immediately.

Fettuccine Florentine

Serves 8

12 ounces fettuccine
1 (10-ounce) package frozen chopped spinach
3 tablespoons olive oil
1 small onion, thinly sliced
1 (16-ounce) container ricotta cheese
1 1/2 cups milk
1 1/2 teaspoons salt
Grated Parmesan cheese
Freshly ground pepper

1. Cook fettuccine in boiling, salted water following package directions; drain. Return to pan, cover, and keep warm.
2. Place frozen spinach in medium bowl, cover with boiling water, and let stand for 5 minutes to thaw; drain spinach well and squeeze dry.
3. Heat oil in frying pan over medium heat; add onion and saute until translucent. Add spinach and cook, stirring frequently, until mixture is heated thoroughly. Add spinach mixture to fettuccine.
4. Add ricotta cheese, milk, and salt; cook over low heat, gently tossing, until heated and well mixed. To serve, sprinkle with grated Parmesan cheese and freshly ground pepper.

Fettuccine Alfredo

Serves 4

1/2 cup unsalted butter, softened
1/2 cup heavy whipping cream
1/2 cup freshly grated Parmesan cheese
1 pound fettuccine
Additional grated Parmesan cheese

1. Cream butter; gradually beat in cream. Blend in 1/2 cup cheese. Cover and set aside.
2. Cook pasta in boiling, salted water until just tender, following package directions; drain.
3. Toss fettuccine with cream mixture. Season with salt and pepper. Serve at once with extra grated Parmesan cheese.

Angel Hair Pasta with Prosciutto

Serves 4

3 tablespoons olive oil
3 tablespoons butter
1/2 pound mushrooms, sliced
3/4 pound prosciutto, chopped
3 medium tomatoes, peeled and finely chopped
1 teaspoon sage
1 cup heavy whipping cream
1 pound angel hair pasta (capellini)
Salt and freshly ground pepper to taste
1/2 cup Parmesan cheese
1/2 cup finely chopped parsley

1. Heat oil and butter together in heavy frying pan. Add mushrooms and saute for 8 minutes, or until lightly browned. Add prosciutto, tomatoes, sage, and cream. Cook over high heat, stirring constantly, for 5 minutes, until sauce begins to thicken. Reduce heat to very low while pasta cooks.
2. Cook fettuccine in boiling, salted water until just tender following package directions; drain. Place in heated serving bowl. Season with salt and pepper, then toss with sauce and Parmesan cheese. Sprinkle with parsley, and serve at once.

Rotelle with Zucchini

Serves 4

1/4 cup butter
1/2 pound mushrooms, sliced
1 1/4 pounds zucchini, cut into julienne strips
1 cup heavy whipping cream
1 pound rotelle
3/4 cup freshly grated Parmesan cheese
1/2 cup chopped parsley
Salt and pepper to taste
Additional grated Parmesan cheese, for garnish

1. Melt butter in large, heavy skillet over moderate heat. Add mushrooms; saute for 4 minutes. Add zucchini and saute for 3 minutes. Add cream and remaining butter, cut into small pieces. Reduce heat to low. Heat thoroughly, stirring gently; simmer while pasta is cooking.
2. Cook rotelle in boiling, salted water following package directions; drain well. Place rotelle in heated serving bowl. Add Parmesan cheese and parsley; toss lightly. Add sauce, salt, and pepper; lightly toss with 2 forks. Sprinkle with Parmesan cheese, and serve.

Gnocchi

Serves 4

**4 medium potatoes, peeled
  and diced**
1 teaspoon salt
1¹/₂ to 1³/₄ cups flour
¹/₄ teaspoon white pepper
¹/₄ cup butter
¹/₄ cup Parmesan cheese

1. Cook potatoes in boiling, salted water until tender, about 20 minutes; drain well. Mash potatoes; immediately add between 1¹/₂ to 1³/₄ cups flour until thick dough forms. Add salt and pepper. Divide dough into 4 equal parts. On floured work surface, roll dough out, a section at a time, into cylinders ¹/₂ inch in diameter. Cut into ¹/₂-inch long pieces.
2. Flour tines of fork; slightly flatten each gnocchi. Place on lightly floured towel until ready to cook. Handle remaining dough in same manner; add more flour if dough becomes sticky.
3. Cook gnocchi in large pot filled with gently boiling, salted water. Drop gnocchi into pot one by one until bottom of pot is covered; cook approximately 5 minutes, until gnocchi float to surface. Remove with slotted spoon; drain well.
4. Butter a well-warmed serving dish thickly. Lay gnocchi on top, sprinkle with grated Parmesan cheese, and dot with remaining butter. Serve hot. Gnocchi may also be served with marinara or meat sauce.

Spinach Gnocchi

Serves 6

**1 (10-ounce) package frozen
  spinach, thawed**
1 pound ricotta cheese
1 egg
**¹/₂ cup grated Parmesan
  cheese**
¹/₂ teaspoon salt
¹/₄ teaspoon pepper
**¹/₄ teaspoon freshly grated
  nutmeg**
³/₄ cup flour
4 cups salted water
Melted butter
**Freshly grated Parmesan
  cheese**

1. Place spinach in sieve; press with back of spoon to push out water. Combine ricotta, spinach, and egg in mixing bowl; mix well. Stir in Parmesan cheese and seasonings. Add ¹/₂ cup flour; mix well.
2. Place ¹/₄ cup flour on plate. Form rounded teaspoons of spinach-cheese mixture into gnocchi dumplings by coating lightly with flour and rolling between palms of hand to form round balls. Place on waxed paper in single layer until ready to cook.
3. Bring salted water to boil in large saucepan. Drop gnocchi one by one into boiling water until bottom of pot is filled with single layer of gnocchi. Cook about 5 minutes. Gnocchi will rise to surface of water when done. Remove with slotted spoon; drain well.
4. Place gnocchi in heated serving bowl. Continue until all gnocchi are cooked. Drizzle with melted butter and sprinkle with grated Parmesan cheese; serve at once.

Tomatoes and Gnocchi

Serves 4

2¹/₂ cups flour
¹/₂ teaspoon salt
3 tablespoons olive oil
**3 cloves garlic, peeled and
  quartered**
**1¹/₂ tablespoons chopped fresh
  basil or 1 teaspoon dried basil**
**3²/₃ cups tomatoes, peeled and
  chopped**
Salt and white pepper to taste
1 teaspoon oregano
4 quarts salted water
**2 tablespoons freshly grated
  Pecorino or Parmesan cheese**

1. Sift flour into bowl; add ¹/₂ teaspoon salt. Gradually add water to form firm dough. Knead dough well. Shape into thin cylinders ¹/₂-inch thick, then cut into 2-inch long pieces.
2. Heat oil in large saucepan; add garlic and saute for 1 minute. Remove garlic from pan and discard. Add basil, tomatoes, salt, and pepper to oil. Stir well and cook over low heat for 30 minutes. Stir in oregano.
3. Cook gnocchi in boiling, salted water for about 5 minutes, or until gnocchi rise to the surface; drain. Place gnocchi in heated serving dish. Spoon tomato mixture on top and sprinkle with grated cheese.

Spaghetti with Tomato Sauce

Serves 4

2 tablespoons olive oil
1 large onion, finely chopped
1 clove garlic, finely chopped
**1 (28-ounce) can Italian-style
  tomatoes, undrained**
1 (6-ounce) can tomato paste
Salt and pepper to taste
1 bay leaf
1 teaspoon basil
1 teaspoon oregano
12 ounces spaghetti

1. Heat oil in saucepan. Add onion and garlic; saute until translucent.

2. Add tomatoes, tomato paste, salt, pepper, bay leaf, basil, and oregano. Bring to a boil, then simmer for 30 minutes.

3. Cook spaghetti in boiling, salted water following package directions; drain.

4. Place spaghetti in heated serving bowl. Pour tomato sauce on top, and serve.

5. To make **SPAGHETTI WITH MEAT SAUCE**, saute 1 pound ground beef until well browned. Pour off excess fat. Add onion and garlic, and follow rest of above instructions beginning with step **2**.

Spaghetti and Meatballs

Serves 4

Meatballs
1 pound lean ground beef
1/2 cup Italian-style bread crumbs
1 egg, slightly beaten
1 tablespoon dried onion flakes
Salt and pepper to taste
3 tablespoons oil

Sauce
2 tablespoons olive oil
1 medium onion, chopped
1 clove garlic, peeled and minced
1 (28-ounce) can Italian-style tomatoes, undrained
1 (6-ounce) can tomato paste
3/4 cup water
1 1/2 teaspoons mixed Italian herbs
1 teaspoon sugar
1/2 cup dry red wine
1/2 cup sliced mushrooms
12 ounces spaghetti
Grated Parmesan cheese

1. To make meatballs, combine beef, bread crumbs, egg, onion flakes, salt, and pepper; mix well. Form into meatballs the size of a walnut. Heat oil in medium skillet; add meatballs and brown on all sides; drain.

2. To make sauce, heat oil in large saucepan. Add onion and garlic; saute for 5 minutes.

3. Puree tomatoes in blender or food processor. Add tomatoes to onion mixture, along with tomato paste, water, seasonings, and wine. Bring to a boil; reduce heat to low. Add meatballs and mushrooms. Cover and simmer for 1 to 1 1/2 hours, or until sauce is thick.

4. Cook spaghetti in boiling, salted water following package directions; drain.

5. To serve, separate meatballs from sauce. Toss sauce and spaghetti together to coat lightly. Serve meatballs and Parmesan cheese separately.

Italian Macaroni and Cheese

Serves 6

1/2 pound ground beef
1 (16-ounce) can tomatoes, undrained
1/3 cup tomato paste
1 tablespoon dried minced onion
1 teaspoon sugar
1/2 teaspoon garlic salt
1/2 teaspoon oregano
Dash of pepper
1 2/3 cups macaroni
1 cup creamed cottage cheese
1 cup shredded sharp Cheddar cheese
2 tablespoons grated Parmesan cheese

1. Cook meat in large, heavy frying pan until it loses red color but is not brown; drain fat. Add tomatoes, tomato paste, onion, and seasonings. Simmer slowly for 30 minutes; stir as needed.

2. Preheat oven to 325 degrees.

3. Cook macaroni in boiling, salted water following package directions; drain. Combine macaroni and cottage cheese.

4. Pour a little meat sauce in bottom of 2 1/2-quart casserole dish. Top with half the macaroni mixture, half the shredded Cheddar cheese, and half the remaining sauce. Repeat layers. Sprinkle Parmesan cheese on top and bake for 40 minutes, or until well heated. Remove from oven, and serve.

Lasagna

Serves 6

8 ounces lasagna noodles
1 pound ground beef
2 mild Italian sausage links, casing removed
1 tablespoon olive oil
1 medium onion, finely diced
1 clove garlic, peeled and minced
1 (28-ounce) can Italian-style tomatoes, drained
1 (6-ounce) can tomato paste
1/2 teaspoon oregano
1/2 teaspoon basil
1 teaspoon sugar
8 ounces ricotta cheese
8 ounces mozzarella cheese, thinly sliced
1/2 cup freshly grated Parmesan cheese

1. Cook lasagna noodles in boiling, salted water following package directions; drain. Rinse with cold water and drain again.

2. Brown beef and sausages in large skillet. Remove from pan and pour off drippings.

3. Add oil to same skillet. Add onion and garlic; cook over low heat for 5 minutes. Add tomatoes, breaking them up with wooden spoon. Add tomato paste and seasonings. Stir well, then add meat to sauce. Cook over low heat for 40 minutes, or until thick.

4. Preheat oven to 350 degrees.

5. Lightly grease 13 x 9 x 2-inch baking dish. Ladle about 3/4 cup sauce into pan. Top with 1/3 of noodles. Dot with half the ricotta and half the mozzarella. Add layer of sauce and 1/3 of noodles, then remaining ricotta and mozzarella. Top with more sauce; add remaining noodles. Top with remaining sauce and sprinkle with Parmesan cheese. Bake for 30 minutes, or until well heated. Remove from oven, and serve.

Lasagna al Forno

Serves 6

¾ **pound ground beef**
2 **onions, finely chopped**
2 **carrots, shredded**
2 **bunches celery, finely**
chopped
10 **tablespoons butter**
Salt and pepper to taste
½ **cup red wine**
1½ **cups beef broth, heated**
1 **tablespoon tomato paste**
2½ **cups milk**
¼ **cup flour**
8 **ounces lasagna noodles**
Pinch of nutmeg
¾ **cup diced mozzarella**
cheese
¼ **cup grated Parmesan**
cheese

1. Mix ground beef and chopped onions, carrots, and celery together. Melt 4 tablespoons butter in saucepan. Add meat mixture and cook until lightly browned. Add salt and pepper to taste. Add wine and beef broth; simmer until liquid is almost absorbed. Add tomato paste, salt, and pepper.
2. Heat ½ cup milk and stir into saucepan; simmer over very low heat for about 1½ hours, stirring occasionally.
3. Meanwhile, make a Bechamel sauce. Melt 4 tablespoons butter in separate saucepan. Add flour and cook, stirring constantly, for 1 minute; do not brown. Gradually add 2 cups milk, stirring constantly. Bring to a boil and simmer for 2 minutes. Season with nutmeg, salt and pepper.
4. Cook lasagna noodles in boiling, salted water following package directions; drain. Rinse with cold water and drain again.
5. Preheat oven to 350 degrees.
6. Butter large, ovenproof dish and spoon in enough meat sauce to cover bottom of dish. Arrange layer of lasagna noodles on top of sauce, followed by layer of Bechamel sauce. Sprinkle some mozzarella and

Parmesan cheese between each layer. Repeat layers until all meat sauce, lasagna noodles, and Bechamel sauce are used, finishing with layer of Bechamel sauce. Sprinkle with any remaining cheese and dot with 2 tablespoons butter. Bake for 30 to 40 minutes, or until golden brown. Remove from oven, and serve.

Linguine with White Clam Sauce

Serves 6

1 **pound linguine**
¼ **cup olive oil**
1 to 2 **teaspoons finely chopped**
garlic
2 **cups clam juice (bottled mixed**
with drained juice from clams)
½ **cup white wine**
1 **teaspoon thyme**
Freshly ground pepper to taste
2½ **cups chopped clams, fresh**
or canned, drained
¼ **cup chopped parsley**
2 **tablespoons grated Parmesan**
cheese

1. Heat oil in saucepan. Add garlic and saute for 1 minute. Add clam juice, wine, thyme, and pepper. Simmer for 10 minutes. Add clams and parsley; simmer until heated thoroughly.
2. Meanwhile, cook linguine in boiling, salted water following package directions; drain.
3. Place hot linguine in heated serving bowl. Spoon on clam sauce, sprinkle with Parmesan cheese, and serve.

Linguine with Red Clam Sauce

Serves 4 to 6

1 **pound linguine**
¼ **cup olive oil**
2 **cloves garlic, peeled and**
minced
1 (28-ounce) **can tomatoes,**
undrained

1 **teaspoon oregano**
3 (10-ounce) **cans clams,**
drained, reserve can liquid
Salt and pepper to taste
Dash of cayenne pepper
Grated Parmesan cheese

1. Cook linguine in boiling, salted water following package directions; drain.
2. Heat oil in saucepan. Add garlic and saute for 2 minutes. Add tomatoes and cook over medium heat for 10 minutes. Add oregano, clams, and ½ cup of reserved clam liquid. Cook over medium heat for 5 minutes longer. Add salt, pepper, and cayenne pepper.
3. Place linguine in heated serving dish. Add clam sauce, sprinkle with Parmesan cheese, and serve at once.

Spaghetti Roma

Serves 6 to 8

3 **tablespoons olive oil**
4 **anchovy fillets, chopped**
1 **clove garlic, peeled and finely**
chopped
1 **dried hot chili pepper, crushed**
1 (1-pound) **can Italian-style**
tomatoes, undrained
½ **cup pitted black olives,**
sliced
1 **tablespoon capers**
1 (7-ounce) **can tuna fish,**
drained
Salt and pepper to taste
1 **teaspoon oregano**
1 **pound thin spaghetti**

1. Heat olive oil in saucepan. Add anchovy fillets, garlic, and chili pepper; saute for 1 minute. Add tomatoes and juice, olives, capers, and tuna fish. Season with salt, pepper, and oregano. Simmer for 10 minutes.
2. Cook spaghetti in boiling, salted water following package directions; drain.
3. Place spaghetti in heated serving dish. Add sauce and toss lightly. Serve immediately.

Fusilli with Clams and Anchovies

Serves 6

3 dozen cherrystone clams
2 tablespoons olive oil
2 white onions, chopped
6 anchovy fillets, drained
2½ cups chopped tomatoes
2 small green peppers, seeded
  and chopped
1 clove garlic, peeled and minced
1 pound fusilli or spaghetti

1. Remove clams from shells, reserving liquid.
2. Heat oil in saucepan; add onions and saute until translucent. Add clam liquid and anchovies. Simmer for 8 minutes. Add tomatoes, green peppers, and garlic. Cook until liquid has been reduced by half, about 30 minutes. Add clams and cook for 5 minutes more.
3. Cook fusilli in boiling, salted water following package directions; drain. Place fusilli in heated serving bowl. Pour sauce on top; toss to mix well, and serve at once.

Seafood Linguine

Serves 4 to 6

¼ pound butter
2 cans minced clams, drained
1 clove garlic, peeled and finely
  minced
1 teaspoon salt
¼ teaspoon pepper
½ pound cooked shrimp,
  shelled and deveined
2 teaspoons lemon juice
1 pound linguine

1. Melt butter in medium frying pan. Add clams, garlic, salt, pepper, shrimp, and lemon juice. Cook on low heat for 15 minutes, stirring occasionally.
2. Cook linguine in boiling, salted water following package directions; drain.
3. Place linguine in warmed serving bowl. Pour seafood sauce over linguine, and serve at once.

Shrimp Marinara

Serves 4

1 quart salted water
1 bay leaf
1 lemon slice
1½ pounds large shrimp,
  shelled and deveined
2 tablespoons olive oil
½ cup chopped onion
1 clove garlic, peeled and
  minced
1½ cups Italian-style tomatoes,
  drained
¼ cup tomato sauce
½ teaspoon sugar
½ teaspoon basil
Salt and pepper to taste
2 tablespoons bread crumbs
2 tablespoons grated Parmesan
  cheese
1 tablespoon finely chopped
  parsley
8 ounces thin spaghetti

1. Place salted water, bay leaf, and lemon in large saucepan; bring a boil. Add shrimp and boil for 5 minutes; drain.
2. Heat oil in heavy frying pan. Add onion and garlic; saute until translucent. Break up tomatoes with wooden spoon and add to frying pan, along with tomato sauce, sugar, basil, salt, and pepper. Simmer for 20 minutes.
3. Preheat oven to 450 degrees.
4. Place shrimp in lightly greased baking dish. Top with tomato sauce. Combine bread crumbs, cheese, and parsley; sprinkle over shrimp and sauce. Bake for 10 minutes.
5. Meanwhile, cook pasta in boiling, salted water following package directions; drain.
6. Place pasta in heated serving dish. Cover with shrimp and sauce, and serve.

Mussels Marinara

Serves 6

5 dozen fresh mussels
½ cup dry white wine
¼ cup olive oil
3 cloves garlic, peeled and
  finely chopped
2 (28-ounce) cans Italian-style
  tomatoes, drained, reserve
  juice
1 teaspoon oregano
½ bay leaf
Salt and pepper to taste
1 pound thin spaghetti
Freshly grated Parmesan
  cheese

1. Scrub mussels well under cold running water; remove beards. Discard any mussels that are opened. Place cleaned mussels in large pot with wine. Cover and cook over high heat for 4 or 5 minutes, or until mussels open. Remove mussels from pot, discarding any that have not opened. Reserve cooking liquid. Set aside a handful of mussels, then remove remaining mussels from shells.
2. Heat oil in large saucepan. Add garlic and saute for 1 minute. Add tomatoes, oregano, bay leaf, pepper, and mussel cooking liquid. Cook over low heat, breaking up tomatoes with fork, for 20 minutes. Add reserved tomato liquid if sauce is too thick.
3. Cook pasta in boiling, salted water following package directions; drain.
4. Add shelled mussels to sauce and cook for 1 minute. Season with salt and pepper. Place spaghetti in heated serving bowl, cover with sauce, and sprinkle with grated cheese. Garnish with mussels left in shells, and serve.

Spaghetti Milanese

Serves 4

6 tablespoons butter
1 slice bacon, chopped
1 small onion, finely chopped
1 carrot, peeled and chopped
3 to 4 tomatoes, skinned and
 quartered
1 cup chicken stock or water
Pepper to taste
Pinch of thyme
1 bay leaf
Dash of lemon juice
1 cup sliced mushrooms
1 cup diced prosciutto
8 to 12 ounces spaghetti
Grated Parmesan or Romano
 cheese

1. Melt 2 tablespoons butter in saucepan. Add bacon and cook just until fat begins to melt. Add onion and carrot; cook for 5 minutes. Add tomatoes, cover, and cook over low heat for 5 minutes. Add stock or water, seasonings, and lemon juice. Cover and simmer for 30 minutes; remove bay leaf.
2. Melt 2 tablespoons butter in frying pan. Add mushrooms and saute until tender.
3. Cook spaghetti in boiling, salted water following package directions; drain well. Toss with remaining 2 tablespoons butter. Add prosciutto and mushrooms to spaghetti.
4. Place spaghetti mixture in heated serving dish. Pour hot tomato sauce on top; sprinkle with grated cheese and serve.

Penne with Sauce Amatrice

Serves 4

2 tablespoons olive oil
2 cloves garlic, peeled and
 minced
¼ pound salt pork, diced
1 small onion, chopped
¼ cup dry white wine
1 (28-ounce) can Italian-style
 tomatoes, drained and minced

1 teaspoon sugar
1 teaspoon chili powder
½ teaspoon paprika
½ teaspoon basil
½ teaspoon oregano
Salt and pepper to taste
12 ounces penne
Freshly grated Parmesan cheese

1. Heat oil in large saucepan. Add garlic, salt pork, and onion. Saute until onion is tender. Add wine; cook until wine evaporates. Add tomatoes and spices. Simmer for 20 minutes.
2. Meanwhile, cook penne in boiling, salted water following package directions; drain.
3. Place penne in heated serving bowl. Top with sauce, sprinkle with grated Parmesan cheese, and serve.

Bracciole with Pasta

Serves 4

2 pounds thinly sliced round
 steak, cut into 2-inch
 wide strips
Salt and pepper to taste
1 large clove garlic, peeled
 and minced
¼ cup finely chopped parsley
½ pound provolone cheese
Grated Romano cheese
½ cup olive oil
1½ cups diced mushrooms
1 green pepper, seeded and
 diced
4 scallions, diced
2 (28-ounce) cans crushed
 tomatoes, undrained
8 ounces pasta of your choice

1. Lay round steak strips flat. Season with salt and pepper; sprinkle with garlic and parsley. Place provolone cheese on each strip; sprinkle with Romano cheese. Roll meat up and tie with string.
2. Heat olive oil in large, heavy frying pan. Add mushrooms, green pepper, and scallions. Simmer for 4 minutes. Add meat rolls to pan. Cook until meat rolls are browned on all sides.

3. Add tomatoes, salt, and pepper. Simmer, partially covered, over medium-low heat for 1 hour.
4. Cook pasta in boiling, salted water following package directions; drain.
5. Place hot pasta on heated serving platter. Remove string from meat, then place meat on top of pasta. Cover with sauce, and serve.

Manicotti with Cheese

Serves 6

12 manicotti shells
1 pound ricotta or pot cheese
1 cup grated mozzarella cheese
7 tablespoons grated Parmesan
 cheese
1 tablespoon parsley flakes
1 egg, lightly beaten
½ teaspoon salt
¼ teaspoon white pepper
¼ teaspoon garlic powder
3 cups marinara sauce
½ cup water

1. Cover manicotti shells with boiling water and let stand for 5 minutes. Drain; rinse in cold water.
2. Combine ricotta, mozzarella, and 4 tablespoons Parmesan cheese; add parsley flakes, egg, salt, pepper, and garlic powder, mixing well.
3. Place marinara sauce and water in medium saucepan. Heat on low while stuffing manicotti.
4. Preheat oven to 375 degrees.
5. Stuff each manicotti shell with ⅓ to ½ cup cheese filling. Pour ¾ cup marinara sauce into bottom of 13 x 9 x 2-inch baking dish. Place stuffed noodles on top of sauce; top with remaining sauce. Cover with foil and bake for 45 minutes. Uncover and sprinkle with 3 tablespoons Parmesan cheese. Bake, uncovered, for 5 minutes longer. Remove from oven, and serve.

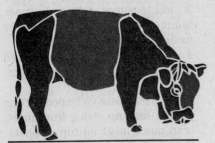

Manicotti with Beef

Serves 6

12 manicotti shells
2 tablespoons olive oil
1 small onion, chopped
1/2 pound ground beef
1/4 pound Italian sweet sausage
3 1/4 cups marinara sauce
1/4 cup Italian-style bread
  crumbs
1 cup grated mozzarella
  cheese
2 tablespoons finely chopped
  parsley
Salt and pepper to taste
1/2 cup water
3 tablespoons grated Parmesan
  cheese

1. Cover manicotti shells with boiling water; let stand for 5 minutes. Drain; rinse in cold water.
2. Heat oil in frying pan. Add onion, ground beef, and sausage. Cook over moderate heat, breaking up meat and sausage with fork, until meat is lightly browned. Remove from heat and drain well. Let meat mixture cool for 5 minutes. Add 1/4 cup marinara sauce, bread crumbs, mozzarella cheese, parsley, salt, and pepper; mix well.
3. Preheat oven to 375 degrees.
4. Heat remaining 3 cups marinara sauce with 1/2 cup water.
5. Stuff each manicotti shell with 1/3 to 1/2 cup filling. Pour 3/4 cup of heated sauce into bottom of 13 x 9 x 2-inch baking dish. Place stuffed manicotti on top of sauce; top with remaining sauce. Cover with foil and bake for 45 minutes. Uncover and sprinkle with Parmesan cheese. Bake, uncovered, for 5 minutes more. Remove from oven, and serve.

Venetian-Style Manicotti

Serves 6 to 8

8 ounces manicotti noodles

Meat Filling

1 pound meatloaf mixture
  (ground pork, beef, and veal)
1 large onion, diced
1 clove garlic, peeled and
  minced
1 egg, well beaten
1 cup bread crumbs
1/4 cup finely chopped parsley
1 teaspoon basil
Salt and pepper to taste

Manicotti Sauce

6 tablespoons butter
6 tablespoons flour
1/2 teaspoon salt
White pepper to taste
1/4 teaspoon nutmeg
1 1/2 cups chicken broth
1 cup light cream
3/4 cup freshly grated Parmesan
  cheese
Additional nutmeg, for
  garnish
Chopped parsley, for garnish

1. Cook manicotti shells in boiling, salted water following package directions; drain and rinse with cold water.
2. Place meatloaf mixture, onion, and garlic in frying pan; cook over low heat until meat is lightly browned. Remove from heat and drain well. Combine meat mixture, egg, bread crumbs, parsley, and seasonings; mix well.
3. Preheat oven to 350 degrees.
4. Stuff manicotti shells with meat filling. Place in lightly greased baking dish.
5. To make sauce, melt butter in large saucepan. Add flour; cook, stirring constantly, until bubbly. Add seasonings, continuing to stir. Add broth and cream all at once. Cook, stirring constantly, until sauce thickens. Remove from heat and stir in Parmesan cheese.

6. Pour sauce evenly over stuffed manicotti noodles. Sprinkle lightly with nutmeg and chopped parsley. Bake for 30 minutes. Remove from oven and serve immediately.

Neapolitan Dinner

Serves 8

1 cup lentils
3 slices bacon, chopped
1/2 cup chopped onion
1 clove garlic, peeled and
  minced
1 red pepper, seeded and
  chopped
1/4 cup chopped celery
1/2 pound Italian sausage or
  salami, sliced
1 teaspoon salt
1/4 teaspoon pepper
4 cups cooked elbow
  macaroni
1 cup tomato sauce
1/4 cup grated Parmesan
  cheese

1. Wash and pick over lentils. Soak lentils in cold water to cover overnight.
2. Drain lentils and reserve soaking liquid.
3. Place bacon in sauce and cook until fat begins to melt. Add onion and garlic; saute with bacon until onion is translucent. Add lentils, 2 1/2 cups reserved soaking liquid, red pepper, celery, sausage, salt, and pepper. Cover and cook over moderate heat for 15 minutes, or until lentils are tender.
4. Preheat oven to 350 degrees.
5. Combine lentil mixture, macaroni, and tomato sauce. Place in greased, 3-quart casserole dish. Sprinkle with Parmesan cheese and bake for 30 minutes. Remove from oven, and serve.

Pasta Primavera

Serves 6

4 quarts salted water
1 pound thin pasta, such as vermicelli or spaghettini
2 cloves garlic, peeled and halved
1 zucchini or yellow crookneck squash, sliced
6 fresh asparagus, cut into 1-inch pieces
1 bunch fresh broccoli, cut into 1-inch florets
2 tablespoons olive oil
2 tablespoons butter
1/2 cup sliced mushrooms
1/2 teaspoon dried red pepper flakes
1 1/2 cups frozen peas, thawed
1 red pepper, seeded and cubed
1 teaspoon basil
Salt and freshly ground pepper to taste
1 1/2 cups heavy whipping cream
1 cup grated Parmesan cheese

1. Place salted water in large saucepan and bring to a boil. Add pasta and garlic; boil for 3 minutes, stirring occasionally. Add zucchini or squash, asparagus, and broccoli; boil for 3 minutes more, or until pasta is just tender and vegetables are crisp-tender. Drain and discard garlic.

2. Meanwhile, heat oil and butter in frying pan. Add mushrooms and red pepper flakes; saute until mushrooms are tender. Remove from pan.

2. Return cooked pasta and vegetables to pan. Add peas, red pepper, mushrooms, and seasonings; toss to mix. Add cream and Parmesan cheese; using 2 large forks, toss pasta until cheese melts and creamy sauce forms. Place in heated serving bowl, sprinkle with freshly ground black pepper, and serve at once.

Pasta Shells with Genoese Sauce

Serves 6

2 tablespoons butter
1/2 cup olive oil
1 1/2 cups finely chopped onions
1 carrot, grated
1/2 cup finely diced celery
1/2 pound fresh mushrooms, finely chopped
1 pound ground veal
2 cups chopped peeled tomatoes
2 tablespoons flour
3/4 cup dry red wine
1 cup beef broth
Salt and freshly ground pepper to taste
1 pound pasta shells

1. Combine butter and oil in heavy frying pan; heat until sizzling. Add onions and saute for 3 minutes. Add carrot, celery, and mushrooms; cook, stirring frequently, about 5 minutes. Add veal; cook, stirring constantly, until well broken up and lightly browned. Add tomatoes; stir to mix well.

2. Sprinkle flour over mixture; stir to mix well. Gradually add wine and then beef broth. Season with salt and pepper. Simmer for 2 hours, stirring occasionally.

3. Cook shells in boiling, salted water following package directions; drain.

4. Place shells in heated serving dish. Pour sauce on top, and serve.

Ravioli

Serves 6 to 8

Ravioli Dough

3 cups flour
1/4 teaspoon salt
2 eggs
1/3 cup water

Meat Filling

3/4 pound meatloaf mix (ground pork, beef, and veal)
1/4 cup bread crumbs
2 tablespoons grated Parmesan cheese
1 egg
1 tablespoon parsley flakes
1/2 teaspoon garlic salt
1/4 teaspoon pepper
Cornmeal for dusting

For Cooking

4 quarts water
1 tablespoon salt
1 tablespoon oil
Melted butter
Freshly grated Parmesan cheese

1. To make dough, stir flour and salt together in mixing bowl; form a well in center. Add eggs to center of well, then blend with flour. Stir in enough water to form very stiff dough. Turn out onto lightly floured work surface. Knead until dough is smooth and elastic, about 10 minutes. Cover and let rest for 10 minutes.

2. Combine filling ingredients, except cornmeal, in bowl; mix well. Refrigerate until ready to use.

3. Divide dough into 8 pieces. Roll one piece at a time on lightly floured surface until paper-thin; keep remaining dough tightly covered until ready to use. Cut dough into 2-inch squares.

4. Place 1 teaspoon meat filling in center of half of the squares. Cover each filled square with an unfilled one; press edges tightly together to seal; moisten edges with a little water to ensure tight seal.

5. Dust cookie sheet lightly with cornmeal. Place ravioli on sheet, cover, and refrigerate for 2 hours.

6. Place water and salt in large saucepan and bring to a boil; float oil on surface of water. Drop ravioli into water a few at a time; stir to prevent ravioli from sticking to bottom of pan. Boil gently for about 12 minutes, or until ravioli are tender; drain.

7. To serve, toss with melted butter and Parmesan cheese. Ravioli can also be served with tomato or meat sauce.

Ravioli with Cheese Filling

Serves 4

6 large eggs
½ teaspoon salt
2 tablespoons oil
4½ cups flour
2 cups freshly grated Parmesan
  cheese
2 cups ricotta cheese
Pinch of white pepper
Pinch of nutmeg
8 to 12 cups salted water
⅔ cup butter

1. Break 4 eggs into bowl. Stir in salt and oil. Add enough flour to form thin dough.
2. Sift remaining flour into separate bowl. Add egg mixture and mix until smooth, elastic dough forms. Place under bowl and let rest for 1 hour.
3. While dough rests, combine ¾ cup Parmesan cheese, ricotta, 2 eggs, salt, pepper, and nutmeg.
4. Roll out pasta dough on lightly floured work surface as thinly as possible; cut into 2-inch squares. Divide cheese filling evenly among squares. Wet edges of squares with water and firmly fold ravioli in half; seal edges together well.
5. Place salted water in large saucepan and bring to a boil. Add ravioli and boil for 5 minutes; drain.
6. Melt butter in frying pan until lightly browned. Stir in remaining Parmesan cheese. Add ravioli and very carefully stir-fry until golden. Remove from pan and serve.

Spaghetti Carbonara

Serves 6

1 pound spaghetti
10 slices bacon, diced
3 eggs
½ cup grated Parmesan cheese
⅓ cup chopped parsley
Salt and freshly ground pepper
  to taste

1. Cook spaghetti in boiling, salted water following package directions; drain.
2. While spaghetti is cooking, cook bacon in frying pan until crisp; drain on paper towels, reserving 2 tablespoons pan drippings.
3. Beat eggs, Parmesan cheese, parsley, salt, pepper, and reserved pan drippings together.
4. Place hot spaghetti in heated serving bowl. Add egg mixture, tossing well. Add bacon, toss again, and serve at once.

Spaghetti Bolognese

Serves 4

3 tablespoons olive oil
10 ounces ground beef
4 ounces ground pork
¼ pound bacon, cut into
  narrow strips
2 onions, finely chopped
1 carrot, diced
2 stalks celery, finely sliced
½ cup chopped parsley
2 tablespoons tomato paste
1¼ cups hot beef broth
2 cups dry white wine
1 bay leaf
½ teaspoon salt
Pinch of pepper
Pinch of sugar
10 ounces spaghetti
2 tablespoons butter
4 ounces chicken livers

1. Heat 2 tablespoons oil in large saucepan. Brown ground beef and pork. Add bacon and onions; cook for 3 minutes more. Add carrot, celery, parsley, tomato paste, stock, wine, bay leaf, salt, pepper, and sugar. Simmer for 30 minutes.
2. Cook spaghetti in boiling, salted water following package directions; drain and toss with 1 tablespoon butter.
3. Saute chicken livers in 1 tablespoon butter until tender; remove from pan, finely chop, and add to sauce.
4. Place spaghetti in heated serving dish. Spoon sauce on top, and serve.

Capellini con Aglio e Olio

Serves 4

¼ cup olive oil
4 cloves garlic, peeled and finely
  chopped
1 small hot red chili
8 ounces capellini (angel hair
  pasta)
¼ cup very finely chopped
  parsley
¼ cup freshly grated Pecorino or
  Parmesan cheese

1. Heat oil in small frying pan. Add garlic and whole chili; saute, stirring constantly, until garlic changes color; be careful not to burn garlic or it will taste bitter. Remove pan from heat, cover, and keep warm.
2. Cook pasta in boiling, salted water following package directions, being careful not to overcook; drain.
3. Discard chili, then toss pasta with garlic-flavored oil in heated serving dish. Sprinkle with parsley and grated cheese, and serve at once.

Linguine Fegato

Serves 6

2 tablespoons olive oil
½ pound pork sausage
1 cup chopped onion
1 clove garlic, peeled and minced
½ pound ground beef liver
3½ cups canned Italian-style tomatoes, drained
1 (6-ounce) can tomato paste
1 cup beef stock
2 tablespoons chopped parsley
½ bay leaf
¼ teaspoon basil
¼ teaspoon thyme
Salt and pepper to taste
1 cup chopped pitted black olives
8 ounces linguine

1. Preheat oven to 350 degrees.
2. Heat oil in saucepan and brown sausage meat. Add onion, garlic, and liver. Cook for 10 minutes. Add tomatoes, tomato paste, stock, parsley, and seasonings; simmer for 1 hour. Add olives.
3. Cook linguine in boiling, salted water following package directions; drain.
4. Spoon sauce over linguine and mix lightly. Turn into greased, shallow, 2½-quart casserole dish. Bake for 30 minutes. Remove from oven, and serve.

Tortellini Alfredo

Serves 4 to 6

1 pound cheese-filled tortellini
½ cup butter
1 cup grated Parmesan cheese
1 cup heavy whipping cream
1 cup chopped parsley
Freshly ground pepper

1. Cook tortellini in boiling, salted water following package directions; drain.
2. Melt butter in saucepan. Add cheese, stirring to mix well. Add cream and parsley. Cook, stirring constantly, until sauce thickens.
3. Toss tortellini with sauce. Top with freshly ground pepper, and serve at once.

Pasta Fagioli

Serves 4

⅓ cup pinto beans
⅓ cup kidney beans
⅓ cup Great Northern or white beans
2 tablespoons oil
1 pound trimmed chuck steak, cut into chunks
3 onions, chopped
4 stalks celery, chopped
1 (16-ounce) can tomatoes, drained
1 large meat bone
¼ cup chopped parsley
Salt and pepper to taste
Italian seasoning to taste
Garlic powder to taste
2 quarts water
1 large meat bone
1 cup macaroni

1. Soak beans overnight in water to cover.
2. Drain beans.
3. Heat oil in large saucepan. Brown meat, onions, and celery. Add tomatoes, meat bone, parsley, salt, pepper, Italian seasoning, garlic powder, beans, and water. Simmer for 2 hours. Add macaroni and cook for 10 minutes more.
4. Cover and refrigerate overnight. Reheat gently, and serve hot.

Jumbo Stuffed Shells

Serves 4

16 jumbo pasta shells
2 tablespoons olive oil
½ cup finely chopped onion
1 clove garlic, peeled and minced
1 (16-ounce) can peeled Italian-style tomatoes, undrained
3 tablespoons tomato paste
½ teaspoon sugar
½ teaspoon mixed Italian seasoning
Salt and pepper to taste
1 (10-ounce) package frozen spinach, thawed
1 pound ricotta cheese
1 egg, slightly beaten
¼ teaspoon nutmeg
½ cup freshly grated Parmesan cheese

1. Cook shells in boiling, salted water following package directions; drain and rinse with cold water.
2. Meanwhile, heat olive oil in medium saucepan. Add onion and garlic; saute until translucent. Puree tomatoes in blender or food processor, then add to saucepan. Add tomato paste, sugar, Italian seasoning, salt, and pepper; mix well. Bring to a boil, then simmer for 30 minutes.
3. Preheat oven to 350 degrees.
4. Press spinach through sieve to remove water. Mix spinach with ricotta, egg, nutmeg, salt, and pepper.
5. Stuff spinach-ricotta mixture into cooked shells. Place shells in single layer in lightly greased, 9 x 9-inch baking pan. Pour sauce over shells; sprinkle with Parmesan cheese. Bake for 30 minutes. Remove from oven, and serve.

Julia's Stuffed Shells

Serves 4

2 teaspoons olive oil
2 cloves garlic, peeled and
  finely chopped
2 (10-ounce) cans condensed
  tomato soup
2 teaspoons salt
1 teaspoon pepper
1 teaspoon oregano
1 teaspoon basil
4 eggs
1 cup ricotta cheese
16 large pasta shells

1. Heat oil in saucepan. Add garlic and saute until lightly browned. Add soup; season with 1 teaspoon salt, ¹/₂ teaspoon pepper, oregano, and basil. Cook over medium heat, stirring occasionally, until sauce thickens.
2. Cook pasta shells in boiling, salted water until slightly hard, following package directions; drain and cool.
3. Preheat oven to 350 degrees.
4. Mix eggs, cheese, and remaining salt and pepper together. Stuff shells with egg-cheese mixture. Place shells in single layer in greased baking dish. Pour tomato sauce on top and bake for 20 minutes. Remove from oven, and serve.

Stuffed Rigatoni

Serves 8

Rigatoni Sauce

¹/₄ cup olive oil
2 pounds meatloaf mixture
  (ground beef, veal, and pork)
4 cloves garlic, peeled and
  chopped
¹/₂ cup finely chopped celery
¹/₂ cup finely chopped carrots
¹/₂ cup finely chopped green
  pepper
¹/₄ cup finely chopped parsley
1 medium onion, finely chopped
1 (6-ounce) can tomato paste
³/₄ cup water

1 (28-ounce) can Italian-style
  tomatoes, undrained
2 teaspoons sugar
1 teaspoon salt
¹/₂ teaspoon pepper
¹/₂ teaspoon basil
¹/₂ teaspoon oregano

Pasta and Filling

1 pound rigatoni
2 (10-ounce) packages frozen
  chopped spinach, thawed
³/₄ cup grated Parmesan cheese
¹/₂ cup bread crumbs
2 eggs
Salt and pepper to taste
1 clove garlic, peeled and
  minced

1. Heat 2 tablespoons olive oil in heavy skillet. Add meatloaf mixture and 3 cloves garlic. Cook over low heat until meat loses its pink color. Drain; reserve half of meat mixture to stuff pasta.
2. Heat remaining olive oil in Dutch oven. Saute celery, carrots, green pepper, parsley, onion, and 1 clove garlic over medium heat until limp. Add tomato paste and water.
3. Puree tomatoes in blender or food processor; add to sauce. Add half of cooked meat, sugar, salt, pepper, basil, and oregano. Bring to a boil. Reduce heat and simmer for 1¹/₂ to 2 hours.
4. Cook rigatoni in boiling, salted water following package directions; drain and rinse with cold water.
5. Push spinach through sieve to remove water. Combine spinach, ¹/₄ cup Parmesan cheese, remaining meat, bread crumbs, eggs, salt, pepper, and garlic; mix well. Stuff rigatoni with mixture using pastry tube or fingers.
6. Preheat oven to 350 degrees. Lightly grease 13 x 9 x 2-inch baking dish. Layer rigatoni and sauce in baking dish. Sprinkle with ¹/₂ cup Parmesan cheese. Bake for 30 to 45 minutes, or until hot and bubbly. Remove from oven, and serve. This can be prepared in advance and refrigerated until baking time.

Baked Ziti

Serves 6

8 ounces ziti
2 tablespoons olive oil
1 pound ground beef
1 onion, chopped
2 cloves garlic, peeled and
  chopped
1 (28-ounce) can crushed
  tomatoes, undrained
1 (16-ounce) can tomato
  sauce
Salt and pepper to taste
1 teaspoon oregano
¹/₂ teaspoon marjoram
¹/₄ cup chopped parsley
¹/₄ pound mozzarella cheese,
  grated
¹/₄ cup grated Parmesan
  cheese

1. Cook ziti in boiling, salted water following package directions; drain.
2. Heat olive oil in saucepan. Add ground beef and onion. Cook until meat is lightly browned. Pour off any excess fat. Add garlic, tomatoes with can liquid, tomato sauce, oregano, and marjoram. Simmer for 15 minutes.
3. Preheat oven to 350 degrees.
4. Mix cooked ziti and sauce together in 2¹/₂-quart casserole dish. Combine mozzarella and Parmesan cheeses; sprinkle over ziti mixture. Sprinkle with chopped parsley and bake for 25 minutes, or until lightly browned and bubbly. Remove from oven, and serve.

Ziti with Sausage and Cream Sauce

Serves 6

2 tablespoons olive oil
3 tablespoons butter
¼ cup chopped onion
1 pound Italian sweet sausage, casing removed
1 cup heavy whipping cream
½ teaspoon salt
¼ teaspoon pepper
1 pound ziti
¼ cup grated Parmesan cheese

1. Heat butter and oil in large frying pan. Add onion and saute for 2 minutes. Add sausage and cook, crumbling with a fork, for 10 minutes, or until lightly browned. Reduce heat to low and add cream, salt, and pepper. Continue to cook, stirring constantly, until sauce thickens; do not boil.
2. Meanwhile, cook ziti in boiling, salted water following package directions; drain well.
3. Place ziti in heated serving dish. Toss with sauce and sprinkle with Parmesan cheese. Serve hot.

Tagliatelle Bolognese

Serves 4

2 tablespoons water
1 tablespoon dry vermouth
1 onion, chopped
1 carrot, diced
1 stalk celery, diced
½ green pepper, seeded and chopped
1 pound lean ground beef
2 (8-ounce) cans tomato sauce
1 clove garlic, peeled and minced
1 bay leaf
1 cup beef broth
½ teaspoon salt
¼ teaspoon pepper
12 ounces tagliatelle
¼ cup grated Parmesan cheese

1. Place water and vermouth in large frying pan. Add onion, carrot, celery, and green pepper; cook until onion becomes translucent. Remove vegetables with slotted spoon and set aside.
2. Brown ground beef in same pan, adding more vermouth if necessary to prevent sticking. Pour off excess fat. Add vegetables, tomato sauce, garlic, bay leaf, broth, salt, and pepper. Simmer for 30 minutes; discard bay leaf.
3. Cook tagliatelle in boiling, salted water following package directions; drain.
4. Place tagliatelle in heated serving dish; pour meat into center. Sprinkle with Parmesan cheese, and serve.

Tagliatelle with Herbs

Serves 4

2¼ cups diced tomatoes
2 cloves garlic, peeled and crushed
½ large onion, finely chopped
1 stalk celery, chopped
1 cup finely chopped parsley
1 cup finely chopped fresh basil
3 tablespoons extra-virgin olive oil
1 teaspoon chopped fresh oregano or ½ teaspoon dried oregano
½ teaspoon salt
Pinch of freshly ground pepper
8 ounces tagliatelle

1. Combine tomatoes, garlic, onion, celery, parsley, basil, olive oil, and oregano. Season vegetable mixture with salt and pepper; refrigerate for 3 hours.
2. Cook tagliatelle in boiling, salted water following package directions; drain. Toss with tomato and herb mixture, and serve immediately.

Tagliatelle alla Emilia-Romagna

Serves 4

12 ounces tagliatelle
1 tablespoon olive oil
2 ounces lean bacon, diced
¼ cup heavy whipping cream
1¼ cups frozen peas, thawed

1. Cook tagliatelle in boiling, salted water following package directions; drain.
2. Heat oil in frying pan. Brown bacon until crisp. Add cream and peas; cook over low heat, stirring constantly, for 5 minutes. Mix pasta and peas in heated serving dish, and serve.

Penne al Pomodoro

Serves 4

½ cup olive oil
1 onion, sliced
2 cloves garlic, peeled and crushed
Salt and pepper to taste
1 teaspoon oregano
1 pound pork shoulder, cubed
1 (28-ounce) can Italian-style tomatoes, undrained
1 (6-ounce) can tomato paste
12 ounces penne

1. Heat olive oil in deep skillet. Add onion, garlic, salt, pepper, and oregano; cook until onion is translucent. Add pork. Cook until pork is browned on all sides; remove pork from pan. Add tomatoes with can liquid and cook for 15 minutes, mashing tomatoes a little as they cook.
2. Add pork to tomato mixture; simmer for 1 hour.
3. Cook penne in boiling, salted water following package directions; drain.
4. Place penne in heated serving bowl. Spoon pork and tomato sauce on top, and serve.

NEW TWISTS ON OLD FAVORITES

Baked Macaroni with Four Cheeses

Serves 4 to 6

1 pound elbow macaroni
2 ounces mozzarella cheese, diced
2 ounces Cheddar cheese, diced
2 ounces Swiss cheese, diced
¼ cup grated Romano or Parmesan cheese
½ cup butter, melted

1. Cook macaroni in boiling, salted water until barely tender, following package directions; drain, reserving ½ cup cooking water. Place macaroni in buttered baking dish.
2. Preheat oven to 400 degrees.
3. Mix mozzarella, Cheddar, and Swiss cheeses together. Add cheese mixture to hot macaroni; toss lightly. Mix butter and reserved hot cooking water together; pour over macaroni.
4. Sprinkle macaroni with grated Romano or Parmesan cheese. Bake for 15 minutes. Remove from heat, and serve.

Debbie's Swiss-Cheese Stuffed Shells

Serves 6

12 jumbo pasta shells
1 (10-ounce) package frozen chopped spinach, cooked and drained
¼ pound Gruyere cheese, shredded
¼ pound Swiss cheese, shredded
¼ cup grated Parmesan cheese
Salt and pepper to taste
1 teaspoon basil
1 teaspoon oregano

1 teaspoon fennel
1 small clove garlic, peeled and minced
¼ cup butter, melted
½ cup dry white wine

1. Cook shells in boiling, salted water following package directions; undercook slightly since pasta will be baked. Drain well.
2. Preheat oven to 350 degrees.
3. Mix spinach, cheeses, seasonings, and garlic together; stuff shells with mixture. Place shells in baking dish and drizzle with melted butter. Cover and bake for 20 minutes. Remove cover, add wine, and cook uncovered for 20 minutes more. Remove from oven, and serve immediately.

Ziti with Three Cheeses

Serves 8

1 pound ziti
1 (15-ounce) container ricotta cheese
2 cups shredded mozzarella cheese
1 egg, lightly beaten
2 tablespoons finely chopped parsley
1 clove garlic, minced
Salt and pepper to taste
½ teaspoon basil
¼ cup grated Parmesan cheese

1. Cook ziti in boiling, salted water following package directions; drain.
2. Preheat oven to 350 degrees.
3. Blend ricotta, 1 cup mozzarella, egg, parsley, garlic, salt, pepper, and basil together in mixing bowl. Place in greased casserole dish. Top with remaining mozzarella and grated Parmesan. Bake for 30 minutes, until golden. Remove from oven, and serve.

Cousin Tillie's Cheese Lasagna

Serves 6

8 ounces lasagna noodles
1 (15-ounce) container ricotta cheese
1 egg
¼ cup finely chopped parsley
¾ cup grated Parmesan cheese
Salt and pepper to taste
2 cups meatless spaghetti sauce
1 cup shredded mozzarella cheese
1 cup shredded provolone cheese

1. Cook lasagna noodles in boiling, salted water following package directions; drain.
2. Combine ricotta, egg, parsley, ¼ cup Parmesan cheese, salt, and pepper; blend until smooth.
3. Preheat oven to 375 degrees.
4. Spread a layer of sauce in bottom of 9-inch square pan. Alternate layers of lasagna noodles, ricotta filling, shredded cheeses, and spaghetti sauce until all ingredients are used; end with layer of noodles and sauce. Sprinkle with ½ cup grated Parmesan cheese. Bake for 30 minutes, until browned. Remove from oven, and serve.

Spaghetti Gorgonzola

Serves 4

3 tablespoons olive oil
1 small onion, finely chopped
1 to 2 cloves garlic, peeled
   and finely chopped
1 teaspoon flour
2 cups heavy whipping cream
½ cup white wine
1¼ cups gorgonzola cheese
¼ cup pine nuts
12 ounces spaghetti
½ teaspoon mixed Italian
   herbs

1. Heat oil in saucepan. Add onion and garlic; saute until translucent. Stir in flour; add cream and white wine, stirring constantly. Add 1¼ cups gorgonzola and pine nuts to sauce, stirring to melt cheese; simmer for 10 minutes.
2. Cook spaghetti in boiling, salted water following package directions; drain.
3. Mix gorgonzola sauce and herbs with pasta. Crumble remaining gorgonzola over top, and serve.

Bow Ties with Cheese

Serves 4 to 6

12 ounces pasta bow ties
1¼ cups heavy whipping cream
⅓ to ½ cup blue-veined cheese,
   crumbled
½ to ⅔ cup grated Parmesan
   cheese
15 walnuts, broken into pieces

1. Cook pasta in boiling, salted water following package directions; drain.
2. Place cream and cheeses in saucepan. Cook over low heat, stirring constantly, until sauce is smooth and thick.
3. Place pasta in heated serving dish. Pour cheese sauce on top, and garnish with walnuts. Serve immediately.

Linguine with Mozzarella

Serves 4

8 ounces linguine
2 tablespoons butter
1 small onion, finely
   chopped
1 clove garlic, peeled and
   minced
2 tablespoons flour
¾ cup milk
½ teaspoon oregano
½ teaspoon basil
2 cups shredded mozzarella
   cheese
¼ cup grated Parmesan
   cheese
1 cup diced prosciutto
¼ cup frozen peas,
   thawed
Salt and pepper to taste

1. Cook linguine in boiling, salted water following package directions; drain.
2. Melt butter in medium saucepan. Add onion and garlic; saute until translucent. Add flour, stirring constantly. Gradually stir in milk; season with oregano and basil. Cook, stirring constantly, over medium heat until sauce boils.
3. Remove saucepan from heat. Add mozzarella and Parmesan cheeses; stir until cheeses melt. Add prosciutto and peas.
4. Return saucepan to heat and cook gently until well heated. Season with salt and pepper. Place linguine in heated serving dish. Pour sauce over linguine, mix well, and serve.

Rotelle with Cheese Sauce

Serves 4

1 pound rotelle
5 tablespoons butter
3 tablespoons flour
1 teaspoon chicken bouillon
   powder
Salt and pepper to taste
2 cups milk
3 cups shredded Cheddar
   cheese
1 teaspoon basil
2 cups hot cooked broccoli
   florets

1. Cook rotelle in boiling, salted water following package directions; drain.
2. While pasta is cooking, melt 3 tablespoons butter in saucepan. Add flour, bouillon powder, salt, and pepper, stirring constantly. Gradually add milk; cook, stirring constantly, over medium heat until boiling. Remove from heat.
3. Add cheese to saucepan, stirring until melted. Keep warm.
4. Toss hot rotelle with 2 tablespoons butter, basil, and hot cooked broccoli. Pour hot cheese sauce on top, and serve.

Pasta Pizza

Serves 6

1 pound spaghetti
4 quarts boiling, salted water
2 green peppers, seeded and
   chopped
½ pound salami, thinly sliced
2¼ cups sliced tomatoes
8 eggs
1½ cups milk
1 tablespoon cornstarch
1 cup grated Parmesan cheese
2 tablespoons mixed Italian
   herbs
1 teaspoon salt
1¼ cups grated Emmenthaler
   cheese
¼ cup olive oil
2 tablespoons chopped chives

1. Cook spaghetti in boiling, salted water for 6 minutes. Add green peppers to spaghetti and cook for 2 minutes more; drain.

2. Preheat oven to 350 degrees.

3. Butter 2 glass or ceramic, 9-inch pie plates. Line bottom of pie plates with spaghetti mixture. Place salami slices on top. Place tomatoes on top of salami.

4. Mix eggs, milk, cornstarch, Parmesan cheese, Italian herbs, and salt together; pour over tomatoes. Sprinkle top with grated Emmenthaler. Pour oil over all. Bake for 30 minutes. Remove from oven, sprinkle with chives, and serve.

Pasta with Meatballs and Lemon Sauce

Serves 4

1 pound lean ground beef
1 onion, finely chopped
1 clove garlic, peeled and crushed
3 tablespoons ground rice
2 tablespoons parsley
¼ teaspoon ground coriander seed
1 egg, well beaten
3 egg yolks
2 lemons
8 ounces pasta of your choice

1. Have butcher grind meat twice. Place meat in bowl with onion and garlic. Place in blender or food processor and blend for a few minutes at high speed. Return to bowl. Mix in ground rice, parsley, and coriander. Add egg. Mix to a very smooth paste with wooden spoon or your hand.

2. Roll meat paste into balls the size of walnuts; simmer in lightly salted water for 20 minutes.

3. While meatballs are cooking, prepare lemon sauce. Beat egg yolks until light and fluffy. Slowly add juice of 2 lemons and ⅔ cup of water. Heat sauce in top of double boiler and cook until thickened. Do not let mixture boil.

4. Drain meatballs; place them in sauce and heat gently.

5. Cook pasta in boiling, salted water following package directions; drain.

6. Place pasta in heated serving dish. Top with meatballs and sauce. Sprinkle with grated rind of 1 lemon, and serve.

Pasta and Swedish Meatballs

Serves 6

6 tablespoons butter
¼ cup chopped onion
1 cup fresh bread crumbs
1 cup milk
1¼ pounds meatloaf mixture (ground beef, pork, and veal)
1 egg
Salt and pepper to taste
½ cup plus 1 tablespoon flour
1 pound tagliatelle
¾ cup heavy whipping cream

1. Melt 2 tablespoons butter in frying pan; add onion and saute until golden. Remove from pan.

2. Place bread crumbs in mixing bowl; pour milk on top and let soak for 1 minute. Add sauteed onion, ground meats, egg, salt, and pepper, mixing well. Shape into balls the size of walnuts; roll in ½ cup flour.

3. Melt remaining butter in large frying pan. Add meatballs and cook over medium heat until well browned. Remove from pan and keep warm.

4. Meanwhile, cook pasta in boiling, salted water following package directions; drain and place in heated serving dish.

5. Blend 1 tablespoon flour with cream; gradually add to pan juices, stirring constantly. Simmer for 3 minutes, stirring. To serve, place meatballs on top of pasta. Spoon sauce on top, and serve.

Grandmother's Meatballs

Serves 6

1½ pounds ground beef
2 slices bread, crumbled
1 egg
¾ cup milk
½ cup finely chopped onion
Salt and pepper to taste
2 tablespoons butter
2 tablespoons flour
1½ cups beef broth
1 tablespoon tomato sauce
1 tablespoon dry sherry
12 ounces egg noodles
⅓ cup sour cream

1. Mix ground beef, bread, egg, milk, ¼ cup onion, salt, and pepper together until well blended. Form into 2 dozen meatballs.

2. Melt butter in large frying pan. Add ¼ cup onion and saute until translucent. Stir in flour, then gradually add beef broth, stirring constantly. Add tomato sauce and sherry. Cook, stirring constantly, until sauce thickens.

3. Add meatballs to sauce and simmer for 5 to 10 minutes, until thoroughly heated.

4. Cook egg noodles in boiling, salted water following package directions; drain.

5. Place egg noodles on heated serving platter. Stir sour cream into sauce, then pour over noodles. Serve at once.

Lucy's Sausage Lasagna

Serves 4

8 ounces lasagna noodles
1 pound Italian sausage
¼ cup finely chopped onion
2 tomatoes, peeled and coarsely
  chopped
2 (10-ounce) cans condensed
  tomato soup
2 cloves garlic, peeled and finely
  chopped
1 teaspoon oregano
Salt and pepper to taste
2 eggs, beaten
1 cup ricotta cheese
¼ cup grated Parmesan cheese
¼ cup chopped parsley
½ cup shredded mozzarella
  cheese

1. Cook lasagna noodles in boiling, salted water following package directions; drain.
2. Cook sausage and onion in frying pan until browned, breaking up sausage as it cooks; pour off excess fat.
3. Combine tomatoes, tomato soup, garlic, oregano, salt, and pepper. Add to sausage mixture; blend well.
4. Preheat oven to 375 degrees.
5. Combine eggs, ricotta and Parmesan cheeses, and parsley. Place a layer of lasagna noodles in bottom of greased baking dish. Alternate layers of sausage mixture, egg-cheese mixture, and noodles until all ingredients are used. End with noodles topped with sausage mixture and sprinkled with mozzarella cheese. Cover with foil and bake for 30 to 35 minutes. Remove from oven, let cool slightly, and serve.

Spaghetti Caruso

Serves 6

1 pound ground beef
½ pound country or sage
  sausage
1 small onion, finely chopped
1 bay leaf
1 (6-ounce) can tomato paste
1 (10-ounce) can condensed
  tomato soup
1 tablespoon chili sauce
1 tablespoon ketchup
1 pound spaghetti

1. Brown ground beef and sausage in large frying pan. Add onion and cook for 5 minutes. Pour off excess fat. Add bay leaf, tomato paste, tomato soup, chili sauce, and ketchup. Bring to a boil; reduce heat and simmer while spaghetti cooks. Remove bay leaf.
2. Cook spaghetti in boiling, salted water following package directions; drain.
3. Place spaghetti in heated serving bowl. Spoon sauce on top, and serve.

Chili Spaghetti

Serves 10

¼ pound butter
1 onion, finely chopped
1 clove garlic, finely cut
2 stalks celery, sliced
1 tablespoon flour
1 pound ground beef
1 (10-ounce) can tomato soup
1 soup-can water
1 (28-ounce) can tomatoes,
  drained
1 teaspoon chili powder
1 cup sliced mushrooms
1 pound spaghetti
Grated Parmesan cheese

1. Melt butter in frying pan. Saute onion, garlic, and celery until soft. Add ground beef; sprinkle with flour and cook until meat browns. Transfer to large pot.

2. Add tomato soup, water, tomatoes, chili powder, and mushrooms. Simmer for 30 minutes.
3. Meanwhile, cook spaghetti in boiling, salted water following package directions; drain.
4. Add spaghetti to meat mixture, mixing well. Serve with Parmesan cheese.

Linguine with Herbed Meat Sauce

Serves 4

½ pound ground beef
1 small onion, finely chopped
1 clove garlic, peeled and finely
  chopped
½ green pepper, seeded and
  finely chopped
½ cup sliced mushrooms
1 (10-ounce) can condensed
  tomato soup
1 (8-ounce) can tomato sauce
½ teaspoon oregano
½ teaspoon basil
⅛ teaspoon marjoram
⅛ teaspoon thyme
1 bay leaf
Salt and pepper to taste
8 ounces linguine
Freshly grated Parmesan cheese

1. Brown meat in large frying pan. Add onion, garlic, green pepper, and mushrooms; saute for 3 minutes. Pour off excess fat.
2. Add soup and tomato sauce to meat, mixing well. Add herbs, salt, and pepper. Cook over medium-high heat until sauce boils. Reduce heat, cover, and simmer for 30 minutes, stirring occasionally.
3. Meanwhile, cook linguine in boiling, salted water following package directions; drain.
4. Place linguine in heated serving bowl. Discard bay leaf, then spoon meat sauce over linguine. Sprinkle with grated Parmesan cheese, and serve.

Mezzani with Spicy Tomato-Meat Sauce

Serves 4

2 quarts salted water
1½ tablespoons salad oil
8 ounces mezzani
1 tablespoon olive oil
1 teaspoon finely chopped
   parsley

Spicy Sauce

½ pound ground beef
½ cup tarragon vinegar
1 teaspoon dry mustard
1 teaspoon paprika
½ teaspoon white pepper
1 clove garlic, peeled and sliced
¾ teaspoon salt
2 bay leaves
¼ teaspoon cayenne pepper
½ cup beef consomme
2 tablespoons butter
1 tablespoon Worcestershire
   sauce
1 (15-ounce) can tomato sauce

1. Bring salted water to a boil; add salad oil. Add mezzani slowly and cook for 14 minutes, or until tender; drain.
2. While pasta is cooking, brown ground beef in skillet. Combine vinegar, mustard, paprika, white pepper, garlic, salt, bay leaves, and cayenne pepper in saucepan. Boil until mixture is reduced by half. Strain through fine sieve, then return to saucepan. Add ground beef, consomme, butter, Worcestershire sauce, and tomato sauce. Simmer for 8 minutes.
3. Place hot pasta in serving dish. Add olive oil and toss lightly. Sprinkle with parsley. Pour sauce on top and serve hot.

Ham Tetrazzini

Serves 6 to 8

8 ounces spaghetti
¼ cup finely chopped onion
½ cup butter
½ pound mushrooms, sliced
⅓ cup flour

2 cups milk
2 cups light cream
3 tablespoons dry sherry
¼ teaspoon salt
Pinch of garlic salt
Pepper to taste
¾ cup grated Parmesan cheese
2 cups diced cooked ham

1. Cook spaghetti in boiling, salted water following package directions; drain.
2. Saute onion in butter until translucent; add mushrooms and saute until tender. Stir in flour, then milk and cream. Cook, stirring constantly, until mixture is smooth and thickened. Add sherry, salt, garlic salt, and pepper.
3. Preheat oven to 375 degrees.
4. Mix ½ cup cheese and spaghetti together in bottom of buttered, 2-quart baking dish. Cover with alternating layers of sauce and ham, ending with sauce. Sprinkle remaining cheese on top. Bake for 20 to 25 minutes, or until browned and bubbly. Remove from oven, and serve.

Greek Macaroni with Meat Sauce

Serves 4

3 tablespoons butter
1 cup chopped onion
2 cloves garlic, peeled and
   minced
1 pound ground beef
1 (6-ounce) can tomato paste
2 cups water
¼ cup red wine
1 teaspoon salt
¼ teaspoon pepper
1 (2-inch) piece cinnamon
¼ teaspoon ground allspice
Pinch of ground cloves
8 ounces macaroni
Grated Kafaloteri cheese

1. Melt butter in large skillet. Add onion, garlic, and beef; cook over medium heat, stirring occasionally, until meat loses its pink color.
2. Combine tomato paste and water; add to meat mixture. Add wine, salt,

pepper, cinnamon stick, allspice, and cloves. Bring to a boil; reduce heat and simmer for 1 hour, stirring occasionally. Remove cinnamon stick.
3. Cook macaroni in boiling, salted water following package directions; drain.
4. Place macaroni in heated serving dish; spoon meat sauce on top. Serve with grated cheese.

Spaghetti in a Skillet

Serves 4

1 pound lean ground beef
1 onion, finely chopped
1 clove garlic, peeled and
   finely chopped
1 green pepper, seeded and
   finely chopped
½ pound mushrooms, sliced
1 (28-ounce) can tomatoes,
   undrained
1 cup water
1 cup spaghetti, broken into
   pieces
1 teaspoon oregano
Salt and pepper to taste
1 cup shredded mozzarella
   cheese

1. Brown beef in large, heavy frying pan. Add onion and garlic, and saute until translucent. Add green pepper and mushrooms; cook over medium heat until vegetables are tender. Pour off excess fat.
2. Add tomatoes and can liquid to pan. Add water, spaghetti, oregano, salt, and pepper. Cook over medium-high heat until sauce boils—break up tomatoes with wooden spoon as they cook. Cover and simmer for 15 minutes, or until spaghetti is cooked; stir occasionally.
3. To serve, place hot spaghetti mixture in serving bowl. Add grated cheese and toss until cheese melts. Serve immediately.

Beef Gulyas with Noodles

Serves 4

3 slices bacon, diced
¹/₂ cup chopped onion
1¹/₂ pounds stew beef, cut
    into 1¹/₂-inch cubes
2 teaspoons paprika
¹/₂ teaspoon caraway seeds
Salt and pepper to taste
2 cups beef broth
2 cups frozen pearl onions
1¹/₂ tablespoons flour
1¹/₂ tablespoons water
8 ounces egg noodles

1. Cook bacon in large, heavy skillet until crisp. Remove with slotted spoon and drain. Add onion to pan; saute until tender in bacon fat. Remove onion from pan and set aside. Add beef to pan and brown well on all sides. Remove pan from heat.
2. Add paprika, caraway seeds, salt, and pepper to meat; stir well. Add reserved onion and beef broth. Cover and bring to a boil over medium heat. Reduce heat to low and cook for 1¹/₂ hours. Add pearl onions and bacon. Simmer for 45 minutes to 1 hour, or until meat is tender.
3. Mix flour and water together to form smooth paste. Slowly stir flour mixture into stew; cook stirring constantly, until sauce thickens.
4. Cook noodles in boiling, salted water following package directions; drain.
5. To serve, place noodles in serving bowl. Spoon stew on top and mix lightly.

Macaroni with Salami and Olives

Serves 6

2 cups shredded sharp Cheddar
    cheese
1 cup undiluted evaporated milk
¹/₂ cup sliced pimento-stuffed
    olives
¹/₂ pound salami, diced
¹/₂ teaspoon salt
¹/₈ teaspoon pepper
1 teaspoon prepared mustard
4 cups cooked elbow macaroni
1 cup fresh bread crumbs, tossed
    with melted butter

1. Preheat oven to 375 degrees.
2. Melt cheese in top of double boiler. Gradually add milk, stirring constantly until sauce is smooth. Add olives, salami, salt, pepper, mustard, and macaroni.
3. Pour into greased 2-quart casserole dish. Sprinkle with crumbs and bake for 20 minutes, or until crumbs are lightly browned. Remove from oven, and serve.

Spinach and Chicken Manicotti

Serves 6

12 manicotti shells
1 medium onion, minced
1 clove garlic, peeled and finely
    chopped
2 tablespoons butter
1 (10-ounce) package frozen
    chopped spinach, thawed
¹/₂ cup finely chopped cooked
    chicken
1 teaspoon lemon juice
¹/₂ teaspoon salt
¹/₄ teaspoon nutmeg
1 pound ricotta cheese
1 egg, lightly beaten
3¹/₂ cups marinara sauce
¹/₄ cup grated Parmesan cheese

1. Cover manicotti shells with boiling water and let stand for 5 minutes; drain and rinse with cold water.
2. Saute onion and garlic in butter until translucent. Press spinach through sieve to remove water. Combine onion, spinach, chicken, lemon juice, salt, nutmeg, ricotta cheese, and egg; mix well.
3. Preheat oven to 375 degrees.
4. Stuff manicotti shells with ¹/₃ to ¹/₂ cup spinach-chicken filling each. Cover bottom of 13 x 9 x 2-inch pan with about ³/₄ cup of marinara sauce. Place stuffed manicotti on top of sauce, then cover with remaining sauce. Cover with foil and bake for 45 minutes. Remove foil and sprinkle with Parmesan cheese; bake, uncovered, for 5 minutes more. Remove from oven, and serve.

Chicken Canalones

Serves 4 to 6

Dough

3 cups flour
¹/₂ teaspoon salt
3 eggs
2 tablespoons olive oil
5 tablespoons water

Filling

2 cloves garlic, peeled and
    minced
2 onions, finely chopped
1 pound diced cooked chicken
2 tablespoons tomato paste
¹/₂ cup dry red wine
1 tablespoon chopped parsley
1 teaspoon salt
Pinch of pepper
1 teaspoon oregano

Sauce

¹/₄ cup olive oil
1 onion, chopped
2 cloves garlic, peeled and
    minced
1 green pepper, seeded and
    chopped
1 cup tomato sauce
¹/₄ cup tomato paste
3 tablespoons dry red wine
1 teaspoon salt
Pepper to taste
1 tablespoon sugar
Garnish
¹/₄ cup grated Parmesan cheese

1. To make dough, sift flour and salt into large bowl; form a well in center. Add remaining dough ingredients to well; blend together using pastry blender. When dough forms into ball, knead for 5 minutes. Cover dough and let rest for 5 minutes. Roll dough out as thinly as possible on floured work surface. Cut into 16, 4½ x 5-inch rectangles.
2. To make filling, combine all filling ingredients. Place filling in center of each pasta rectangle. Roll up firmly; seal seams and ends tightly, moistening with water to fasten.
3. Drop filled pasta into large saucepan of gently boiling, salted water; cook for 10 minutes. Remove with slotted spoon. Place filled pasta seam side down in greased, shallow baking dish.
4. Preheat oven to 400 degrees.
5. To make sauce, heat olive oil in saucepan. Add onion, garlic, and green pepper; saute for 5 minutes. Add remaining sauce ingredients and simmer for 20 minutes.
6. Spread sauce over pasta. Sprinkle with grated Parmesan and bake for 15 minutes. Remove from oven, and serve.

Chicken and Pasta Primavera

Serves 6

1 pound vermicelli
3 tablespoons butter
¼ cup grated Parmesan cheese
¼ cup olive oil
1 clove garlic, peeled and minced
2 boneless chicken breasts, cut into thin strips
¾ cup tomato sauce
¾ cup chicken broth
Salt and pepper to taste
2 cups broccoli florets
1 cup sliced zucchini
2 carrots, sliced
1 red pepper, seeded and sliced

1. Cook vermicelli in boiling, salted water following package directions; drain. Toss with butter and Parmesan cheese.
2. While vermicelli is cooking, heat olive oil in saucepan. Add garlic and chicken; saute until browned. Add all remaining ingredients, mixing well. Simmer for 10 minutes, stirring occasionally.
3. Place vermicelli in heated serving bowl. Spoon chicken mixture on top, and serve at once.

Turkey Lasagna

Serves 4

½ cup chopped onion
¼ cup olive oil
2 to 3 cloves garlic, peeled and crushed
½ pound ground turkey
1 teaspoon salt
1 teaspoon basil
1 teaspoon oregano
1 (8-ounce) can tomato sauce
1 egg
1 cup cottage cheese
4 cooked lasagna noodles
1 cup chopped cooked spinach
1½ cups shredded mozzarella cheese

1. Saute onion in olive oil until translucent. Add garlic and turkey; cook until lightly browned. Remove from pan and set aside.
2. Stir salt, basil, and oregano into tomato sauce; beat egg with cottage cheese.
3. Preheat oven to 350 degrees.
4. In 8-inch square baking pan, lay 3 cooked lasagna noodles across the bottom, letting ends of noodles hang over edge of pan. Spread ground turkey mixture over noodles, then cover with half the tomato sauce.

Spread spinach over sauce, and cover with cottage cheese mixture and ½ cup shredded mozzarella. Fold over remaining part of lasagna noodles and use extra noodle to cover filling.
5. Pour remaining tomato sauce on top and cover with remaining shredded mozzarella. Cover pan lightly with foil and bake for 20 minutes. Remove from oven, and serve.

Turkey Piccata

Serves 4

8 ounces thin spaghetti
½ cup flour
Freshly ground pepper to taste
1¼ pounds turkey breast cutlets
2 tablespoons butter
2 tablespoons olive oil
½ cup fresh lemon juice
Parsley sprigs, for garnish
1 lemon, thinly sliced

1. Cook spaghetti in boiling, salted water following package directions; drain.
2. Season flour with pepper. Coat turkey with flour on both sides.
3. Heat butter and oil in large frying pan. Add turkey and cook over high heat until golden on both sides. Remove from pan and keep warm.
4. Place spaghetti on heated serving platter. Arrange turkey cutlets on top. Add lemon juice to frying pan, stirring to deglaze pan; pour on top of turkey. Garnish with parsley and lemon slices, and serve.

Linguine and Broccoli

Serves 4

8 ounces linguine
2 (8-ounce) packages frozen
   broccoli in cheese sauce
¼ cup butter
¾ cup diced cooked ham
1 cup heavy whipping cream
2 eggs, beaten
½ teaspoon oregano
¼ cup grated Parmesan
   cheese

1. Cook linguine in boiling, salted water following package directions; drain.
2. Cook broccoli following package directions; drain.
3. Melt butter in saucepan. Add diced ham and drained linguine. Cook over medium heat, stirring constantly, until well heated. Remove from heat.
4. Add broccoli to saucepan, mixing well. Mix cream, eggs and oregano together, then stir into saucepan. Cook over low heat, stirring constantly, until sauce thickens.
5. Transfer linguine mixture to heated serving bowl. Sprinkle with grated Parmesan cheese, and serve.

Cannelloni with Vegetable Filling

Serves 4

12 tablespoons olive oil
1 large onion, finely chopped
2 carrots, peeled and cut into
   julienne strips
1 small kohlrabi, peeled and
   diced
1¼ cups frozen peas
3 tablespoons chopped parsley
1 tablespoon chopped fresh
   thyme or ½ teaspoon dried
   thyme
1 tablespoon chopped fresh
   basil or ½ teaspoon dried
   basil
5 tablespoons dry white wine
8 ounces cannelloni noodles
Salt and white pepper to taste

1 cup heavy whipping cream
1¼ cups freshly grated Pecorino
   or Parmesan cheese
¼ cup butter

1. Heat oil in saucepan. Add onion and saute until translucent. Add carrots, kohlrabi, peas, herbs, and wine; saute for 5 minutes. Remove from pan and let cool.
2. Preheat oven to 450 degrees.
3. Precook pasta if necessary, following package instructions; drain.
4. Mix vegetable mixture with salt, pepper, cream, and ¼ cup grated cheese. Fill cannelloni with mixture. Lay cannelloni in single layer in buttered baking dish. Top with remaining grated cheese, dot with butter, and bake for 20 minutes. Remove from oven, and serve.

Spinach Fettuccine

Serves 8

8 ounces egg noodles
2 tablespoons butter
2 small cloves garlic, peeled
   and minced
1 (10-ounce) package frozen
   chopped spinach, thawed
8 ounces creamed cottage
   cheese, at room temperature
2 tablespoons grated Parmesan
   cheese
¼ cup chopped parsley
1 teaspoon basil
Salt and pepper to taste

1. Cook noodles in boiling, salted water following package directions; drain.
2. Combine butter and garlic in nonstick skillet and cook over moderate heat until garlic is golden. Add spinach and cook over low heat until heated thoroughly.
3. Combine hot, drained noodles, spinach mixture, and cottage cheese. Add remaining ingredients and toss lightly to combine. Serve immediately.

Lasagna with Spinach

Serves 4

3 cups spinach
2 cups water
½ teaspoon salt
¼ cup butter
½ cup flour
1 cup milk
Pinch of nutmeg
Pinch of white pepper
1 cup ricotta cheese
1 cup Pecorino or Parmesan
   cheese, chopped into small
   pieces
2 large tomatoes, sliced
8 ounces lasagna noodles
½ teaspoon oregano

1. Cook spinach in boiling, salted water for 2 minutes; drain well, reserving 1 cup cooking liquid.
2. To make sauce, melt butter in saucepan. Stir in flour, then milk. Add reserved spinach liquid, nutmeg, and pepper. Stir in ricotta cheese.
3. Cook lasagna noodles in boiling, salted water following package directions; drain.
4. Preheat oven to 400 degrees.
5. Line bottom of large, buttered ovenproof dish with lasagna noodles. Layer some spinach over noodles, top with tomatoes, and sprinkle with oregano and Pecorino or Parmesan cheese. Pour some ßsauce on top. Repeat layers. Finish with a layer of noodles, then pour any remaining sauce on top. Bake for 30 minutes. Remove from oven, and serve.

Lasagna with Savoy Cabbage

Serves 4

2¼ cups chopped savoy cabbage
1 onion, finely chopped
1 clove garlic, peeled and finely chopped
2 tablespoons oil
1 pound ground beef
1/2 teaspoon thyme
1 teaspoon salt
Pinch of pepper
8 ounces lasagna noodles
3 tablespoons butter
3 tablespoons flour
1 cup milk
1 cup ricotta cheese
4 large tomatoes, sliced
½ cup grated Pecorino or Parmesan cheese

1. Cook cabbage in saucepan of boiling, salted water for 2 minutes; drain, reserving 1 cup cooking liquid.
2. Saute onion and garlic in oil. Add ground beef, thyme, salt, and pepper. Cook until beef is browned. Remove from heat.
3. Cook lasagna noodles in boiling, salted water following package directions; drain.
4. Preheat oven to 400 degrees.
5. Melt butter in saucepan. Add flour, reserved cooking liquid, and milk; bring to a boil, stirring constantly. Stir in ricotta. Mix cabbage, tomatoes, and grated cheese with half the sauce.
6. Pour a little sauce on bottom of buttered ovenproof dish. Repeat layers of noodles, cabbage, ground beef, tomatoes, and cheese, beginning and ending with noodles. Pour remaining sauce on top and bake for 40 minutes. Remove from oven, and serve.

Mary's Spaghetti and Zucchini Sauce

Serves 4 to 6

¼ cup olive oil
1 clove garlic, peeled and minced
1 small onion, chopped
½ pound ground beef
1 (28-ounce) can tomatoes, undrained
Salt and pepper to taste
1 teaspoon basil
⅛ teaspoon marjoram
3 zucchini, thickly sliced
½ cup sliced mushrooms
1 pound thin spaghetti
¼ cup grated Parmesan cheese

1. Heat 2 tablespoons olive oil in large saucepan. Add garlic, onion, and ground beef; cook until browned. Pour off excess fat.
2. Add tomatoes, salt, pepper, basil, and marjoram to meat mixture; break up tomatoes with wooden spoon as they cook. Cover and simmer for 15 minutes.
3. Heat 2 tablespoons olive oil in large frying pan. Add zucchini and mushrooms; saute until just tender. Stir zucchini and mushrooms into meat mixture.
4. Cook spaghetti in boiling, salted water following package directions; drain.
5. Place spaghetti in heated serving bowl. Spoon meat-zucchini sauce on top. Sprinkle with Parmesan cheese, and serve.

Fusilli with Sun-Dried Tomato Pesto

Serves 6

1 pound fusilli
3 cups sun-dried tomato halves, not packed in oil
1½ cups extra-virgin olive oil
1 cup grated Parmesan cheese
½ cup chopped parsley
4 medium cloves garlic, peeled
½ cup chopped walnuts
Hot water

1. Cook pasta in boiling, salted water following package directions; drain.
2. Cook tomatoes in boiling water to cover for 1 minute; drain.
3. Puree remaining ingredients together in blender or food processor. Add hot water, a little at a time, until pesto is sauce consistency.
4. Toss hot pasta with sauce, and serve at once.

Pasta with Bean Sprouts

Serves 4

12 ounces vermicelli
3 tablespoons sesame oil
2 tablespoons finely chopped, peeled fresh ginger
10 ounces pork filet, cut into ¼-inch strips
1½ cups bean sprouts, rinsed and drained
2 fresh chili peppers, seeded and cut into rings
2 scallions, cut into rings
3 tablespoons soy sauce
Salt and pepper to taste

1. Cook vermicelli in boiling, salted water following package directions; drain.
2. Heat oil in wok or large saucepan. Add ginger and stir-fry, stirring constantly, for 1 minute. Add pork and stir-fry for 2 minutes more. Add bean sprouts, chilies, and scallions; stir-fry for 3 minutes.
3. Stir pasta into bean sprout mixture; cook for 3 minutes, stirring constantly. Season with soy sauce, salt, and pepper. Transfer to serving platter. Serve with soy sauce.

Twists with Eggplant

Serves 4

¼ cup olive oil
2 cloves garlic, peeled and crushed
2 small eggplants, diced
4 ripe tomatoes, peeled and chopped
2 yellow peppers, seeded and cut into strips
2 anchovies, finely chopped
1 tablespoon capers
½ cup sliced pitted green olives
½ cup chopped fresh basil or 2 teaspoons dried basil
½ cup hot chicken broth
Salt and pepper to taste
1 pound pasta twists

1. Heat oil in large frying pan. Add garlic and saute until browned; discard garlic. Add eggplant to frying pan and saute for 2 minutes. Add tomatoes, pepper strips, anchovies, capers, olives, basil, and chicken broth. Simmer for 30 minutes, adding more broth if needed. Season with salt and pepper.
2. Cook pasta in boiling, salted water following package directions; drain.
3. Place pasta in heated serving bowl. Toss with vegetable mixture, and serve.

Ratatouille with Pasta

Serves 4

¼ cup oil
2 large onions, finely chopped
3 cloves garlic, peeled and finely chopped
1 eggplant, cubed
1 cup chopped green pepper
1¼ cups chopped zucchini
2 teaspoons instant vegetable bouillon powder
2 teaspoons paprika
Pinch of cayenne pepper

1 tablespoon finely chopped fresh basil or 1 teaspoon dried basil
2¼ cups chopped tomatoes
8 ounces whole-wheat pasta twists
2 tablespoons chopped chives

1. Heat oil in large frying pan. Add onions and garlic; cook over low heat until translucent. Add eggplant, green pepper, and zucchini to onions. Add vegetable bouillon powder, paprika, cayenne pepper, and half the basil; simmer for 15 minutes.
2. Add tomatoes to vegetables and simmer for 5 minutes more.
3. Cook pasta in boiling, salted water until just tender, following package directions; drain. Toss with remaining basil and chives.
4. Place pasta in heated serving bowl. Add vegetables; mix lightly, and serve.

Tagliatelle with Eggplant

Serves 4

1 onion, chopped
1 clove garlic, peeled and minced
1 medium eggplant, peeled and chopped
1 (15-ounce) can tomato sauce
1 teaspoon basil
1 teaspoon oregano
1 teaspoon chopped parsley
Pinch of red pepper flakes
2 tablespoons red wine
1 pound spaghetti
1 tablespoon butter
½ cup grated Parmesan cheese

1. Saute onion and garlic in oil. Add eggplant and brown lightly. Add tomato sauce, herbs, pepper, and wine; simmer for 20 minutes, or until tender.
2. Cook spaghetti in boiling, salted water following package directions; drain. Toss with butter.
3. Place spaghetti in heated serving dish. Pour sauce over spaghetti; sprinkle with Parmesan cheese, and serve.

Vegetarian Spaghetti

Serves 8

2 tablespoons olive oil
1 small onion, finely chopped
3 cloves garlic, peeled and finely chopped
1 (28-ounce) can Italian-style tomatoes, undrained
2 ripe tomatoes, chopped
1 (6-ounce) can tomato paste
½ cup sliced mushrooms
½ zucchini or yellow squash, sliced
½ green pepper, seeded and diced
1 teaspoon oregano
½ teaspoon basil
⅛ teaspoon cinnamon
Pinch of nutmeg
1 bay leaf
Salt and pepper to taste
12 ounces spaghetti

1. Heat olive oil in large saucepan. Add onion and garlic; saute until translucent. Stir in tomatoes and tomato paste, blending well. Add mushrooms, zucchini or squash, green pepper, herbs, and seasonings. Simmer, stirring frequently, for 1 hour.
2. Cook spaghetti in boiling, salted water following package directions; drain.
3. Place spaghetti in heated serving dish. Top with vegetable mixture, and serve.

Vegetable-Filled Manicotti

Serves 4

8 manicotti shells
2 tablespoons olive oil
1 onion, finely chopped
1 clove garlic, peeled and
   crushed
1/2 cup chopped celery
1 tablespoon whole-wheat
   flour
2 ripe tomatoes, peeled and
   chopped
1/2 cup chopped mushrooms
1 tablespoon tomato paste
1/2 teaspoon basil
Salt and pepper to taste
1/2 cup finely chopped filberts
1/4 cup finely chopped parsley
2 cups canned vegetable juice

1. Cook manicotti in boiling, salted water following package directions; drain.
2. Heat oil in saucepan. Add onion and garlic; saute until translucent. Add celery and saute for 2 minutes more. Sprinkle in flour, stirring to blend. Add tomatoes, mushrooms, tomato, basil, salt, and pepper. Bring to a boil. Reduce heat and simmer for 15 minutes, stirring occasionally. Add nuts and parsley, blending well.
3. Preheat oven to 400 degrees.
4. Using pastry or your hands, fill manicotti with vegetable mixture. Pour small amount of vegetable juice on bottom of greased baking dish. Lay filled manicotti in single layer over juice. Pour remaining juice on top and bake for 20 minutes. Remove from oven, and serve.

Penne with Creamed Artichokes

Serves 4

12 ounces penne
1 cup cooked frozen artichoke
   hearts
1 cup cream cheese, softened
2 tablespoons olive oil
Salt and pepper to taste

1. Cook penne in boiling, salted water until just tender, following package directions; drain, reserving cooking water.
2. Pass artichokes through sieve or puree in blender or food processor. Soften cream cheese over hot water, then beat until smooth and creamy. Slowly blend in olive oil, and season with salt and pepper. Mix in artichoke puree. Gradually stir in enough pasta cooking water to make cheese sauce smooth and creamy.
3. Place pasta in heated serving dish. Add cream sauce, mixing well. Serve at once.

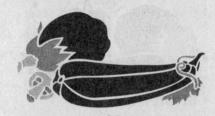

Eggplant Lasagna

Serves 4 to 6

8 ounces lasagna noodles
1 medium eggplant, unpeeled
   and cut into 1/4-inch rounds
Oil for frying
1 (6-ounce) can tomato paste
1 cup red wine
1/2 cup hot water
1 clove garlic, peeled and
   crushed
1 teaspoon basil
1 teaspoon turmeric
Salt and pepper to taste
2 cups chopped green pepper
10 pitted black olives,
   chopped
1/2 cup grated Parmesan cheese

1. Cook lasagna noodles in boiling, salted water following package directions; drain.
2. Fry eggplant on both sides in hot oil until tender. (They cook quickly and absorb considerable oil; add more oil when needed.) Drain eggplant on paper towels.
3. Combine tomato paste, wine, water, garlic, basil, turmeric, salt, and pepper; simmer for 5 minutes. Add green pepper and olives; simmer for 5 minutes more.
4. Preheat oven to 350 degrees.
5. Arrange layer of lasagna in buttered, shallow baking dish. Cover with layer of eggplant slices and several spoonfuls of sauce. Sprinkle with cheese. Repeat until all ingredients are used. Bake for 30 minutes. Remove from oven, and serve.

Spaghetti with Basil Sauce

Serves 4

12 ounces spaghetti
2 tablespoons olive oil
2 shallots, finely chopped
1 to 2 cloves garlic, peeled
   and finely chopped
2 1/4 cups light cream
1 cup chopped fresh basil
Salt and freshly ground
   pepper to taste
1 to 2 teaspoons lemon juice
1 egg yolk

1. Cook spaghetti in boiling, salted water following package directions; drain.
2. While spaghetti cooks, heat oil in saucepan. Add shallots and garlic; saute until translucent. Add cream, stirring constantly. Stir in basil, salt, pepper, lemon juice, and egg yolk. Cook, stirring constantly, until smooth and well heated.
3. Combine sauce with drained spaghetti, and serve at once.

Fettuccine with Herbs and Vegetables

Serves 4

7 tablespoons extra-virgin olive oil
4 onions, cut into strips
1¼ cups sliced zucchini
2 green peppers, seeded and shredded
1¼ cups sliced mushrooms
1 teaspoon chicken bouillon powder
Salt and pepper to taste
2 sprigs fresh tarragon
½ cup chopped parsley
½ cup chopped fresh dill
½ cup chopped fresh basil
6 sage leaves
2 cloves garlic, peeled and crushed
2 tablespoons flaked almonds
1 tablespoon lemon juice
2 tomatoes, skinned and diced
12 ounces fettuccine

1. Heat 4 tablespoons olive oil in saucepan. Add onions and saute until translucent. Add zucchini, green pepper, and mushrooms; saute for 5 minutes. Sprinkle vegetables with bouillon powder and pepper; cover and cook over low heat for 10 minutes.
2. Combine herbs, garlic, and almonds. Add salt, pepper, lemon juice, and remaining olive oil. Set aside.
3. Stir tomatoes into vegetable mixture and simmer to allow liquid to evaporate a little.
4. Cook fettuccine in boiling, salted water following package directions; drain. Toss fettuccine, vegetables, and herb mixture together, and serve.

Parsley Pesto and Capellini

Serves 4

8 ounces angel hair pasta (capellini)
1½ cups parsley leaves
1 large clove garlic, peeled and chopped
3 tablespoons freshly grated Asiago or Parmesan cheese
1 tablespoon red wine vinegar
¼ cup extra-virgin olive oil
Freshly ground pepper to taste

1. Cook pasta in boiling, salted water following package directions; drain.
2. While pasta is cooking, puree parsley, garlic, cheese, and vinegar together in food processor or blender. Scrape down sides of work bowl. With food processor or blender running, slowly add olive oil in steady stream.
3. Place pasta in heated serving bowl. Toss with parsley pesto and top with freshly grated black pepper. Serve at once.

Tortellini with Chervil and Cheese Sauce

Serves 4 to 6

1 pound tortellini stuffed with meat
2 tablespoons butter
1 onion, chopped
1 heaping tablespoon flour
½ cup hot beef broth
½ cup dry white wine
1 cup heavy whipping cream
Salt and pepper to taste
Pinch of nutmeg
1 cup mozzarella, cut into small pieces
½ cup chopped fresh chervil
1 egg yolk

1. Cook tortellini in boiling, salted water following package directions; drain.

2. Melt butter in saucepan. Add onion and saute until translucent. Add flour and cook, stirring constantly, until golden. Gradually add stock. Bring to a boil, stirring constantly. Reduce heat to low; add wine and cream, stirring constantly. Season with salt, pepper, and nutmeg.
3. Place mozzarella cheese in sauce and cook over low heat, stirring constantly, until cheese melts. Stir chervil into sauce.
4. Beat egg yolk with 2 tablespoons hot sauce, then stir into egg yolk mixture into saucepan with remaining sauce. Add tortellini, mixing to coat well with sauce. Transfer to heated serving bowl, and serve.

Pasta with Walnut and Almond Pesto

Serves 6

1 pound pasta of your choice
¼ cup butter
1½ cups chopped parsley
4 teaspoons chopped fresh basil
½ teaspoon salt
Freshly ground pepper to taste
1 clove garlic, peeled and crushed
2 ounces almonds
2 ounces walnuts
1 cup olive oil
¼ cup grated Parmesan cheese

1. Cook pasta in boiling, salted water following package directions; drain. Toss lightly with butter.
2. While pasta is cooking, combine parsley, basil, salt, pepper, garlic, almond, walnuts, and oil in blender or food processor. Blend on high speed until very smooth. Stir in grated cheese.
3. Toss pasta with pesto. Serve with extra grated Parmesan cheese, if desired.

Amelia's Fresh Salmon Spaghetti

Serves 4

1/2 cup dry white wine
1/2 teaspoon salt
1/2 teaspoon whole peppercorns
2 sprigs fresh tarragon or
   1 teaspoon dried tarragon
12 ounces fresh salmon
2 cups light cream
3/4 cup carrots, thinly sliced
12 ounces spaghetti
1 tablespoon butter

1. Place wine, salt, peppercorns, and 1 sprig fresh tarragon or 1/2 teaspoon dried tarragon in large saucepan. Add salmon and cook for 3 to 5 minutes. Remove salmon from pan, cool, and flake. Strain stock and boil down to half the quantity.
2. Add cream to reduced stock and cook over high heat until reduced by half.
3. Cook carrots in boiling water to cover for 2 minutes; drain.
4. Cook spaghetti in boiling, salted water following package directions; drain.
5. Finely chop remaining sprig fresh tarragon, if used; mix into cream sauce, or add 1/2 teaspoon dried tarragon instead. Add butter, a teaspoon at a time. Place salmon and carrots in sauce, and reheat gently.
6. Place spaghetti in heated serving bowl. Spoon salmon sauce on top, and serve.

Farfalle with Salmon Sauce

Serves 4 to 6

12 ounces farfalle
2 tablespoons dry white wine
1 1/2 to 2 tablespoons lemon
   juice
1 cup heavy whipping cream
3 tablespoons finely chopped
   fresh dill
Salt and pepper to taste
1/4 pound smoked salmon,
   cut into thin strips

1. Cook farfalle in boiling, salted water following package directions; drain.
2. Place wine and lemon juice in saucepan and heat until a little evaporates. Add cream; simmer, stirring constantly, for 10 minutes, or until sauce thickens and becomes very creamy. Season with fresh dill, salt, and pepper. Add salmon and simmer until heated.
3. Pour sauce over pasta in heated serving dish. Serve at once.

Linguine with Salmon

Serves 6

1 pound linguine
2 cloves garlic, peeled and
   minced
1/4 cup butter
1/4 cup olive oil
1 teaspoon coarsely ground
   pepper
Bottled clam juice
1 (7 3/4-ounce) can salmon,
   drained, flaked, and liquid
   reserved
2 tablespoons chopped
   parsley

1. Cook linguine in boiling, salted water following package directions; drain.
2. While pasta is cooking, saute garlic in butter and oil until lightly browned; add pepper. Add enough clam juice to reserved salmon liquid to make 1 cup; add to garlic mixture, along with flaked salmon. Simmer until well heated.
3. Place pasta in heated serving dish. Pour salmon sauce over linguine, sprinkle with parsley, and serve.

Vermicelli with Tuna Sauce

Serves 4

6 tablespoons butter
6 tablespoons olive oil
2 (7-ounce) cans tuna
   packed in oil, drained
   and finely chopped
1/3 cup chopped parsley
2 tablespoons chopped capers
2 tablespoons lemon juice
1/4 cup chicken broth
Salt and pepper to taste
1 pound vermicelli

1. Heat butter and oil in heavy skillet over medium heat. Add tuna, parsley, and capers. Cook until well heated, stirring occasionally. Stir in lemon juice, broth, salt, and pepper. Simmer while pasta is cooking.
2. Cook vermicelli in boiling, salted water following package directions; drain.
3. Place pasta in large heated serving bowl. Add sauce; toss gently. Serve immediately.

Tuna Lasagna

Serves 8

1 pound lasagna noodles
1 cup chopped onion
2 cloves garlic, peeled and
  minced
¼ cup butter
4 (7-ounce) cans tuna fish,
  drained and flaked
2 (10-ounce) cans condensed
  cream of celery soup
⅔ cup milk
1 teaspoon oregano
¼ teaspoon pepper
8 ounces sliced mozzarella
  cheese
16 slices processed American
  cheese
1 cup grated Parmesan
  cheese

1. Cook lasagna noodles in boiling, salted water following package directions; drain.
2. Preheat oven to 350 degrees.
3. Sauté onion and garlic in butter until translucent. Add tuna, celery soup, milk, oregano, and pepper. In 2 buttered baking dishes, alternate layers of noodles, tuna sauce, mozzarella cheese slices, American cheese slices, and grated Parmesan cheese. End with layer of noodles. Cover tightly and bake for 30 minutes. Remove from oven, and serve.

Spaghetti with Tuna Tomato Sauce

Serves 6

1 (28-ounce) can Italian-style
  tomatoes, drained
¼ cup oil
¼ cup chopped green pepper
¼ cup chopped onion
3 cloves garlic, peeled and
  minced
1 (8-ounce) can tomato sauce
1 (6-ounce) can tomato paste
⅔ cup water
½ teaspoon salt
½ teaspoon oregano
½ teaspoon basil
¼ teaspoon nutmeg
¼ teaspoon sugar
⅛ teaspoon pepper
1 (7-ounce) can solid white
  tuna fish, drained and
  flaked
1 pound spaghetti

1. Puree tomatoes in blender or food processor until smooth; set aside.
2. Heat oil in Dutch oven. Add green pepper, onion, and garlic; saute for 5 minutes over medium heat. Increase heat to high, then stir in pureed tomatoes, tomato sauce, tomato paste, water, and seasonings. Bring to a boil. Reduce heat to low, cover, and simmer for 35 minutes. Add tuna and simmer for 10 minutes longer.
3. Cook spaghetti in boiling, salted water following package directions; drain.
4. Place spaghetti in heated serving bowl. Pour sauce on top, and serve.

Shrimp Macaroni

Serves 4

10 ounces macaroni
1 (10-ounce) can shrimp,
  drained
Juice of 1 lemon
2 tablespoons butter
1 small onion, diced
18 ounces tomato paste

2 tablespoons pickle relish
½ cup beef broth
Salt and pepper to taste
Pinch of dried red pepper flakes
½ bunch parsley, finely chopped
2 ounces Swiss cheese, grated

1. Cook macaroni in boiling, salted water following package directions; drain.
2. Place shrimp in bowl; sprinkle with lemon juice.
3. Melt butter in frying pan. Add onion and saute until golden. Add shrimp, tomato paste, relish, and bouillon. Season with salt, pepper, and red pepper flakes. Simmer for 10 minutes.
4. Place macaroni in heated serving bowl. Stir in shrimp sauce. Sprinkle with parsley. Serve cheese in separate bowl.

Shrimp Tagliatelle

Serves 4

1 quart salted water
1 bay leaf
1 slice lemon
1 pound large shrimp, shelled
  and deveined
2 tablespoons olive oil
⅓ cup chopped onion
1 clove garlic, peeled and
  minced
1½ cups Italian-style tomatoes,
  drained
¼ cup tomato sauce
½ teaspoon sugar
½ teaspoon basil
Salt and pepper to taste
2 tablespoons bread crumbs
2 tablespoons grated Parmesan
  cheese
1 tablespoon finely chopped
  parsley
8 ounces tagliatelle

1. Place salted water, bay leaf, and lemon slice in large saucepan; bring to a boil. Add shrimp and boil rapidly for 5 minutes; drain.
2. Heat olive oil in heavy skillet. Add onion and garlic; saute until tender. Break up tomatoes and add to skillet along with tomato sauce and seasonings. Reduce heat to low and cook for 20 minutes.
3. Preheat oven to 450 degrees.
4. Place shrimp in lightly greased baking dish. Top with sauce. Combine bread crumbs, Parmesan cheese, and parsley; sprinkle over shrimp. Bake for 10 minutes.
5. While shrimp is baking, cook pasta in boiling, salted water following package directions; drain.
6. Serve shrimp and marinara sauce on bed of pasta. Sprinkle with more grated Parmesan cheese, if desired.

Vermicelli and Shrimp

Serves 2

3½ tablespoons butter
2 cloves garlic, peeled and minced
½ pound shrimp, shelled and deveined
2 tablespoons chopped parsley
2 tablespoons dry white wine
4 ounces vermicelli
¼ cup freshly grated Parmesan cheese
½ cup heavy whipping cream
Freshly ground pepper to taste
¾ cup tiny frozen peas, cooked until just tender

1. Melt 1 tablespoon butter in large frying pan. Add garlic and saute for 1 minute, stirring constantly. Add shrimp, parsley, and wine. Cook until shrimp turn pink, about 2 to 3 minutes. Transfer mixture to bowl.
2. Cook pasta in boiling, salted water following package directions, being careful not to overcook; drain.

3. Add remaining butter to same pan in which shrimp were cooked; heat until melted. Add Parmesan cheese, cream, and pepper. Cook over low heat until cheese melts and sauce is smooth. Remove from heat.
4. Add pasta, peas, and shrimp mixture to sauce. Gently mix until well blended.

Shrimp-Filled Tortellini

Serves 4

2½ cups flour
3 eggs
Salt
4 tablespoons plus 1 teaspoon oil
3 shallots, peeled and diced
2 tomatoes, skinned and diced
3 tablespoons sour cream
1 teaspoon cornstarch
3 tablespoons dry white wine
Freshly ground pepper to taste
1 tablespoon lemon juice
¾ pound cooked shrimp, shelled, deveined, and chopped
2 teaspoons dill
3 quarts water

1. Mix flour, eggs, pinch of salt, and 3 tablespoons oil together to form dough. Cover and let rest for 1 hour.
2. Heat 1 tablespoon oil in saucepan. Add shallots and saute until translucent. Add tomatoes and sour cream. Cook over medium heat for 5 minutes, stirring constantly.
3. Blend cornstarch and wine together; add to saucepan along with salt, pepper, and lemon juice. Remove sauce from heat and let cool.

4. Stir shrimp and dill into cooled sauce.
5. Divide dough into 4 equal portions and roll out a portion at a time as thinly as possible on lightly floured board; keep remaining dough covered until ready to use. Cut dough into 3-inch circles; dampen edges with water. Divide filling among dough circles, then fold in half, pressing edges together firmly.
6. Place water, 1 teaspoon salt, and 1 teaspoon oil in large saucepan and bring to a boil. Add tortellini and cook for 6 minutes. Drain and serve.

Spinach Noodles with Clams

Serves 4

2 tablespoons butter
1 large clove garlic, peeled and finely chopped
2 tablespoons parsley
2 tablespoons flour
2 cups canned chopped clams, drained, reserve can liquid
8 ounces green noodles

1. Melt butter in saucepan. Add garlic, parsley, and flour; cook over low heat, stirring constantly, until well blended. Add reserved clam liquid. Simmer for 10 minutes.
2. Cook noodles in boiling, salted water following package directions; drain.
3. Add clams to sauce; simmer until clams are heated but not overcooked.
4. Place noodles in heated serving dish. Pour clam sauce over noodles, and serve.

Linguine with Mushroom-Tuna Sauce

Serves 6

1/2 cup butter
3 cloves garlic, peeled and
    minced
1 pound fresh mushrooms, sliced
1 (7-ounce) can tuna fish,
    undrained
1/2 cup chopped parsley
1 teaspoon salt
1/4 teaspoon pepper
1 pound linguine

1. Melt butter in large frying pan.
Add garlic; saute until golden. Add
mushrooms, tuna and can liquid,
parsley, salt, and pepper; simmer
until mushrooms are tender.
2. Cook linguine in boiling, salted
water following package directions;
drain.
3. Add mushroom-tuna mixture to
linguine, toss well, and serve.

Ziti with Sardine Sauce

Serves 6

2 tablespoons butter
2 tablespoons olive oil
2 small white onions, minced
2 fresh basil leaves, minced, or
    1/2 teaspoon dried basil
4 ripe tomatoes, skinned and
    diced
1 pound fresh sardines, cut
    into 2-inch pieces
1/2 teaspoon salt
Freshly ground pepper to taste
1/2 cup clam juice
6 large pitted black olives,
    sliced
1 tablespoon pine nuts
1 pound ziti

1. Heat butter and oil in medium
saucepan. Add onions, basil, and
tomatoes; simmer until onions are

soft. Add sardine pieces; use
wooden spoon to break up tomatoes
and sardines as they cook. Season
with salt and pepper. Add clam juice
a little at a time, stirring to blend
well. Simmer for 25 minutes. Add
olives and pine nuts; simmer for 10
minutes more.
2. While sauce simmers, cook ziti in
boiling, salted water following
package directions; drain. Place in
heated serving bowl.
3. Add half of sauce to ziti; toss
gently to blend. Spoon into
individual portions, then spoon
remaining sauce on top.

Shells with Mediterranean Sauce

Serves 4 to 6

12 ounces pasta shells
1 large red onion, chopped
1 green pepper, seeded and
    cubed
1 small eggplant, sliced
Olive oil for frying
2 cloves garlic, peeled and
    crushed
Salt and pepper to taste
2 teaspoons thyme
1/2 teaspoon curry
1 teaspoon cayenne pepper
1 (28-ounce) can crushed
    tomatoes, undrained
1 pound cooked shrimp, shelled
    and deveined

1. Cook pasta in boiling, salted
water following package directions;
drain.
2. Brown onion, green pepper, and
eggplant separately in olive oil; drain
and place in large saucepan. Add
garlic, salt, pepper, thyme, curry,
and a pinch of cayenne pepper. Add
tomatoes. Simmer until sauce
thickens, about 15 minutes. Add
shrimp and simmer until well
heated.
3. Place pasta in heated serving
bowl. Top with sauce, and serve at
once.

Shrimp Linguine

Serves 4 to 6

1/4 pound butter
1 clove garlic, peeled and minced
1 teaspoon salt
1/4 teaspoon pepper
1 1/2 pounds cooked shrimp,
    shelled and deveined
2 teaspoons lemon juice
1 pound linguine
1/4 cup chopped parsley

1. Melt butter in medium frying pan.
Add garlic, salt, pepper, shrimp, and
lemon juice. Cook over low heat for
15 minutes, stirring occasionally.
2. Meanwhile, cook linguine in
boiling, salted water following
package directions; drain.
3. Place linguine in heated serving
bowl. Pour seafood sauce on top,
sprinkle with parsley, and serve.

Whole-Wheat Spaghetti with Tofu Bolognese

Serves 4

1 1/4 cups tofu
1 tablespoon soy sauce
1/8 teaspoon oregano
1/8 teaspoon basil
1/8 teaspoon pepper
6 tablespoons olive oil
2 onions, finely chopped
3 cloves garlic, peeled and finely
    chopped
1 small green pepper, seeded
    and cut into thin strips
2 1/4 cups diced tomatoes
1/4 cup chopped parsley
1/2 cup light cream
12 ounces whole-wheat spaghetti
10 pitted black olives,
    chopped
2 tablespoons chopped chives
1/2 teaspoon paprika
Pinch of cayenne pepper

1. Mash tofu with fork and combine with soy sauce, oregano, basil, and pepper.
2. Heat oil in frying pan. Add onion and garlic; saute until translucent. Add tofu and saute for 2 minutes. Add green pepper and tomatoes; saute for 1 minute longer. Add parsley and cream; cover and simmer for 10 minutes.
3. Cook spaghetti in boiling, salted water following package directions; drain.
4. Add olives, chives, paprika, and cayenne to tofu sauce. Place spaghetti in heated serving dish. Spoon sauce over spaghetti, and serve.

Manicotti with Tofu

Serves 4

1 pound tofu
2 cups shredded mozzarella cheese
1/2 cup grated Parmesan cheese
1/4 cup finely chopped parsley
Salt and pepper to taste
1/4 teaspoon basil
8 ounces manicotti shells
1 (32-ounce) jar spaghetti sauce

1. Preheat oven to 400 degrees.
2. Combine tofu, mozzarella, 1/4 cup Parmesan cheese, parsley, salt, pepper, and basil. Fill uncooked manicotti shells with tofu mixture.
3. Cover bottom of 13 x 9-inch baking pan with spaghetti sauce. Lay stuffed manicotti in single layer on top of sauce. Pour remaining sauce on top. Cover with foil and bake for 40 minutes. Remove foil and sprinkle with 1/4 cup Parmesan cheese; bake, uncovered, for 10 minutes. Remove from oven, and serve.

Spinach and Tofu Filled Manicotti

Serves 4

8 manicotti shells

Filling

1/4 cup minced onion
2 tablespoons oil
1 tablespoon minced parsley
1 large clove garlic, peeled and crushed
1/2 teaspoon basil
1/2 teaspoon oregano
1 pound tofu
1 (10-ounce) package frozen spinach, thawed
1 egg, beaten
Salt and pepper to taste

Sauce

3 large tomatoes, skinned and finely chopped
2 teaspoons oil
2 tablespoons basil
2 tablespoons thyme
1/2 cup grated Parmesan cheese

1. Cook manicotti in boiling, salted water following package directions; drain.
2. Preheat oven to 350 degrees.
3. Saute onion in oil until translucent. Add parsley, garlic, basil, and oregano.
4. Mash tofu with potato masher. Squeeze excess water out of spinach, then combine with tofu. Add sauteed onion and seasonings and egg. Mix well; season with salt and pepper.
5. To make sauce, place tomatoes, oil, basil, and thyme in saucepan. Cook over medium heat for 10 minutes, or until thickened.
6. Stuff manicotti shells with tofu mixture. Place shells close together in shallow baking pan. Pour sauce on top. Sprinkle with grated Parmesan cheese, cover with foil, and bake for 20 minutes. Remove from oven, and serve immediately.

Crabmeat Louisa

Serves 8

8 ounces linguine
2 tablespoons butter
1 onion, finely chopped
1/4 cup chopped green pepper
1 cup sliced mushrooms
1 (10-ounce) can condensed tomato soup
1 (18-ounce) can tomato juice
1 pound fresh crabmeat
1/2 teaspoon seafood seasoning
1 (8-ounce) package sharp cheese spread

1. Cook pasta in boiling, salted water following package directions; drain.
2. Preheat oven to 350 degrees.
3. Melt butter in saucepan. Add onion, green pepper, and mushrooms; saute for 5 minutes. Stir in tomato soup, tomato juice, crabmeat, and seafood seasoning. Blend in linguine and 3/4 of cheese spread.
4. Transfer crab mixture to greased casserole dish. Dot with remaining cheese spread and bake for 30 to 45 minutes, or until browned and hot. Remove from oven, and serve.

Tuna Noodle Casserole

Serves 4 to 6

1 package of ready-to-make
   macaroni and cheese
   (with powdered cheese)
1 (10-ounce) can concentrated
   cream of mushroom soup
¼ cup milk
1 (7-ounce) can tuna fish,
   drained and flaked
Crushed potato chips or fried
   onions to taste

1. Cook macaroni in boiling, salted water until just tender, following package directions; drain.
2. Preheat oven to 350 degrees.
3. Mix most of powdered cheese with soup and milk. Stir in tuna fish. Toss macaroni with tuna mixture and turn into greased casserole dish. Sprinkle remaining cheese on top. Top with crushed potato chips or fried onions. Bake for 45 minutes, or until browned and bubbly. Remove from oven, and serve.

Tuna Noodle Stroganoff

Serves 6

8 ounces egg noodles
1 (10-ounce) can condensed
   cream of mushroom soup
1 cup sour cream
¼ cup milk
1 cup frozen peas, thawed
⅓ cup diced celery
⅓ cup minced onion
2 (7-ounce) cans tuna fish,
   drained
½ teaspoon salt
Pepper to taste
½ cup bread crumbs

1. Cook noodles in boiling, salted water until just tender, following package directions; drain.
2. Preheat oven to 325 degrees.
3. Mix soup, sour cream, and milk together until smooth. Combine with peas, celery, onion, and tuna. Season with salt and pepper. Toss with noodles, then place in casserole dish. Top with bread crumbs and bake for 40 minutes. Remove from oven, and serve.

Tuna Fish Dish

Serves 4

8 ounces elbow macaroni
¾ cup fresh bread crumbs
¼ cup melted butter
1 tablespoon parsley
1 small onion, finely
   chopped
1 teaspoon salt
1 teaspoon chopped
   pimentos
2 (7-ounce) cans tuna fish,
   drained
3 eggs
2½ cups milk

1. Cook macaroni in boiling, salted water following package directions; drain.
2. Preheat oven to 350 degrees.
3. Mix macaroni, bread crumbs, melted butter, parsley, onion, salt, pimentos, and tuna together in buttered casserole dish. Beat eggs and milk together; pour over macaroni mixture. Bake 30 or 40 minutes. Remove from oven, and serve.

CONVENIENT CASSEROLES

Tortellini Casserole

Serves 4

8 ounces cheese-filled tortellini
1 (1.8-ounce) envelope white
  sauce mix
Salt and pepper to taste
Pinch of nutmeg
1 cup grated Swiss cheese
1 cup frozen peas, thawed
1/2 cup sliced mushrooms
1 cup diced leftover meatloaf

1. Cook tortellini in boiling, salted water following package directions; drain.
2. Preheat oven to 400 degrees.
3. In saucepan, prepare white sauce mix following package instructions. Season with salt, pepper, and nutmeg. Gradually add 3/4 cup grated cheese; cook, stirring constantly, until cheese melts.
4. Combine tortellini, peas, mushrooms, and meatloaf in buttered 1-quart casserole dish. Pour cheese sauce on top; toss gently to coat all ingredients with sauce. Sprinkle with remaining cheese and bake for 25 minutes, or until golden brown and bubbly. Remove from oven, and serve.

Baked Macaroni Supreme

Serves 6

8 ounces macaroni, broken into
  pieces
1/2 cup chopped green pepper
1/4 cup chopped onion
3 tablespoons butter
1/2 cup sliced pimento-stuffed
  olives
1/2 cup sliced mushrooms

1 1/2 cups cubed cooked ham
1 cup grated sharp Cheddar
  cheese
1 (10-ounce) can condensed
  tomato soup
3 strips bacon

1. Cook macaroni in boiling, salted water following package directions; drain;.
2. Preheat oven to 400 degrees.
3. Saute green pepper and onion in butter for 5 minutes. Combine macaroni, green pepper, onion, olives, mushrooms, ham, cheese, and tomato soup. Place in greased casserole dish. Top with bacon strips.
4. Bake for 20 minutes, or until bubbly and bacon is cooked. Remove from oven, and serve.

Penne and Ham Casserole

Serves 4

8 ounces penne
3 tablespoons butter
2 tablespoons flour
1 cup milk
1 cup shredded American cheese
1 teaspoon salt
2 tablespoons ketchup
1 tablespoon white horseradish
1 cup frozen peas, thawed
2 cups diced cooked ham
1/4 cup bread crumbs

1. Cook penne in boiling, salted water following package directions; drain.
2. Preheat oven to 350 degrees.
3. Melt 2 tablespoons butter in saucepan. Blend in flour. Add milk; cook, stirring constantly, until sauce

is thick and smooth. Add cheese; cook, stirring constantly, until cheese is melted. Add salt, ketchup, horseradish, peas, ham, and penne; blend well.
4. Transfer mixture to 1-quart casserole dish. Sprinkle with bread crumbs and dot with butter. Bake for 30 minutes, or until top is browned. Remove from oven, and serve.

Rigatoni Casserole

Serves 4

12 ounces rigatoni
1 small onion
2 eggs, well beaten
Pinch of nutmeg
Salt and pepper to taste
2 cups milk
1/2 teaspoon cornstarch
1/2 pound cooked ham, diced
1/4 cup grated Emmenthaler
  cheese
1/4 cup bread crumbs
2 tablespoons butter

1. Cook rigatoni and peeled onion in boiling, salted water until pasta is just tender, following package directions; drain.
2. Beat eggs with nutmeg, salt, pepper, milk, and cornstarch.
3. Preheat oven to 450 degrees.
4. Mix pasta with diced ham in well-buttered casserole dish. Pour egg mixture on top. Sprinkle with grated cheese and bread crumbs. Dot with butter. Bake for 30 minutes, or until golden brown. Remove from oven, and serve.

Ham Casserole

Serves 4

3 tablespoons butter
2 tablespoons flour
1 cup light cream
1 cup shredded Cheddar cheese
1 tablespoon prepared white
  horseradish
1 cup cooked peas
1 cup diced cooked ham
1½ cups cooked egg noodles
¼ cup bread crumbs

1. Preheat oven to 350 degrees.
2. Melt 2 tablespoons butter in saucepan. Blend flour into melted butter to form paste. Add cream, stirring constantly until smooth, thick sauce forms. Add cheese; stir sauce until cheese melts. Add horseradish, peas, ham, and noodles; mix well.
3. Pour noodle mixture into greased, 1-quart casserole dish. Top with bread crumbs; dot with remaining butter. Bake for 30 minutes, or until thoroughly heated. Remove from oven, and serve.

Tagliatelle Pie

Serves 4

10 ounces tagliatelle
1 fennel, cut into thin strips
3 tablespoons butter
½ cup light cream
½ cup chopped mixed fresh
  herbs, such as chervil,
  sage, dill or ¼ teaspoon each
  dried chervil, sage, and dill
¼ pound cooked ham,
  diced
3 tomatoes, sliced
⅔ cup sour cream
½ cup milk
2 eggs, beaten
Salt and pepper to taste
2 tablespoons bread crumbs
Fennel leaves, for garnish

1. Cook tagliatelle in boiling, salted water following package directions; drain.
2. Saute fennel in 1 tablespoon butter; add cream, herbs, and ham.
3. Preheat oven to 400 degrees.
4. Set aside a few tomato slices for garnish. Place pasta, fennel, and remaining tomatoes in layers in buttered casserole dish. Beat sour cream, milk, eggs, salt, and pepper together; pour over casserole. Sprinkle with bread crumbs and dot with remaining butter. Bake for 20 to 30 minutes. Remove from oven and garnish with tomato slices and fennel leaves.

Chopped Ham and Noodle Bake

Serves 4 to 6

¼ cup chopped onion
¼ cup butter or margarine
2 cups cubed cooked ham
2 cups cooked egg noodles
½ cup sliced pitted black olives
1 (11-ounce) can Cheddar cheese
  soup
1 cup bread crumbs

1. Preheat oven to 375 degrees.
2. Saute onion in 2 tablespoons butter until translucent. Add chopped ham, noodles, olives, and soup. Transfer to 1½-quart casserole dish.
3. Melt remaining butter in small saucepan; mix with bread crumbs. Sprinkle bread crumb mixture on top of casserole. Bake for 30 minutes. Remove from oven, and serve.

Pork and Noodle Casserole

Serves 4

1 medium onion, sliced
1 green pepper, seeded and
  diced
3 tablespoons butter
2 pounds lean ground pork
3 cups canned tomatoes, drained
8 ounces cooked egg noodles
1 cup chopped American cheese
Salt and pepper to taste

1. Saute onion and green pepper in butter until soft. Add pork and cook, stirring constantly until lightly browned. Add tomatoes, noodles, and cheese. Season with salt and pepper; mix well.
2. Preheat oven to 350 degrees.
3. Place pork mixture in buttered baking dish. Bake for 1 hour. Remove from oven, and serve.

Rustica Casserole

Serves 4

8 ounces tagliatelle, cut in half
2 tablespoons olive oil
½ pound Italian sweet sausage,
  thinly sliced
½ cup shredded mozzarella
  cheese
¼ cup grated Parmesan cheese
3 eggs, lightly beaten
½ pound prosciutto, diced
2 tablespoons salt
2 tablespoons chopped parsley

1. Cook tagliatelle in boiling, salted water until almost tender, following package directions; drain.
2. Preheat oven to 350 degrees.
3. Heat oil in frying pan. Add sausage and cook for 5 minutes, until lightly browned. Remove from heat and combine with cheeses, eggs, prosciutto, pasta, and salt. Turn mixture into buttered, 9-inch round casserole dish. Cover with foil and bake for 45 minutes. Remove from oven, sprinkle with parsley, and serve.

Frankfurters Monterey

Serves 6

8 ounces egg noodles
1 onion, chopped
1 green pepper, seeded and
  chopped
3 tablespoons salad oil
1 tablespoon Worcestershire
  sauce
2 tablespoons brown sugar
$1/2$ teaspoon salt
$1/8$ teaspoon pepper
Juice of 1 lemon
1 thin strip lemon rind
1 pound frankfurters

1. Preheat oven to 375 degrees.
2. Cook noodles in boiling, salted water following package directions; drain.
3. Saute onion and green pepper in oil until soft. Add Worcestershire sauce, brown sugar, salt, pepper, lemon juice, and lemon rind. Simmer for 15 minutes, stirring occasionally. Remove lemon rind.
4. Arrange frankfurters over noodles in large, greased baking dish. Pour sauce on top. Bake for 30 minutes. Remove from oven, and serve.

Jollini Casserole

Serves 4

$2^{1}/4$ cups pasta twists
$2^{1}/4$ cups frozen peas
1/4 pound salami, cut into thin
  slices
1 cup diced zucchini
$1/4$ cup chopped fresh chives or
  1 tablespoon dried chives
1 cup sour cream
2 eggs, well beaten
$1/2$ teaspoon salt
$1/4$ cup grated fontina cheese
2 tablespoons butter

1. Cook pasta in boiling, salted water until just tender, following package directions; drain.
2. Boil peas in $1/4$ cup salted water for 5 minutes; drain.
3. Preheat oven to 400 degrees.
4. Combine pasta, salami, peas, zucchini, and chives in well-buttered casserole dish. Beat sour cream, eggs, and salt together; pour over pasta mixture. Sprinkle with grated cheese and dot with butter. Bake for 30 minutes, or until golden brown. Remove from oven, and serve.

Spaghetti and Salami Casserole

Serves 4

12 ounces spaghetti
1 (8-ounce) can peeled tomatoes,
  drained
1 teaspoon oregano
Salt and pepper to taste
2 onions, cut into rings
2 ounces salami, cut into thin
  slices
$1^{3}/4$ cups sour cream
1 clove garlic, peeled and finely
  chopped
1 tablespoon olive oil
3 tablespoons grated Parmesan
  cheese
2 tablespoons bread crumbs

1. Cook spaghetti in boiling, salted water until just tender, following package directions; drain.
2. Mash tomatoes. Add oregano, salt, and pepper.
3. Preheat oven to 400 degrees.
4. Toss spaghetti and crushed tomatoes together in casserole dish greased with olive oil. Put onion rings on top. Add layer of salami slices.
5. Mix sour cream, garlic, and oil together; pour over salami. Sprinkle with cheese and bread crumbs. Bake for 30 minutes. Remove from oven, and serve.

Ground Beef Noodle Casserole

Serves 8

1 pound egg noodles
2 tablespoons butter
$1^{1}/2$ pounds ground beef
1 cup chopped celery
1 green pepper, seeded and
  finely chopped
1 tablespoon flour
1 (10-ounce) can condensed
  tomato soup
1 (10-ounce) can condensed
  onion soup
$1/2$ cup red wine
$1^{1}/2$ cups grated Cheddar
  cheese
1 (4-ounce) can mushroom
  stems and pieces, drained
2 tablespoons Worcestershire
  sauce
Salt and pepper to taste

1. Cook noodles in boiling, salted water until just tender, following package directions; drain and toss with butter.
2. Place ground beef in heavy skillet with celery and green pepper; cook until meat is lightly browned. Stir in flour. Add soups and red wine. Cook, stirring constantly, until sauce boils.
3. Reduce heat to low. Add $1/2$ cup Cheddar cheese, stirring until cheese melts. Stir in mushrooms, Worcestershire sauce, salt, and pepper; mix well.
4. Preheat oven to 350 degrees.
5. Combine meat mixture with noodles; transfer to casserole dish. Bake for 45 minutes. Sprinkle with remaining Cheddar cheese and bake for 15 minutes more. Remove from oven; let cool briefly before serving.

Pharaoh's Wheel

Serves 4 to 6

8 ounces thin egg noodles
2¹/₂ cups meat gravy
¹/₂ pound thinly sliced salami
¹/₂ cup raisins
¹/₂ cup pine nuts

1. Cook noodles in boiling, salted water following package directions; drain.
2. Preheat oven to 400 degrees.
3. Alternate layers of noodles, gravy, salami slices, raisins, and nuts in greased 2-quart casserole dish; end with noodle layer and a few slices of salami. Bake for 15 to 20 minutes. Remove from oven, and serve.

Sara's Noodle Casserole

Serves 4

8 ounces pasta shells
1 pound ground beef
1 tablespoon margarine
Salt and pepper to taste
¹/₄ teaspoon garlic salt
1 (10-ounce) can condensed vegetable soup
1 (8-ounce) can tomato sauce

1. Cook pasta in boiling, salted water following package directions; drain.
2. Preheat oven to 350 degrees.
3. Brown meat in margarine. Add salt, pepper, garlic salt, soup, and tomato sauce. Stir in noodles. Place in greased casserole dish and bake for 45 minutes. Remove from oven, and serve.

Noodle Bliss

Serves 4

8 ounces egg noodles
2 tablespoons oil
1 pound ground beef
1 onion, chopped
1 cup chopped green pepper
1 envelope spaghetti sauce mix

1. Cook noodles in boiling, salted water following package directions; drain.
2. Preheat oven to 350 degrees.
3. Heat oil in frying pan. Add ground beef, onion, and green pepper; cook until meat is browned, separating with fork as it cooks. Pour off excess fast. Remove from heat and stir in spaghetti sauce mix.
4. Combine meat mixture with noodles. Place in greased casserole dish and bake for 30 minutes. Remove from oven, and serve.

Mazetti

Serves 10

2 pounds ground beef
2¹/₂ cups finely chopped celery with leaves
2 cups chopped onions
2 cloves garlic, peeled and finely chopped
1 tablespoon water
8 ounces thin egg noodles
2 (10-ounce) cans condensed tomato soup
1 (6-ounce) can mushrooms, undrained
2 teaspoons salt
¹/₂ teaspoon pepper
2 cups grated sharp Cheddar cheese

1. Brown meat in a skillet; add celery, onions, garlic, and water. Cover and cook until vegetables are tender. Remove from heat.
2. Cook noodles in boiling, salted water following package directions; drain.
3. Preheat oven to 300 degrees.
4. Combine noodles and ground beef mixture; add soup, undrained mushrooms, salt, and pepper. Spread mixture in 3-quart casserole. Sprinkle with cheese. Bake for 1 hour, or until bubbly. Remove from oven, and serve.

Greek Macaroni Casserole

Serves 6

7 tablespoons olive oil
1 eggplant, diced
4 medium tomatoes, skinned and quartered
2 cloves garlic, peeled and chopped
¹/₂ teaspoon salt
¹/₄ teaspoon pepper
1 stick cinnamon
¹/₄ teaspoon allspice
¹/₂ cup red wine
3 tablespoons tomato paste
8 ounces elbow macaroni
1 pound meatloaf mixture (ground beef, pork, and veal)
2 onions, chopped
¹/₄ cup grated Kafaloteri cheese
2 tablespoons butter

1. Heat 5 tablespoons oil in large skillet. Saute eggplant, tomatoes, and garlic for 5 minutes, stirring occasionally. Add salt, pepper, cinnamon stick, allspice, wine, and tomato paste. Simmer for 15 minutes.
2. Cook macaroni in boiling, salted water following package directions; drain.
3. Preheat oven to 350 degrees.
4. Heat remaining 3 tablespoons oil. Brown meat and onions; combine with eggplant mixture. Remove cinnamon stick.
5. Place macaroni in bottom of greased, 13 x 9 x 2-inch baking dish. Add half the cheese, and mix well. Top with vegetable-meat mixture and remaining cheese. Dot with butter. Bake for 30 minutes. Remove from oven, and serve.

Macaroni Casserole in Earthenware Dish

Serves 4

¼ cup butter
3 onions, chopped
2 cloves garlic, peeled and chopped
1 leek, diced
1 stalk celery, diced
1 carrot, peeled and diced
1 pound ground lamb
½ cup chopped parsley
½ teaspoon salt
Freshly ground pepper
½ cup dry red wine
1 cup beef broth, heated
12 ounces macaroni
2¼ cups peeled and chopped tomatoes
½ cup grated Kafaloteri cheese

1. Melt half the butter in saucepan. Add onions and saute until translucent. Add garlic, leek, celery, and carrots; saute for 1 minute more. Add ground lamb and cook until browned, separating with fork as meat cooks. Stir in parsley, salt, pepper, and red wine. Simmer until liquid evaporates. Add beef broth and simmer for 30 minutes.
2. Cook macaroni in boiling, salted water until just tender, following package directions; drain.
3. Rinse earthenware dish in cold water.
4. Place half the macaroni in earthenware dish. Add ground lamb sauce. Put remaining macaroni on top. Season with salt and pepper; add tomatoes.
5. Cover dish and put into cold oven. Turn heat to 450 degrees and bake for 30 minutes. Sprinkle grated cheese on top, dot with remaining butter, and bake uncovered for 15 minutes more, or until golden brown. Remove from oven, and serve.

Lamb Casserole

Serves 4

8 ounces egg noodles
6 tablespoons butter
3 eggs
½ cup pine nuts
1 large onion, finely chopped
1 pound ground lamb
1 teaspoon garlic powder
1 teaspoon oregano
2 tablespoons finely chopped parsley
½ teaspoon thyme
Salt and pepper to taste

1. Cook noodles in boiling, salted water following package directions; drain. Toss with 2 tablespoons butter and 2 beaten eggs.
2. Preheat oven to 350 degrees.
3. Melt 2 tablespoons butter in frying pan. Add pine nuts and saute until golden; remove from pan. Add onion; saute until translucent. Add ground meat and cook until browned. Simmer for 5 minutes; pour off excess fat. Add pine nuts, garlic powder, oregano, parsley, thyme, salt, and pepper to meat. Stir in remaining egg.
4. Cover bottom of greased casserole dish with layer of noodles. Cover with meat mixture, then top with remaining noodles. Dot with remaining butter. Bake for 45 minutes; remove from oven, and serve.

Veal Macaroni Bake

Serves 4

1¼ pounds veal scallops
¼ cup oil
2 bay leaves
½ cup dry white wine
½ cup sour cream
5 eggs
Salt and pepper to taste
1 teaspoon tarragon
8 ounces macaroni
½ cup grated Emmenthaler cheese
½ cup chopped parsley
1 onion, diced
½ cup light cream

1. Saute veal in 2 tablespoons oil. Add bay leaves and wine. Cover and cook for 30 minutes. Remove meat from sauce, let cool, and chop finely. Add sour cream and 1 egg to chopped meat. Season with salt, pepper, and tarragon.
2. Cook macaroni in boiling, salted water following package directions; drain. Toss macaroni with remaining oil.
3. Preheat oven to 400 degrees.
4. Place half the macaroni in bottom of buttered casserole dish. Add chopped meat and sprinkle with parsley. Place onions and half the cheese on top of meat. Add remaining macaroni.
5. Mix remaining eggs with cream. Add salt and pepper, then pour over macaroni. Bake for 30 minutes. Sprinkle remaining cheese on top and bake for 10 to 15 minutes longer, or until golden brown and crispy. Remove from oven, and serve.

Fettuccine Chicken Casserole

Serves 4

8 ounces fettuccine
3 tablespoons butter
2 tablespoons grated Parmesan
  cheese
1/2 cup heavy whipping cream
1/2 cup shredded cooked chicken
1/2 pound fontina cheese,
  chopped
Pinch of nutmeg
Salt and freshly ground pepper to
  taste
1/4 cup bread crumbs

1. Cook fettuccine in boiling, salted water until just tender, following package directions; drain. Toss with 3 tablespoons butter, Parmesan cheese, cream, chicken, fontina cheese, nutmeg, salt, and pepper.
2. Preheat oven to 350 degrees.
3. Add pasta mixture to buttered casserole dish. Melt remaining 2 tablespoons butter and toss with bread crumbs; sprinkle over casserole. Bake for 20 minutes, or until bread crumbs are browned. Remove from oven, and serve.

Chicken and Shell Hash

Serves 4

8 ounces pasta shells
2 cups hot scalded milk
1 (20-ounce) can mixed
  vegetables, drained, liquid
  reserved
1 cup diced cooked chicken
1 (8-ounce) can mushroom sauce
1/2 cup grated Parmesan cheese
1 teaspoon seasoned salt

1. Preheat oven to 450 degrees.
2. Combine pasta shells and hot milk in buttered, 2-quart casserole dish. Cover and let stand for 5 minutes. Add reserved can liquid, chicken, mushroom sauce, cheese, and seasoned salt. Cover and bake for 10 minutes.

3. Stir vegetables into casserole. Reduce heat to 375 degrees, cover, and bake for 20 minutes more. Remove from oven, and serve.

Chicken Noodle Casserole

Serves 8

1 (5-pound) hen
1 onion
1 stalk celery
Salt and pepper to taste
1 cup butter, melted
3/4 cup flour
1 cup chicken broth
1 cup milk
1 cup finely chopped celery
1/2 cup sliced mushrooms
1 (8-ounce) can tomato sauce
1/4 cup chopped pimentos
1 cup grated American cheese
2 cloves garlic, peeled and
  chopped
1 pound broad egg noodles

1. Place chicken in large pot in water to cover; add onion, celery stalk, salt, and pepper. Bring to a boil, skimming as needed. Simmer until chicken is tender, about 1 hour. Remove chicken from broth and let cool. Remove meat from bones and cut into small pieces. Strain broth.
2. Combine butter and flour in saucepan. Add chicken broth and milk. Cook, stirring constantly, until sauce thickens. Add celery, mushrooms, tomato sauce, pimentos, cheese, garlic, salt, and pepper. Simmer, stirring constantly, until cheese melts.
3. Preheat oven to 350 degrees.
4. Cook noodles in boiling, salted water until just tender following package directions; drain.
5. Combine noodles, chicken, and sauce; mix well. Transfer to greased casserole dish. Bake for 45 minutes. Remove from oven, and serve.

Turkey Noodle Bake

Serves 6

4 ounces egg noodles
1/4 cup flour
1 (4-ounce) can mushroom stems
  and pieces, drained, liquid
  reserved, and chopped
2 chicken bouillon cubes
Salt and pepper to taste
1/2 teaspoon sage
2 cups diced cooked turkey
3/4 cup grated sharp Cheddar
  cheese
1/2 cup bread crumbs
2 tablespoons butter

1. Cook noodles in boiling, salted water following package directions; drain.
2. Blend flour with enough reserved mushroom liquid to make paste. Mix remaining mushroom liquid with enough water to make 2 cups; place in saucepan and heat. Gradually blend in flour paste, stirring constantly. Add bouillon cubes, salt, pepper, and sage. Cook, stirring constantly, until mixture boils. Reduce heat and simmer for 1 minute, stirring occasionally. Add mushrooms.
3. Preheat oven to 350 degrees.
4. Place half the noodles in bottom of buttered, 2-quart casserole dish. Cover with half the turkey, then half the sauce. Repeat layers, ending with sauce. Sprinkle with grated cheese and bread crumbs; dot with butter. Bake for 30 to 40 minutes, or until browned and bubbly.

Turkey Noodle Cocottes

Serves 4

8 ounces egg noodles
2 tablespoons butter
2½ cups diced cooked turkey
1 (10-ounce) can condensed
  cream of mushroom soup
1 cup light cream
2 tablespoons capers
½ cup grated Cheddar cheese
Paprika

1. Cook noodles in boiling, salted water following package directions; drain and toss with butter.
2. Preheat oven to 325 degrees.
3. Grease 4 individual casserole dishes and line with noodles. Combine turkey, mushroom soup, cream, and capers; spoon over noodles. Sprinkle with grated cheese and paprika. Bake for 25 minutes, or until golden brown. Remove from oven, and serve.

Turkey Casserole

Serves 4

1 tablespoon butter
2 tablespoons finely chopped
  onion
1 (10-ounce) can condensed
  mushroom soup
1 pimento, chopped
1 hot green chili pepper,
  seeded and finely chopped
1 cup diced cooked turkey
2½ cups cooked noodles
Salt and pepper to taste
½ cup grated sharp Cheddar
  cheese

1. Preheat oven to 350 degrees.
2. Melt butter in saucepan. Add onion and saute until translucent. Add soup, pimento, and chili pepper.
3. Arrange layer of turkey, noodles, and soup mixture in casserole dish. Sprinkle lightly with salt, pepper, and grated cheese. Repeat layers. Sprinkle remaining cheese on top and bake for 30 to 40 minutes. Remove from oven, and serve.

Macaroni and Cheese Casserole

Serves 8

1 pound elbow macaroni
1 (1-pound) can whole tomatoes,
  drained
1 small onion, grated
1 clove garlic, peeled and
  minced
¼ green pepper, seeded and
  chopped
Salt and pepper to taste
2 cups grated sharp Cheddar
  cheese

1. Cook macaroni in boiling, salted water following package directions; drain.
2. Combine tomatoes, onion, garlic, green pepper, salt, and pepper in saucepan. Simmer until green pepper and onion are soft.
3. Preheat oven to 350 degrees.
4. Grease large, oblong baking dish with butter. Alternate layers of macaroni, cheese, and tomatoes. Season with salt and pepper between layers. Bake for 1 hour, or until browned on top. Remove from oven, and serve.

Baked Macaroni and Cheese

Serves 6

1½ cups elbow macaroni
1 to 2 cups shredded sharp
  natural Cheddar cheese
1 to 2 cups shredded processed
  Cheddar cheese
2 eggs, beaten
2 cups milk, whole or skim
1 teaspoon finely chopped
  onion
½ teaspoon salt
¼ teaspoon white pepper
¼ cup cornflake crumbs

1. Cook macaroni in boiling, salted water until almost tender following package instructions; drain.
2. Preheat oven to 350 degrees.

3. Grease 1½-quart casserole dish. Cover bottom of dish with half the macaroni. Combine cheeses; sprinkle half of cheese mixture over macaroni in casserole. Repeat layers.
4. Combine eggs with milk, onion, salt, and pepper. Pour over macaroni and cheese. Sprinkle top with cornflake crumbs. Set casserole in pan of hot water.
5. Bake for 45 minutes to 1 hour, until browned and almost set in center. Remove from oven and let cool for 10 minutes before serving.

Baked Spaghetti

Serves 6

8 ounces spaghetti
2 tablespoons butter
1½ tablespoons chopped
  onion
1½ tablespoons chopped
  green pepper
2 cups canned tomatoes,
  drained
1 teaspoon salt
¼ teaspoon pepper
⅛ teaspoon paprika
1 tablespoon sugar
1 cup grated Parmesan cheese

1. Cook spaghetti in boiling, salted water following package directions; drain.
2. Preheat oven to 400 degrees.
3. Melt butter in saucepan; saute onion and green pepper until soft. Add tomatoes, salt, pepper, paprika, and sugar; simmer for 10 minutes. Add spaghetti; mix well. Add ½ cup cheese. Turn into greased baking dish. Sprinkle with remaining cheese and bake for 20 to 25 minutes, until cheese is browned. Remove from oven, and serve.

Savory Kugel Casserole

Serves 12

1 pound broad noodles,
  preferably spinach noodles
1 bunch fresh broccoli
½ head cauliflower
1 pound cottage cheese
1 cup grated Cheddar cheese
¼ cup butter, softened
½ teaspoon garlic salt
1 teaspoon tarragon
½ teaspoon dry mustard
Pepper to taste
1 onion, sliced
¼ pound sliced mushrooms

1. Cook noodles in boiling, salted water following package directions; drain.
2. Meanwhile, cook broccoli and cauliflower; dice.
3. Preheat oven to 350 degrees.
4. Mix noodles, cottage cheese, ½ cup Cheddar cheese, butter, garlic salt, tarragon, mustard, pepper, broccoli, cauliflower, onion, and most of the mushrooms together. Place in greased casserole dish. Top with remaining Cheddar cheese and mushroom slices. Bake for 30 minutes, or until cheese is browned. Remove from oven, and serve.

Gratin Vegetables and Noodles

Serves 4 to 6

2 tablespoons butter
2 onions, sliced
2 green peppers, seeded and
  diced
1 yellow squash, sliced
4 ripe tomatoes, skinned
  and chopped
2 cloves garlic, peeled and
  crushed
2 to 3 tablespoons chili sauce
1 teaspoon salt
1 teaspoon thyme
8 ounces egg noodles
1 cup grated Parmesan
  cheese

1. Melt butter in large saucepan. Add onion and saute until translucent. Add green peppers, squash, tomatoes, garlic, chili sauce, salt, and thyme. Stir well, then cover and simmer for 10 to 15 minutes. Uncover and simmer for 15 minutes longer.
2. Meanwhile, cook noodles in boiling, salted water following package directions; drain.
3. Preheat oven to 425 degrees.
4. Place half the noodles in bottom of greased baking dish. Cover with vegetable mixture. Place remaining noodles on top of vegetables and top with grated cheese. Bake for 10 minutes, or until browned.

Ditalini Casserole with Eggplant

Serves 4

1 tablespoon salt
3 small eggplants, cut into
  ½-inch strips
12 ounces ditalini or macaroni
3 scallions, finely chopped
2 carrots, finely chopped
¾ cup finely chopped celery
1 sprig fresh thyme or ½
  teaspoon dried thyme
½ cup olive oil
1 (28-ounce) can tomatoes,
  drained
½ cup grated Pecorino or
  Parmesan cheese
4 ounces mozzarella cheese,
  sliced

1. Lightly salt eggplants and leave for 20 minutes.
2. Cook pasta in boiling, salted water until just tender, following package directions; drain.
3. Saute scallions, carrots, celery, and thyme in 2 tablespoons oil. Add tomatoes and simmer for 10 minutes.
4. Preheat oven to 425 degrees.
5. Rinse and dry eggplants; cook in remaining oil until browned.
6. Place half the ditalini in buttered casserole dish. Sprinkle with 2 tablespoons grated cheese. Pour on tomato sauce. Add eggplant, then remaining pasta. Finish with layer of mozzarella cheese slices. Sprinkle with remaining grated cheese. Bake for 30 minutes. Remove from oven, and serve.

Lasagna Casserole

Serves 4

8 ounces lasagna noodles
Salt and pepper to taste
½ cup seedless raisins
1 to 2 tablespoons rum
1 cup sour cream
1 cup cottage cheese
2 to 3 tablespoons blanched
  slivered almonds

1. Cook lasagna in boiling, salted water until just tender, following package directions; drain. Place in deep, buttered casserole dish. Sprinkle with salt and pepper.
2. Preheat oven to 350 degrees.
3. Soak raisins in rum for 5 minutes.
4. Mix sour cream with cottage cheese and raisins; pour over lasagna noodles and toss together lightly. Sprinkle with almonds and bake for 20 minutes. Remove from oven, and serve.

Pasta Twists and Mushroom Casserole

Serves 4

12 ounces pasta twists
2 tablespoons oil
1 clove garlic, peeled
1¼ cups broccoli florets
1¼ cups mushrooms
2 eggs, separated
2 cups milk
⅛ teaspoon salt
⅛ teaspoon paprika
Pinch of nutmeg
1 cup grated Parmesan cheese
1 tablespoon almond flakes
1 tablespoon sesame seeds
1 tablespoon melted butter

1. Cook pasta in boiling, salted water until just tender, following package directions; drain.
2. Heat 1 tablespoon oil in skillet. Add garlic and saute briefly; add broccoli and cook over low heat for 3 minutes, stirring constantly. Remove from pan.
3. Heat remaining oil in same pan; add mushrooms and saute until golden brown. Remove from pan.
4. Preheat oven to 450 degrees.
5. Combine pasta, broccoli, and mushrooms in well-buttered casserole dish.
6. Beat egg yolks well, then beat in milk, salt, paprika, nutmeg, and Parmesan cheese. Whisk egg whites until gentle peaks form. Fold egg whites into egg yolk mixture; pour over pasta. Sprinkle casserole with almonds and sesame seeds. Pour melted butter on top and bake for 40 minutes. Remove from oven, and serve.

Whole-Wheat Pasta with Fennel

Serves 4

2¼ cups fennel, cut into thin strips
12 ounces whole-wheat pasta shells
2½ quarts water
1 teaspoon salt
4 eggs
1 cup heavy whipping cream
2 tablespoons whole-wheat flour
6 tablespoons tomato paste
Freshly ground pepper to taste
2 teaspoons sea salt
¼ cup chopped parsley
1 cup sliced Gouda cheese
¼ cup butter

1. Cook fennel and pasta together in boiling, salted water for 8 minutes, or until tender; drain.
2. Beat eggs with cream, flour, tomato paste, pepper, sea salt, and 2 teaspoons parsley.
3. Preheat oven to 350 degrees.
4. Place pasta and fennel in buttered casserole dish. Pour egg mixture on top and bake for 20 minutes. Place cheese slices on top and dot with butter; bake for 10 minutes more. Remove from oven and garnish with remaining parsley.

Macaroni Casserole with Onions

Serves 4

12 ounces macaroni
3 tablespoons oil
2¼ cups chopped onions
1 clove garlic, peeled and chopped
Salt and pepper to taste
4 eggs
1 cup grated Emmenthaler cheese
1 cup sour cream
2 tablespoons chopped parsley
2 teaspoons paprika

1. Cook macaroni in boiling, salted water following package directions; drain.
2. Heat oil in frying pan. Add onions and garlic; saute until translucent. Season with salt and pepper.
3. Preheat oven to 400 degrees.
4. Whisk eggs, grated cheese, sour cream, parsley, and paprika together in mixing bowl. Place half the sauteed onions in buttered casserole dish. Add macaroni and put remaining onions on top. Pour creamy cheese mixture on top. Bake for 30 minutes, or until golden brown and crispy. Remove from oven, and serve.

Spaghetti Casserole

Serves 4

8 ounces thin spaghetti
6 tablespoons butter
½ cup sliced mushrooms
½ cup sliced pitted black olives
1 (1-pound) can tomatoes, drained
1 onion, diced
1 green pepper, seeded and diced
¼ cup diced celery
Salt and pepper to taste
2 tablespoons flour
1 cup half and half
¾ cup grated Parmesan cheese

1. Cook spaghetti in boiling, salted water until almost tender, following package directions; drain.
2. Melt 4 tablespoons butter in large frying pan. Add mushrooms, olives, tomatoes, onion, green pepper, and celery. Season with salt and pepper. Simmer for 40 minutes.
3. Preheat oven to 350 degrees.
4. Melt 2 tablespoons butter in saucepan. Stir in flour until well blended, then stir in half and half; cook, stirring constantly, until sauce thickens. Stir in cheese.
5. Toss spaghetti, vegetables, and sauce together. Place in buttered casserole dish. Sprinkle with a little more Parmesan cheese and bake for 1 hour. Remove from oven, and serve.

Quick Noodle Casserole

Serves 4

1 (10-ounce) can beef broth
½ soup can water
8 ounces egg noodles
1 cup grated American
  cheese
1 (3-ounce) can sliced
  mushrooms, undrained
Salt and pepper to taste

1. Preheat oven to 325 degrees.
2. Bring broth and water to boil in saucepan. Add noodles and cook for 8 to 10 minutes, or until liquid is absorbed. Stir in cheese and mushrooms. Season with salt and pepper.
3. Bake for 20 minutes, or until cheese is melted and casserole is hot.

Macaroni Caprice

Serves 4 to 6

4 cups cooked macaroni
2 cups cooked green beans,
  cut into 1-inch pieces
1 cup chopped cooked ham
1 (10-ounce) can condensed
  cream of celery soup
1 tablespoon steak sauce
⅛ teaspoon pepper
¾ cup milk
1 cup grated American
  cheese
½ cup buttered whole-wheat
  bread crumbs

1. Preheat oven to 375 degrees.
2. Place 2 cups macaroni in bottom of buttered, 2½-quart casserole dish. Cover with layer of green beans, a layer of ham, and remaining macaroni.
3. Beat soup, seasonings, milk, and cheese together until smooth; pour over macaroni. Top with buttered crumbs. Bake for 30 minutes, or until lightly browned and bubbly. Remove from oven, and serve.

Neapolitan Casserole

Serves 4

2 eggplants, sliced
2 teaspoons salt
6 tablespoons olive oil
1 onion, chopped
1 carrot, grated
1 stalk celery, chopped
2¼ cups peeled and chopped
  tomatoes
Salt and pepper to taste
½ cup chopped fresh basil
  or 1 teaspoon dried basil
12 ounces macaroni
1 cup grated Pecorino or
  Parmesan cheese
1¾ cups shredded mozzarella
  cheese

1. Sprinkle eggplant slices with salt and set aside for 30 minutes.
2. Heat 2 tablespoons oil in frying pan. Add onion, carrot, and celery; saute until tender. Add tomatoes, salt, pepper, and basil. Simmer, stirring occasionally, until sauce thickens.
3. Rinse and dry eggplant. Heat remaining oil in separate frying pan; cook eggplant until browned.
4. Cook macaroni in boiling, salted water following package directions; drain.
5. Preheat oven to 450 degrees.
6. Place macaroni with half the sauce in well-buttered casserole dish. Add half the grated cheese. Cover with half the eggplant and sprinkle with half the mozzarella. Repeat layers of macaroni, grated cheese, eggplant, and mozzarella. Pour remaining sauce on top and bake for 20 to 30 minutes. Remove from heat, and serve.

Penne Super Casserole

Serves 6

8 ounces penne
2 tablespoons oil
3 cups frozen pearl onions,
  thawed
1 clove garlic, peeled and
  crushed
1 (1-pound) can tomatoes,
  undrained
1 (6-ounce) can tomato
  paste
2 teaspoons sugar
Salt to taste
2 eggs
1 (16-ounce) container
  creamed cottage cheese
2 (10-ounce) packaged frozen
  chopped spinach, thawed
  and well drained
3 cups grated Cheddar
  cheese
1 teaspoon sage

1. Cook penne in boiling, salted water following package directions; drain.
2. Heat oil in large saucepan. Add onions and garlic; saute over medium heat, stirring constantly, for 3 minutes. Stir in tomatoes and can liquid; break up tomatoes with wooden spoon. Stir in tomato paste, sugar, and salt.
3. In large bowl, beat eggs until fluffy; stir in cottage cheese, spinach, ½ cup grated Cheddar cheese, sage, and salt; mix well.
4. Preheat oven to 400 degrees.
5. Place ⅓ of tomato sauce in bottom of ungreased, 13 x 9 x 2-inch baking dish. Cover with half the macaroni, ⅓ of grated cheese, and half the spinach mixture. Repeat layers. Spread remaining sauce on final spinach layer. Sprinkle remaining cheese around edges of casserole. Cover with foil and bake for 25 minutes. Uncover and bake for 5 minutes more, or until mixture is hot and bubbly, and cheese melted. Remove from oven, and serve.

Pasta Twists with Swiss Cheese

Serves 4

12 ounces pasta twists
1 cup heavy whipping cream
Pinch of salt
Pinch of nutmeg
1 egg yolk
1³/₄ cups grated Gruyere
  cheese
2 tablespoons butter
2 tablespoons chopped
  parsley

1. Cook pasta in boiling, salted water until just tender, following package directions; drain.
2. Preheat oven to 400 degrees.
3. Whisk cream, salt, nutmeg, and egg yolk together until thick. Place half the pasta in buttered casserole dish. Add grated cheese and then remaining pasta. Pour cream on top. Dot with butter. Bake for 20 to 25 minutes, until golden. Remove from oven, sprinkle with parsley, and serve.

Russian Casserole

Serves 4

8 ounces tagliatelle
¹/₂ pound lean bacon, cut into
  small pieces
2 onions, chopped
1/2 teaspoon marjoram
1³/₄ cups ricotta cheese
2 eggs
¹/₂ cup light cream
Salt and pepper to taste
¹/₄ cup bread crumbs
5 tablespoons butter
2 tablespoons chopped parsley

1. Cook pasta in boiling salted water until just tender, following package directions; drain.

2. Cook bacon in frying pan until crisp; remove from pan. Pour off all but 2 tablespoons fat. Add onions and saute until translucent. Combine pasta, bacon, onions, and marjoram.
3. Preheat oven to 350 degrees.
4. Whisk ricotta cheese, eggs, and cream together. Season with salt and pepper. Place three-quarters of pasta mixture in casserole dish. Add ricotta mixture and top with remaining pasta. Sprinkle with bread crumbs and dot with butter. Bake for 30 minutes. Place casserole under broiler and cook until crispy. Sprinkle with parsley, and serve.

Wagon Wheel Casserole

Serves 4

4 ounces pasta in shape of
  wheels, or pasta of your
  choice
¹/₂ cup dry white wine
1¹/₂ cups grated Cheddar
  cheese
¹/₄ cup butter
¹/₄ cup finely chopped onion
1¹/₂ tablespoons flour
1 cup milk
¹/₈ teaspoon salt
¹/₈ teaspoon curry powder
Pepper to taste
¹/₄ cup sliced pimento-stuffed
  olives
1 large ripe tomato, sliced
¹/₄ cup bread crumbs

1. Cook pasta in boiling, salted water until barely tender, following package directions; drain.
2. Heat wine in saucepan. Add cheese and stir until melted. Blend in 2 tablespoons butter, onion, and flour, stirring constantly. Gradually add milk; cook, stirring constantly,

until mixture thickens. Add salt, curry powder, and pepper. Add pasta and olives; simmer for 10 minutes.
3. Preheat broiler.
4. Place pasta mixture in casserole dish. Arrange tomato slices on top. Melt 2 tablespoons butter and pour over bread crumbs; sprinkle buttered crumbs on top of casserole. Broil for 4 or 5 minutes, or until crumbs are golden brown. Remove from oven, and serve.

Turkish Pasta Pie

Serves 4

12 ounces macaroni
¹/₄ cup butter
3 tablespoons flour
2¹/₄ cups milk
3 eggs, beaten
Pinch of freshly ground white
  pepper
¹/₄ cup chopped walnuts
¹/₄ cup chopped Pecorino or
  Parmesan cheese

1. Cook macaroni in boiling, salted water until just tender, following package directions; drain.
2. Melt butter in saucepan. Add flour and saute, stirring constantly, until light yellow. Gradually stir in milk; simmer, stirring constantly, for 10 minutes. Remove from heat.
3. Preheat oven to 400 degrees.
4. Mix eggs and pepper together; stir into cooled sauce. Cover bottom of buttered ovenproof dish with sauce. Place pasta on top. Sprinkle with walnuts. Cover with remaining sauce and cheese. Bake for 30 minutes, or until golden brown. Remove from oven, and serve.

Salmon and Spaghetti Casserole

Serves 5 to 6

8 ounces spaghetti
$^1/_2$ cup butter
$^1/_2$ cup flour
2 cups hot chicken broth
Salt and pepper
Pinch of nutmeg
$^1/_4$ cup dry sherry
1 (15-ounce) can salmon, drained and flaked, reserve liquid
$^1/_4$ cup light cream
2 cups sliced mushrooms
$^1/_2$ cup grated Parmesan cheese
$^1/_2$ cup bread crumbs

1. Cook spaghetti in boiling, salted water following package directions; drain.
2. Preheat oven to 350 degrees.
3. Melt half the butter in saucepan. Stir in flour, then chicken stock. Season with salt, pepper, and nutmeg. Add sherry and liquid from salmon; simmer for 5 minutes. Stir in cream and adjust seasoning.
4. Saute mushrooms in remaining butter and add to sauce. Toss half the sauce with spaghetti. Transfer to shallow casserole dish. Mix salmon with remaining sauce and pour over spaghetti.
5. Mix grated cheese and bread crumbs together; sprinkle over casserole. Bake for 20 minutes, or until well browned. Remove from oven, and serve.

Green Noodles and Crabmeat

Serves 6 to 8

$^1/_2$ pound mushrooms, sliced
$1^1/_4$ cup butter
2 cups crabmeat

6 cups cooked green noodles
2 pimentos, diced
1 teaspoon salt
$^1/_4$ teaspoon pepper
1 clove garlic, peeled and halved
1 tablespoon oil
3 eggs
1 cup milk
$^1/_4$ cup bread crumbs
$^1/_4$ cup grated Swiss cheese

1. Preheat oven to 350 degrees.
2. Saute mushrooms in 2 tablespoons butter until soft. Mix crabmeat with mushrooms, noodles, pimentos, salt, and pepper.
3. Rub 3-quart casserole dish with cut clove of garlic and oil. Place crab mixture in casserole dish. Beat eggs and milk together; pour over crab.
4. Melt remaining butter in small saucepan; toss with bread crumbs and grated cheese. Sprinkle bread crumb mixture over casserole and bake for 30 minutes, or until delicately browned. Remove from oven, and serve.

Clam Shell Casserole

Serves 8

3 cups small pasta shells
1 (7-ounce) can minced clams, drained, liquid reserved
1 cup diced cooked ham
1 green pepper, seeded and chopped
$^1/_4$ cup butter
1 teaspoon seasoned salt
$^1/_4$ teaspoon pepper
$^1/_2$ teaspoon paprika
1 cup grated American cheese
1 clove garlic, peeled and halved
1 (8-ounce) can tomato sauce
1 cup bread crumbs

1. Preheat oven to 400 degrees.
2. Cook pasta in boiling, salted water following package directions; drain.
3. Lightly toss macaroni, clams, ham, green pepper, 2 tablespoons butter, seasoned salt, pepper, paprika, and $^1/_2$ cup grated cheese together.

4. Rub a $2^1/_2$-quart casserole dish with cut garlic clove and butter it. Turn macaroni mixture into casserole. Mix reserved clam liquid and tomato sauce together; pour into casserole. Melt remaining butter and toss with bread crumbs; sprinkle over casserole. Top with remaining cheese and bake for 30 minutes, or until crumbs are golden brown. Remove from oven, and serve.

Salmon-Rotelle Casserole

Serves 4

12 ounces rotelle
$^1/_4$ cup butter
$^1/_4$ cup finely chopped onion
$^1/_4$ cup finely chopped celery
1 (10-ounce) can condensed cream of celery soup
$^1/_2$ cup milk
2 tablespoons chopped parsley
Salt and pepper to taste
1 (15-ounce) can pink salmon, drained and flaked
1 cup bread crumbs
Paprika

1. Cook rotelle in boiling, salted water until almost tender, following package directions; drain.
2. Preheat oven to 350 degrees.
3. Melt 2 tablespoons butter in frying pan. Add onions and celery; saute until soft. Combine soup, milk, onion, celery, parsley, salt, pepper, and salmon.
4. Mix pasta and salmon mixture together well in greased, 3- quart casserole dish. Melt remaining 2 tablespoons butter and toss with bread crumbs; sprinkle on top of casserole. Bake for 30 minutes, or until browned and bubbly. Remove from oven, and serve.

INDEX